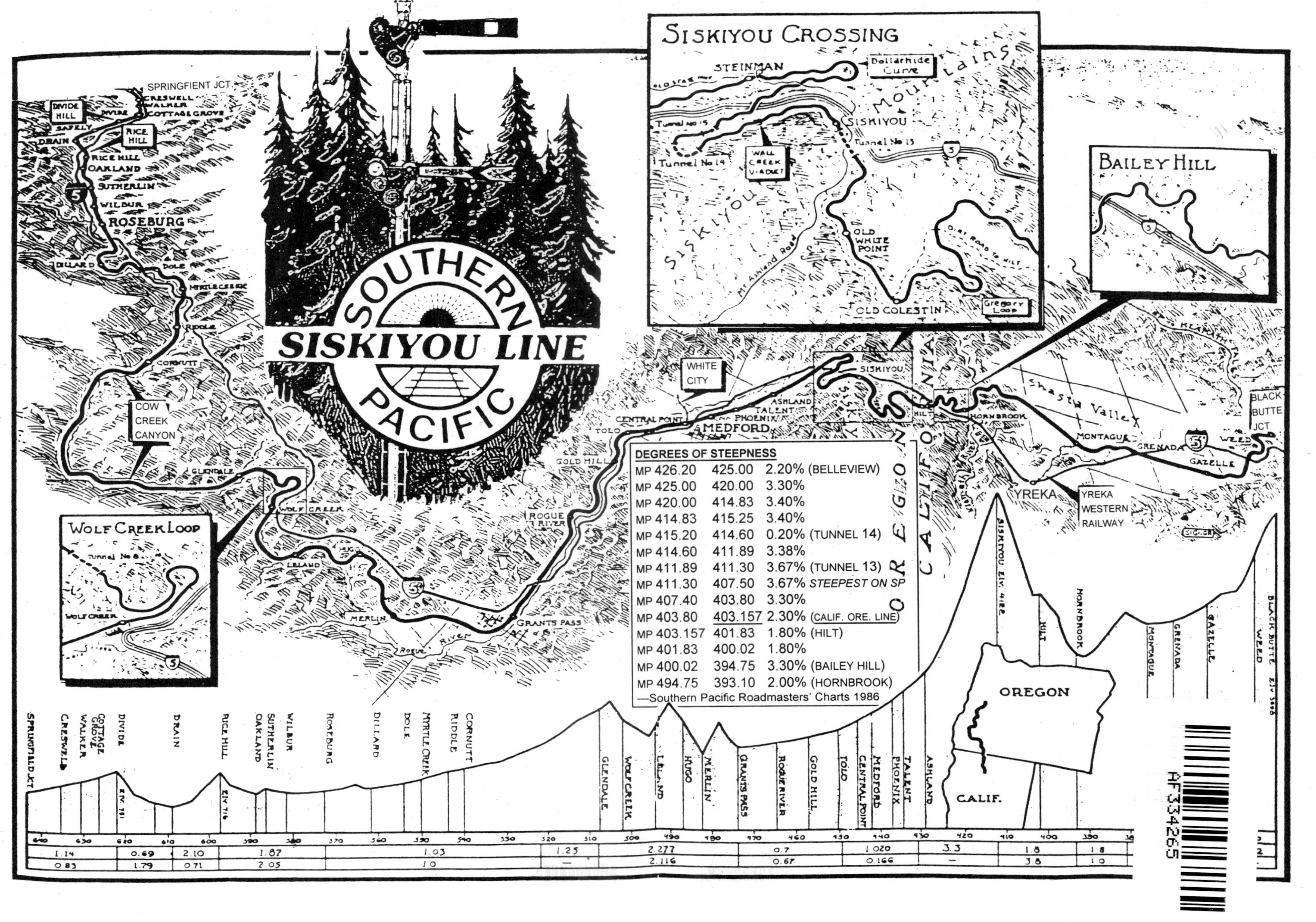

DEGREES OF STEEPNESS

MP		Grade	
MP 426.20	425.00	2.20%	(BELLEVIEW)
MP 425.00	420.00	3.30%	
MP 420.00	414.83	3.40%	
MP 414.83	415.25	3.40%	
MP 415.20	414.60	0.20%	(TUNNEL 14)
MP 414.60	411.89	3.38%	
MP 411.89	411.30	3.67%	(TUNNEL 13)
MP 411.30	407.50	3.67%	STEEPEST ON SP
MP 407.40	403.80	3.30%	
MP 403.80	403.157	2.30%	(CALIF. ORE. LINE)
MP 403.157	401.83	1.80%	(HILT)
MP 401.83	400.02	1.80%	
MP 400.02	394.75	3.30%	(BAILEY HILL)
MP 494.75	393.10	2.00%	(HORNBROOK)

—Southern Pacific Roadmasters' Charts 1986

Famous Southern Pacific *Daylight* locomotive No. 4449 roars through Oregon 's Rogue River Valley between Central Point and Medford on a rare visit December 15-16 1988. The engine, round-housed in Portland, is owned by the City of Portland. It is serviced and operated by a crew of exceptional volunteers. The bellow of its whistle is so distinctive that when No. 4449 is heard, it can be said that rail enthusiasts stop whatever they are doing and look toward the sound. "It is thrilling. It is magnificent. It is pristine sound. It is like a breath of fresh air," exclaimed a fellow who stood near the cameraman. No. 4449 is a 4-8-4, Class GS-4 built by Lima in 1941. During World War II (1941-1945), forty 4-8-4 passenger locomotives, as shown, and ninety cab-forward locomotives were purchased, these the last new steamers on the Southern Pacific. The last second-hand locomotives purchased were ten 4-8-4's from the Saint Louis Southwestern in 1953. During the war, many of these locomotives ran without their skirts and were painted black. Of this class locomotive, only No. 4449 remains.

Photographed about 1 mile north of Medford yard, December 15, 1988
—Bert Webber photos

The Siskiyou Line

Central Oregon & Pacific Railroad GP-38 diesel-electric locomotive at Medford yard.

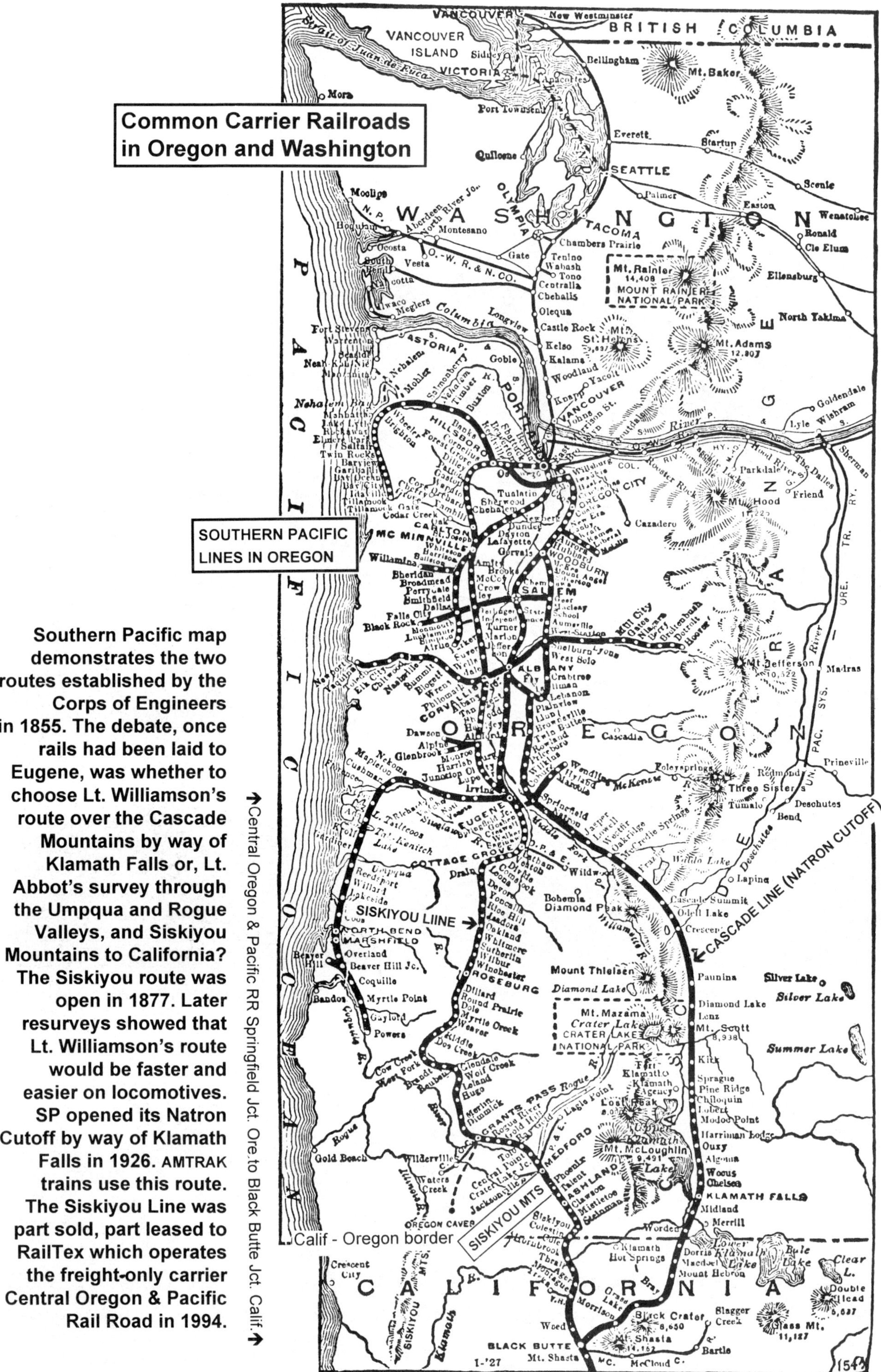

Common Carrier Railroads
in Oregon and Washington

SOUTHERN PACIFIC
LINES IN OREGON

SISKIYOU LIINE

SISKIYOU MTS.

CASCADE LINE (NATRON CUTOFF)

Calif - Oregon border

Central Oregon & Pacific RR Springfield Jct. Ore. to Black Butte Jct. Calif.

BRITISH COLUMBIA
WASHINGTON
OREGON
CALIFORNIA
PACIFIC OCEAN

VANCOUVER
VANCOUVER ISLAND
VICTORIA
SEATTLE
TACOMA
OLYMPIA
PORTLAND
ASTORIA
SALEM
ALBANY
CORVALLIS
EUGENE
COTTAGE GROVE
ROSEBURG
GRANTS PASS
MEDFORD
ASHLAND
KLAMATH FALLS
McMINNVILLE
HILLSBORO
CARLTON
WOODBURN
NORTH BEND
MARSHFIELD
MOUNT RAINIER NATIONAL PARK
Mt. Rainier 14,408
Mt. Baker
Mt. Adams 12,307
Mt. Hood 11,225
Mt. Jefferson 10,522
Three Sisters
Mt. Thielsen
Diamond Peak
CRATER LAKE NATIONAL PARK
Mt. Mazama Crater Lake
Mt. Scott 8,938
Mt. McLoughlin 9,491
Mt. Shasta 14,162
BLACK BUTTE
Silver Lake
Summer Lake
Columbia River
Strait of Juan de Fuca

Southern Pacific map
demonstrates the two
routes established by the
Corps of Engineers
in 1855. The debate, once
rails had been laid to
Eugene, was whether to
choose Lt. Williamson's
route over the Cascade
Mountains by way of
Klamath Falls or, Lt.
Abbot's survey through
the Umpqua and Rogue
Valleys, and Siskiyou
Mountains to California?
The Siskiyou route was
open in 1877. Later
resurveys showed that
Lt. Williamson's route
would be faster and
easier on locomotives.
SP opened its Natron
Cutoff by way of Klamath
Falls in 1926. AMTRAK
trains use this route.
The Siskiyou Line was
part sold, part leased to
RailTex which operates
the freight-only carrier
Central Oregon & Pacific
Rail Road in 1994.

The Siskiyou Line

—Documentary—

Bert and Margie Webber

WEBB RESEARCH GROUP PUBLISHERS
Books About the Oregon Country

Published by
WEBB RESEARCH GROUP PUBLISHERS
Books About the Oregon Country
P. O. Box 314
Medford, Oregon 97501

Photographs made by the authors, and photographs from the authors' collections are not credited except on pages of multi-photographs when those by the authors are credited to avoid confusion..
Photographs from others are credited under each picture.
We trust that no omissions of credit have occurred for if so is was surely not intentional.

The Covers:

<u>Front Cover:</u>
Central Oregon & Pacific train leaves Tunnel 2 and enters a 1905 bridge in the Cow Creek Canyon of Douglas County Oregon.
Photograph by Keith J. Johnson

<u>Back Cover:</u>
Unfortunately, wrecks are a part of the risk of operating all railroads. Wreck shown was in summer 1996 in Cottonwood Creek Valley south of the Siskiyou summit. No one was hurt. Bert Webber, life-long Research Photojournalist, continues to demonstrate his prowess with cameras in this book.

Title Page picture:
Southern Pacific track at Gold Ray Dam on the Rogue River,
Jackson County Oregon summer 1978.
This line is now operated by Central Oregon & Pacific Railroad.
Table Rocks in background. The temperature was about 98 F.
Photo by Bert Webber

<u>Library of Congress Cataloging-in-Publication Data</u>
Webber, Bert.
   The Siskiyou Line : adventure in railroading : documentary / Bert and Margie Webber.
      p.   cm.
   Includes bibliographical references (p.   -   ) and index.
   ISBN 0-936738-04-9 paperback
   ISBN 0-936738-49-9 hardback
   1. Central Oregon & Pacific Railroad. 2. Railroads—Oregon 3. Railroads—California
   I. Webber, Margie. II. Title
TF25.C395W43   1997
385'.0979—dc21   97-4373   CIP

Contents

(TOP) **Oregon & California Rail Road depot at Medford looking northeasterly from Main and Fir Streets. Date unknown. The two men (ARROW) walking the track which is nearly covered with mud from the unpaved street. During this period, there were no "pooper-scoopers" that followed horses.**

Introduction

THE INTENTION OF THE PRESENT BOOK IS to consider that part of the north-south railroad in Oregon from Springfield Junction to the California border, then south to Black Butte Junction near year-around snow-covered Mt. Shasta in California. This is the 300.3 miles of track we call *The Siskiyou Line*. In addition, we will include the various railroads that switch into this main line – those in the past we have been able to discover – and lines presently operating.

For an overview of the intrigue in getting a railroad built from Portland south, of which *The Siskiyou Line* is but a section, refer to Bancroft Vol. II. pages 695-706. Although the Bancroft was published in 1888, it can be found in many libraries and copies are often available from book-sellers as it was recently reprinted. Other books are listed in our Bibliography.

We highly recommend the *Encyclopedia of Western Railroad History* by Donald B. Robertson and *Backwoods Railroads* by C. Jesse Burkhardt. These gentlemen offer concise material about a number of the railroads included in this book, but not all of them. We have traded some correspondence with each of these researchers and we appreciate their input.

Some "Pertinences," as we have titled them, about the O&C railroad will be found on the next page.

Another book that needs to be mentioned is Lewis L. McArthur's *Oregon Geographic Names*. This is a volume, occasionally updated, that should be at the elbow of all Oregon writers, and the existence of which general readers will want to know about. Any bookstore has or can get copies and most Oregon public libraries have it.

A matter of some importance to those writers of history who seek accuracy, is a proper name for that unique valley through which this railroad runs on the south slope of the Siskiyou Mountains. In summer 1996, there were a couple of derailments along here in the vicinity of the site of the once famous Colestin Mineral Springs Hotel. The hotel was so important as a station on the SP, that the Colestin, Oregon post office operated there between 1892 and 1943.

The rankle comes about due to some young television-age reporters who seem to have a tendency to call a place anything that comes to mind. Therefore, all summer long as the saga of the train wrecks continued, it was "Colestin Valley" this and the "Colestin Valley" that.

As most valleys seem to be named for the stream that runs through a valley's cleavage, and the reporters

Oregon & California Rail Road Company
–Pertinences–

The firm was incorporated as *Oregon & California Rail Road Company* March 17, 1870 but many other forms of the name appear and are accepted. It operated from September 5, 1870 until January 3, 1927 when it was sold to Southern Pacific. (The O&C was leased to SP on July 1, 1887 then "conveyed by deed on January 3, 1927.") At its peak, it had 680.25 miles of standard gauge (56.5-inch) track between Portland and the California border. Of this distance, it laid 402 miles and acquired by purchase of other lines, 309.6 miles of track of which about 29 miles were later abandoned. The company used mostly 50 and 56-pound rail on the main line and 35-pound rail on sidings. The steepest portion of the line is in the Siskiyou Mountains where for a five mile stretch the grade is 3.67 percent.*

Its predecessors were two:

1.The Oregon Central *Railroad* with 46.78 miles of track operated from Portland via west side of Willamette River to end-of-track at St. Joseph in Yamhill County. (November 21, 1866 to October 6, 1880).

2. The Oregon Central *Rail Road* with 20.8 miles of track operated on the east side of the Willamette River to New Era by way of Oregon City (operated between April 22, 1867 and March 29, 1870).

In its early days, the O&C bought four lines. These were, Portland & Yamhill Railroad, 28.34 miles of track; Oregonian Railroad Company, 153.11 miles; Albany & Lebanon Railroad with 11.58 miles, and Western Oregon Railroad Company 49.70 miles of track.

The railroads purchased all had short tenure. From date of incorporation:

Portland & Yamhill	(36-inch gauge)	1 year 8 days	(June 14, 1892 - July 22, 1893)
Oregonian:	(36-inch gauge)	3 years, 3 months 12 days	(April 19, 1890 - July 31, 1893)
Albany & Lebanon:	(56.5-inch gauge)	1 year, 2 months, 8 days	(February 28, 1880 - May 6, 1881)
Western Oregon:	(56.5-inch gauge)	1 year, 8 months, 12 days	(January 27, 1879 - October 9, 1880)

Various sections of the track were completed on dates shown: A work train was usually only a few lengths of rail behind the workers, therefore, it is presumed a train arrived at the various towns on the same dates the track to each location was reached. A train with fare-paying passengers usually followed in a day or two.

September 29, 1870	Salem
December 25, 1870	Albany
October 5, 1871	Eugene City
December 3, 1872	Roseburg
December 2, 1883	Grants Pass
February 23 (approx.)	Medford
February 25, 1884	Phoenix
May 4, 1884	Ashland
December 17, 1887	California border

One of the greatest advances in safety for trains was George Westinghouse's invention of the air brake in 1869. Of the O&C's inventory of locomotives, by the end of June 1890, 44 of the 49 engines had air brakes as did all 57 passenger cars, all 24 fresh produce cars and 165 of its 707 freight cars.

---

* The steepest grade of 3.67 is for 5 miles running south from the north end of Tunnel #13. The 3.0 to 3.3 mentioned in many publications is correct for several other sections between Dollarhide Curve and the south end of Bailey Hill. –Data from Roadmasters Charts, 1986.

(including the local newspaper's) talked and wrote about the formaldehyde leaking tank car whose goo did not run into *Cottonwood Creek* because of quick action by Fire Chief Steve Avgeris and his volunteer fire fighters, why didn't these graduate reporters date line their stories as "Cottonwood Creek Valley"? Or just "Colestin" as that site was just a snort away?

Avgeris, Chief of the Colestin Rural Fire District, who lives on the site of the historic Colestin Hotel thought about this naming affair and told the authors, "I have lived here all my life and this valley never had an official name." He said the "Colestin Valley" name seems to have started in the 1970's by some writers "but I don't know why."

The name "Colestin" is identified by McArthur in his *Oregon Geographic Names,* as is the forerunner post office, White Point, also a station in the SP, about one mile away. McArthur mentions the Cottonwood Creek Valley under his entry "White Point" but does not associate it with Colestin.

After all this flap, the authors go on record by naming this beautiful valley, where will be found the railroad's sweeping bands of steel on which trains gracefully round Gregory Loop then enter California:

"COTTONWOOD CREEK VALLEY"

We wish to thank special people who helped by providing information and pictures that were essential to this book.

Larry Bacon, General Manager of the Yerka Western Railroad, willingly opened his archives to us, answered questions and read part of the manuscript.

Steve Avgeris, already mentioned.

DeAnn Carlton, White City Railroad Company, fielded our questions and pointed out where we might find material.

Dr. William L. Barnum, DDS (ret.) provided first-hand information and loaned priceless artifacts for our look into the fascinating history of the Rogue River Valley Railroad.

Dan Wilkinson, Grants Pass, a railroad fancier of great repute, who owns a fully reconditioned and working Santa Fe caboose, has provided essential information on railroads to us for a number of years. We appreciate Dan's knowledge and willing help.

Brian Patrick Webber observed and reported the age of the bridge at Myrtle Creek (1906) when we went there to photograph it.

Ben Truwe was a keen observer on the trip when we investigated and rode on the Yreka Western's "Blue Goose." He was also along on an inspection of the Central Oregon & Pacific right-of-way in the Cottonwood Creek Valley, then we went to the north mouth of Tunnel 13. That was an exciting day!

Norm VanManen, a man of intellect and many skills, was hiker-researcher companion in the Siskiyous for the trip to photograph out-of-the-way tunnels 14 and 15. He also reviewed the manuscript.

Larry McLane, who wrote *First There Was Two-good*, permitted our use of his private photographs of early railroading in Northern Josephine County.

Ted Wharton of the Gold Hill Historical Society allowed us use of some of the original photographs from the Society's collection.

Keith Johnson, Myrtle Creek, was of substantial assistance in assembling photographs from his collections for use here, and for his diligence in obtaining information about the Glenbrook Nickel Company and its unique shortline operation.

Dennis Carlton of Superior Lumber Company, jockeyed the BB/GE switcher out of a dark shed and into the sunlight, with the author on board, for photographs. He has worked there for 25 years and with his brother Jim, 30 years, both mechanics, keep the switcher going. They also fix trucks.

Tom Mell, Glendale, Oregon, long retired from Superior as General Manager, who also worked for predecessors, provided exciting tales of his fifty years in the timber business including being an engineer of gear-driven locomotives. Mell was able to clear some misunderstandings among some writers who insist that the Robert Dollar Company logging short line (now Superior Lumber Company), went up Cow Creek. Mell distinctly recalls the route was along Windy Creek and pointed to it on a map.

A number of personnel of the Central Oregon & Pacific Railroad went out of their ways to be helpful. These included but are not limited to Robert W. Libby, General Manager; Gerald L. Carter, Operations Manager; James R. Becker, Supervisor of Locomotive Engineers in the Roseburg headquarters.

In the Medford sub-office we are indebted to Roger Greidanus, Assistant General Manager, Bruce Pfleiger Assistant Operations Manager who arranged a trip for us to go "over the hill," the Siskiyou Mountains, sharing the cab of GP-40 #3084 with Engineer Tom Moore, and Conductor Ron Kneebone. The trip was an exciting experience and allowed the making of photographs that could not have been made in any other manner.

In detailed visits with Bob Libby, and later with Roger Greidanus, each revealed that a position the Central Oregon & Pacific Railroad has assumed is to support the local communities in which the company

Henry Larcom Abbot, U.S.A.

operates.

Dale Matheny, Medford Agent for CORP, and a former assistant road master with SP on the Siskiyou Line, assisted us over many weeks during the course of this project. He shared his first-hand knowledge acquired over the years.

Gary Michener, who spends his days eye-balling track conditions, a Track Supervisor, CORP, drives a flange-wheeled pickup truck up to 160 miles a day at track speed, usually about 10 mph. He willingly helped us by identifying safety concerns about track, ties, spikes, and a number of allied matters. These included his experiences with wild animals in the Siskiyous, and his throwing rocks at great icicles that dangerously hang from tunnel portals in the dead of winter.

And there were many more who took time to answer our questions, as did Doris Hubbard of Sutherlin, who went out of her way to be helpful especially with the Weyerhaeuser material. Also, retired locomo-

tive engineer George W. Norman, Klamath Falls, who loaned early photos and replied by letter with many answers.

In writing acknowledgments it would be unseemly not to mention that the reference librarians at the Jackson County Library in Medford fielded many questions during the course of this project. We appreciate the willingness and thoroughness of these professionals in helping us with many tough inquiries.

We are indebted to friendly and helpful folks as all of these, and others, who have assisted to make this book a success. We thanked each of them individually, and now we do so collectively in these pages.

Constructive comments about this book can be sent to us in care of the publisher whose address will be found on page *vi,* but it may be that every letter cannot be personally acknowledged.

Bert and Margie Webber
Central Point, Oregon

The Pacific Railroad Survey

Prologue to the Establishment of a North-South Railroad Route in Oregon

The Field Reconnaissance of 1855

ON MAY 1, 1855, Lieutenant Robert Stockton Williamson, Unites States Army Corps of Topographical Engineers, received written orders directly from the Honorable Jefferson Davis, Secretary of War. The lieutenant, then in Washington, D. C., was to proceed immediately to Benicia, California where he was to:

> Make such explorations and surveys as will determine the practicability, or otherwise, of connecting the Sacramento Valley, in California, with the Columbia River, Oregon Territory by railroad, either by the Willamette Valley or (if this route should prove impractical) by the valley of the Des Chutes River....

> **Benicia is on the Sacramento River upstream a few miles from where the river flows first into San Pablo Bay then into San Francisco Bay. Benicia is about 30 miles by water from San Francisco. It is about 5 miles east by highway from Vallejo. Benicia Barracks, founded in 1849, a year before California statehood, was the first United States military installation on the west coast. Today Benicia has a military museum. The city is termed a "bedroom" community of San Francisco. —Editor**

Lt. Williamson's orders contained some lines that suggested the Deschutes route was likely "improbable," but he was to check it out. Further, as soon as this mission was completed, he would proceed with surveys over the Sierra Nevada mountains in an effort to locate a route for rails to connect Salt Lake City with San Francisco.

On the same day, 2nd Lieutenant Henry Larcom Abbot, also of the Topographical Engineers, was ordered to join the expedition as second in command.

It was understood should illness overtake Lt. Williamson, Lt. Abbot would assume command as it was the desire of the Congress that the surveys not be delayed. There was also provision for detaching Lt. Williamson back to Washington, or he could stay in the field and send Lt. Abbot to Washington, to write reports.

We must understand that very little was known in the United States about these "wilds of the far west," as some journalists referred to the Oregon Territory. Accordingly, the official report of the survey was to include geological information and acute observations of the country, nature of difficulties encountered and the quality and extent of building materials to be found. Further:

> Your attention will be directed to the botany and natural history...and to such other objects as tend to illustrate its...condition. You are authorized to hire a geologist, a civil engineer, a computer [mathematical astronomer], a draughtsman, and a physician who will at the same time perform as a naturalist or geologist....

Also permitted in his orders was provision for hiring a number of packers and extra hands as needed. Lt. Williamson was to draw stores from the Quartermaster and to receive from the inventory of the Topographical Engineers such scientific equipment as required for such a mission. If the Engineers did not have such instruments as Lt. Williamson required to carry out his orders, as well as maps, books, camp and garrison equipment, smaller instruments and animals, he was authorized to procure them by purchase.

Here was a party of a handful of scientists, with some helpers, outfitted for a survey of the topography of the land to see if a railroad could be installed. Could Lt. Williamson's first reaction to his orders suggested to him that this unique study group would be on a comfortable hike into the woods to last a few weeks? Could an enjoyable time be expected with early mornings spent fishing, and evenings telling yarns around a campfire – yes?

Wrong !

The country into which this Corps of exploration would venture was a wild, unsettled land where there were Indians. Some were friendly but most had to be presumed to be unfriendly.

The Commanding General of the Pacific Department was ordered to provide an escort of 100 men plus regimental officers and an assistant surgeon as "a large escort will be required to protect the exploring party in Oregon...."

There was a further order on the Quartermaster to "furnish horses, mules, equipments" as requisitioned. The detachment for doing this railroad survey was getting pretty large but all this was still not the end of the order.

The Ordnance Department "will furnish arms, accouterments and a mountain artillery forge."

But an admonishment that even today hassles Army officers was contained not once but twice within the orders, stated here in jocular form:

"If you lose any of this stuff or bust it, we're gonna take it oudda your pay"!

The orders continued: Lt. Williamson was to draw a cash purse, the money to be used to purchase – "for the purpose of trafficking with the Indians and compensating them for their services" – such articles of Indian goods as are most desirable for such purposes but he was not to spend more than $300 for these articles.

In all, Lt. Williamson was authorized to spend up to $42,000 for his survey.

The Secretary of War did not foresee any delays in the field, at least from his desk in Washington, D. C., therefore, he ended his orders saying when the duty was completed, Lt. Williamson was to sell the outfit and then quickly get back to Washington to write his reports. Whoa – not quite that easy! The lieutenant was to "make usual monthly reports and besides, advise from time-to-time of progress and results."

Lt. Williamson, and his assistant, Lt. Abbot, would have their hands full just keeping track of "all that stuff." Nevertheless, these professional survey officers would have adequate time each day to attend to the purpose of the trip: Recommend a place to plant a railroad.

So ordered, Lt. Williamson, with Lt. Abbot, set out for San Francisco to organize his expedition.

—000—

Robert Stockton Williamson was not new to field trips as a Topographical Engineer. He was an expert at organization therefore on his arrival at Benicia, he set about quickly to assemble his expedition and get under way. While the authors have not discovered exactly how many people were on this trip, it is estimated to have been about 150. The cooks and bakers would be pressed to prepare 450 meals a day while the troupe kept on the move.

> We left camp near Benicia on the 10th of July [1855] and traveled thirteen miles, camping on a small stream…Suison Creek which is about thirty feet wide. This is a fine place where a bridge will be required. [Then] through low, rolling hills…to Putos Creek…would require a bridge 130 feet long.

His reports were detailed, as the Secretary of War directed and as the Congress, in approving the Act ordering these surveys, expected.

Each time a camp was made, the location was charted and numbered. If the camp that night was on a side trek led by Lt. Williamson, the letter "W" appeared on the chart with the camp number. The letter "A" appeared if it was an Abbot bivouac. Every night, soldiers on guard duty patrolled the sleepers' area to guard them against any intrusion. Nevertheless, during the night of August 5th, a mule was stolen by Indians.

The days were anything but routine. On arising one morning, a soldier let out a *whoop* on discovery of a huge rattlesnake under a blanket. On another, a fire was started when someone slipped and slid down a hill on tinder-dry grass. The fire spread rapidly and Lt. Abbot recorded: "It took the united exertion of the whole command to put it out." And there were hazards of the work. Barometers were broken and had to be refilled. A chronometer was damaged. The soldiers not only walked guard posts at night, but had to maintain their patrols in daytime as well for at times, Indians were seen at a distance, or close by peering at the expedition through nearby trees. These Indians did not seem to be in a fighting mood, but were curious as to what manner of men were these strangers dressed in strange garments and doing strange things. A conclusion could be reached that the Indians were "casing the place," because often during the dark hours, after some scurrying in the nearby underbrush, mules were stolen.

All sorts of wild game were sighted – grizzly bears and rabbits and beavers. While it seems doubtful that the entire command suppered on fresh trout, at least the handful of officers did, and there is mention on at least one occasion "many crawfish which when cooked were scarcely inferior to lobster" were the main course. On another occasion, the entree was venison.

There were side trips. On August 28th, Lt. Williamson and certain of the scientists, packers and a detachment under command of Lt. Philip Sheridan, carried seven day's provisions and started their first exploration of the Cascade Mountains. This group ascended to an elevation of 6,303 feet above sea level then went down into a valley where they met some Indians, some of whom spoke a little Chinook, as did Lt. Williamson. When an Indian and his woman were encountered on a trail on September 1, a conversation in Chinook ensued that provided the surveyors with directions.

But Indian trails, as well as striking out through rough country, can be dangerous to man and equipment. Slipping and falling was not uncommon. Lt. Williamson noted, "Our barometer was unfortunately broken today." Of Oregon weather he inscribed: "It rained and we did not leave camp."

In due time, the two topographical officers were back together comparing notes. It was decided that Lt. Williamson would back track to take a wagon road near Diamond Peak and Crescent Lake into the Willamette Valley as suggested by the Indians.

> ### Williamson's Route
> #### Today's AMTRAK and Southern Pacific Mainline Between Eugene and Sacramento Closely Follows 1855 Survey
>
> On today's maps, note the town of Crescent on Highway 97. This is about where Lt. Williamson turned west. He then proceeded by way of Crescent Lake down the Middle Fork of the Willamette River along what is now highway 58 through Oakridge and Lowell to Eugene. Years later, a railroad, today's Southern Pacific's Natron cutoff, would follow Lt. Williamson's route from Eugene past lakes Odell and Crescent to Chemult, Kirk, along the banks of Upper Klamath Lake to the city of Klamath Falls then into California and on to Redding and south.

From their rendezvous, the two officers made plans for continuing the exploration. Lt. Williamson, and his detachment, would proceed to the Willamette Valley then north to Oregon City, then on to the Columbia River to make camp across from Fort Vancouver.

Lt. Abbot was ordered to continue north along the east side of the Cascade Mountains to Fort Dalles (pron: Dalz) on today's maps as the City of The Dalles on the Columbia River. Then he would go west to Lt. Williamson's camp. He recorded:

> Sept 6. I left camp 40 to day [with three assistants] and
> eight packers [for our] train…. My instruments consisted
> of a Gambrey sextant and mercurial horizon, a Green's
> cistern barometer No. 1089, a thermometer, and a pris-
> matic compass. As we were about to start, a horse,
> becoming entangled in the cords of the office tent, threw
> down and broke the barometer. I sent the rest of the party
> forward and Mr. Anderson, Dr. Sterling [and I] remained
> to repair it. As this detained us about two hours, we were
> compelled to travel rapidly to overtake the train.

Lt. Abbot's route was through the thick forests of pon-
derosa pine, across prairies and along streams. He came
upon a large river at the bottom of an "immense canyon,"
the river called *Mpto-ly-as* by the Indians. This became the
Metolius River and Lt. Abbot's viewing of it is believed to
be the first time a white man saw it. (On today's maps, this
area is about ten miles north of Camp Sherman off highway
20.) It was here that the detachment saw Indians spearing
salmon. Lt. Abbot bought one that weighed about 25
pounds. So large were these fish that a member of the party
shot one with his pistol.

**A well-dressed "dragoon" of the
United States Army in the 1850's.**

Early in October, with the weather turning cold, on reaching a settler's cabin, the party was met
with the alarming news that a general Indian war had started. Lt. Abbot wrote:

> To guard against any sudden attack [that night], I had the animals carefully tied to a strong fence
> and [set] three watches, [taking] one myself. It was very dark and cloudy, with occasionally a few
> drops of rain. I could not but feel our prospects were rather gloomy.

In the morning, the party moved along trying to locate a reported pass through the mountains
south of Mt. Hood into the Willamette Valley. (On a topographic or road map see Clear Lake and
Frying Pan Lake in Clackamas County, and highway 224 by way of Estacada (pron: ess-tuh KAY-
duh) to Oregon City.)

When the expedition reached the Willamette Valley, Lt. Abbot noted that many of the settlers
were abandoning their places for fear of an Indian attack. He wrote, "a general panic prevailed…."
On being handed a newspaper, "We had the rare pleasure of reading an account of our own massacre
in the mountains."

In a few days, the expedition reached Oregon City "in a drenching rain," and there he learned of
Lt. Williamson's departure for San Francisco by steamship. It was late in the season and Commanding Officer, Lt. Williamson had to prepare for the contemplated venture into the Sierra Nevada.

Almost immediately upon arriving at Oregon City, on orders from Major G. J. Rains, 4th United
States Infantry, commanding the district, the survey parties, both Lt. Williamson's and Lt. Abbot's,
lost their military escort as these troops were needed to fight Indians. Lt. Williamson had sent a letter
of protest to the Major and asked for reconsideration, but no answer was forthcoming. With the
departure of Lt. Williamson, Lt. Abbot was now in charge. He too applied for return of his escort as

> …an Indian war had broken out in the Rogue Valley, through which our route lay and all
> [travel] between Fort Lane and the Upper Umpqua Valley was now cut off except for strong and
> well armed parties. Our party consisted of Lt. Crook and myself, [plus six civilian assistants] with
> twenty packers, ten of whom were Mexicans. Several of [us] were unarmed, others had a few
> pistols [and] I think five rifles….

No answer came from his remonstrance to Major Rains. Lt. Abbot's responsibility was to con-
duct a topographical survey and try to stay on schedule, there being no provision for waiting out an
Indian war nearly 250 miles away. He was determined to continue the survey with or without an

armed escort, therefore he tightened his grip over his new command and announced that his party would proceed without delay.

—oOo—

Lieutenant Henry Larcom Abbot was a man whose shoulders were heavily burdened as he headed south from Oregon City on October 22, 1855. He first concern was for the safety of his men for now he had no military escort. He was certain there were hostile Indians in his path. Would he accidentally lead his party into a massacre far from rescuers? What about his responsibility for all the scientific notes in his charge since Lt. Williamson had departed? He had pleaded with Major Rains for an escort of dragoons using the security of the papers as part of his argument. Further, there was a potential serious delay for the overall plan assigned by the Congress, through the Secretary of War to the Topographical Engineers. His and Lt. Williamson's survey of Oregon was only a part of the Congressional Act to explore for transcontinental railway routes. If Abbot's mission to complete the survey in Oregon was delayed by the Indian war in the Rogue River Valley, this could seriously jeopardize the next phase already planned for a survey in the Sierra Nevada Mountains. And it was late in the year. There being no reply from Major Rains, a question arose: Did the letters of request ever reach him? *

Henry Abbot was born in Massachusetts and grew up there. He graduated from West Point Military Academy at age 23 as a 2nd Lieutenant in the Corps of Topographical Engineers. The Oregon reconnaissance was his first assignment. Now 24, he had his hands full. He accepted his responsibility as an Army Officer and ordered his men to move out.

On the second day, he stopped to visit with the Surveyor General of Oregon Territory at Salem where they compared professional notes. Next he went through Corvallis without stopping, remarking in his diary that it was "a little town consisting principally of one street lined by several stores and dwellings…." Of Eugene City, he wrote: "… a small village near the junction of the Coast and Middle Forks of the Willamette."

As the group trudged on, they learned that the reports of hostilities in the Rogue River Valley were real. While camping at the village of Winchester along the North Umpqua River, he learned that only the strongest parties could get through to Fort Lane on the Rogue River. A call for volunteers was then taking place at Roseburg and a camp had been established at Canyonville – a "town" of exactly one house and one barn. Major Martin, in charge of the volunteers, offered to escort the mapping party through the canyon and his offer was promptly accepted. Their route was up a steep canyon covered with dense forest and the lively Canyon Creek to the divide at about 1,450 feet elevation. Lt. Abbot recorded: "We were compelled, after crossing the creek about thirty times, to travel part of the way in its bed." **

The Indians of Southern Oregon were well-armed and the party first noted the devastation of the raids the next day – November 1. Lt. Abbot recorded:

> We passed a team on the road; the oxen lay shot in the yoke, and the dark blood stains upon the seat of the wagon told the fate of the driver. Even the hay stacks and grain in the fields had been burned.

The route (now near Azalea), led up Cow Creek for a short way then the surveyors and the escort crossed the divide to Wolf Creek. Here, Major Martin, itching to get into the fight, announced his departure. Lt. Abbot:

---

* The Special Collections Department of the West Point Military Academy Archives has the records on Major Gabriel James Rains, Class of 1827. The Major had his hands full with the Yakima Indian War in October 1855 and he was in the field commanding 350 soldiers. Because communication in the west during this period between field operations under war conditions and any headquarters, Fort Dalles (The Dalles, Oregon), in this case, was very poor, archivists have found no correspondence naming Rains, Williamson, Abbot on this matter. This strongly suggests the Major never received either Lt. Williamson's or Lt. Abbot's letters. What happened to the letters remains undiscovered in April 1997. —Editor.

** Luckily, the usual heavy fall rains had not yet started when this party of exploration climbed the steep Canyon Creek Valley. Nine years earlier, when the first wagon train on the Applegate Trail was proceeding in the opposite direction, the rains started and the large party was inundated with disaster. For this account refer to *Over the Applegate Trail to Oregon in 1846* in bibliography. This route was first established by the Army in 1853 then it became Highway 99 and later Interstate-5.

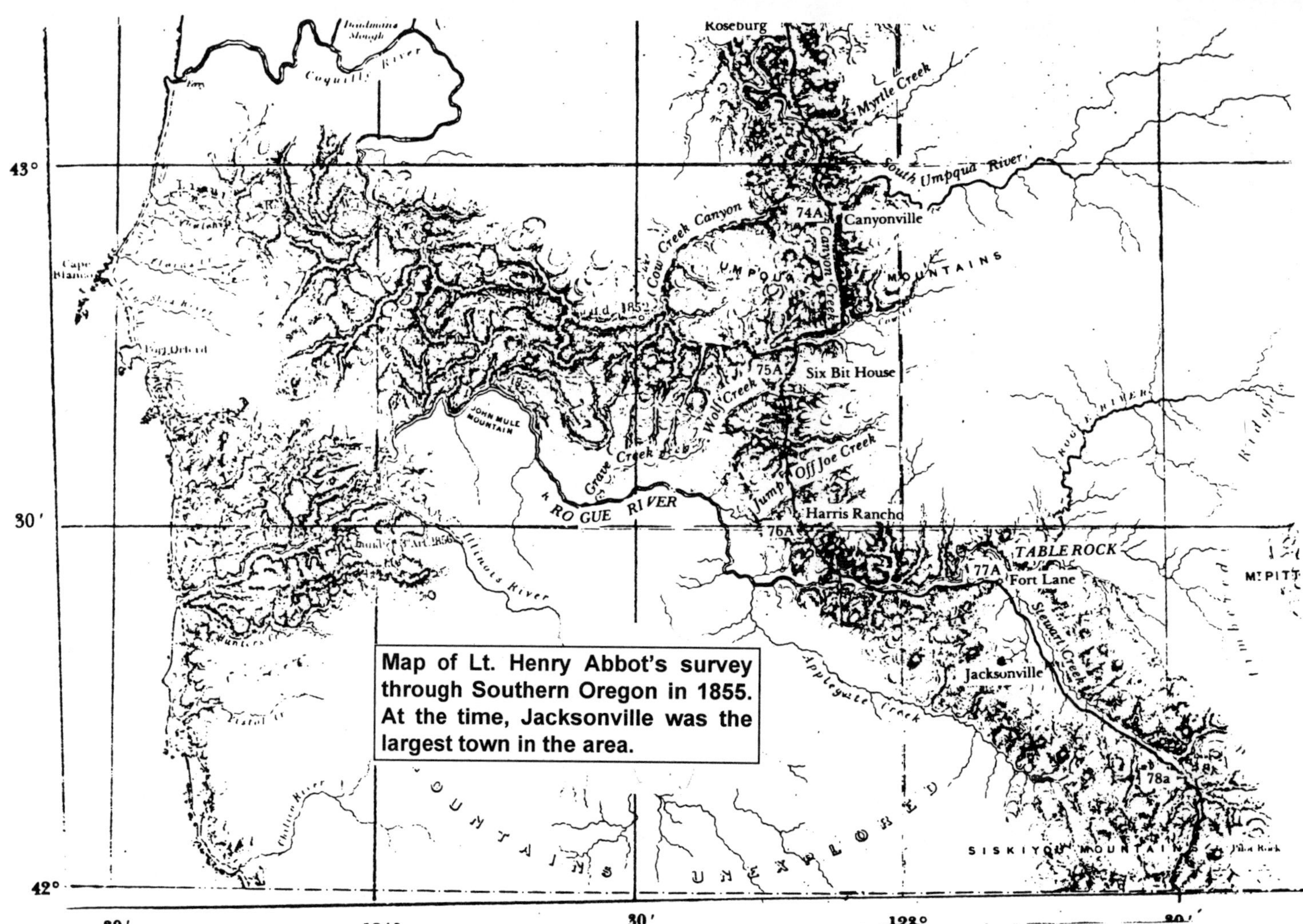

He could not spare us an escort [so] we determined to press forward as rapidly as possible toward Fort Lane. We trusted that the Indians would be too busy [elsewhere] to attack our party.

By nightfall, some stragglers from the major's unit made their way back with the tale that their provisions were consumed, their gunpowder nearly gone and that the Indians were strongly posted – very many of them. Further, whites were being attacked at random.

An allied matter faced the young lieutenant. The Indians had burned the forage along the route therefore "our animals suffered much for want of food."

Another officer, a Major Morgan, came through the engineers' camp in command of another assemblage of volunteers also on their way south. This officer agreed to escort the surveyors, so the entire group broke camp quickly and moved along.

The situation was complex as well as fluid. There was general lack of communication between volunteer groups and units of the regular army and many of the volunteers, single, and in groups, were zealous in their desire to protect the countryside. Most of the volunteers were untrained, had no uniforms, lacked supplies of the most basic nature, had no medicines or knowledge of medical aid, and probably the most challenging of all, had no "intelligence" of where the Indians might be. Further, these "volunteers" frequently came and went on short notice. Major Morgan's force didn't stay with the engineers very long for at Wolf Creek, the surveyors were once again without escort. But not for long.

At Wolf Creek, Lt. Abbot found a Captain Smith with a small band about ready to leave for Fort Lane. The lieutenant inquired if these troops would provide escort, got agreement and "in less than fifteen minutes we were again on our way."

Between Grave Creek and Jump Off Joe Creek, the party witnessed many incidents of Indian attacks including a scene where a man had been killed along with a large number of pigs he had been

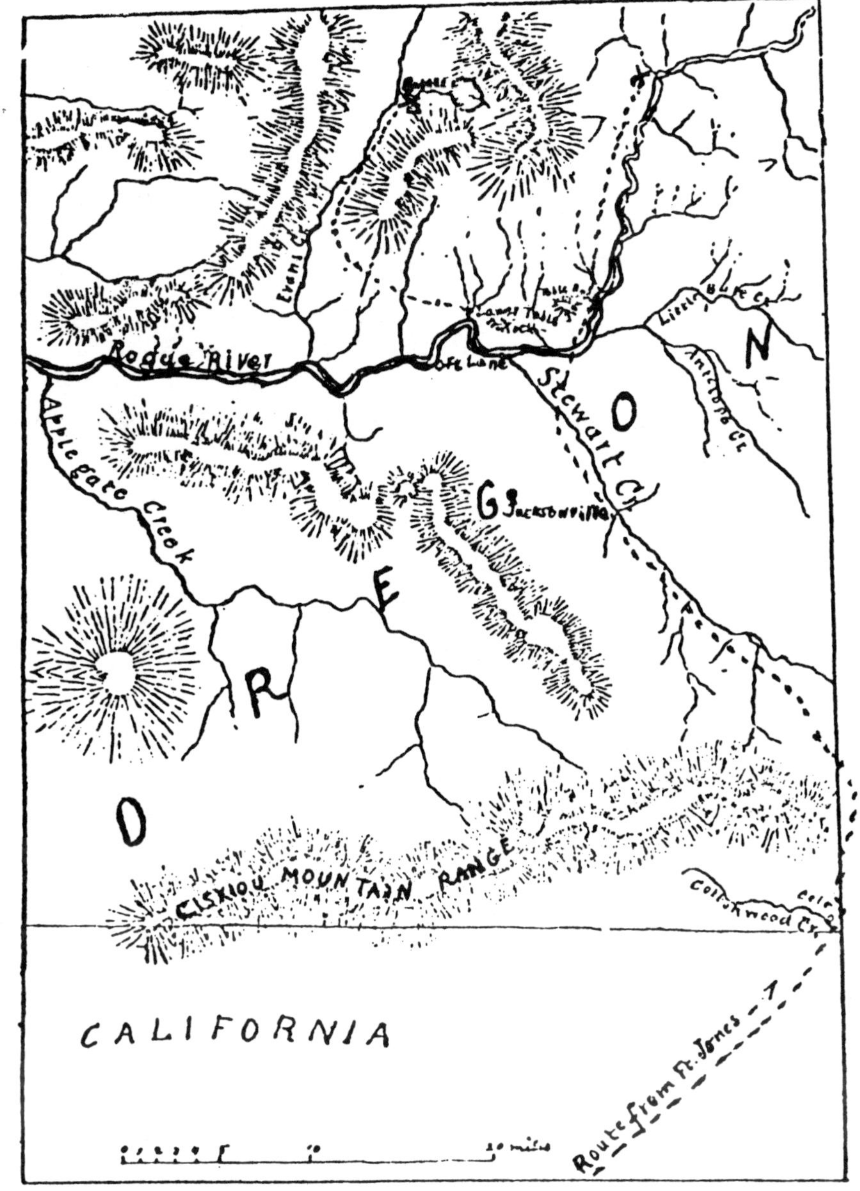

This map is believed to be the earliest map of Bear Creek drainage and Rogue River.

Map of Captain Thomas Jefferson Cram, U. S. Army Corps of Topographical Engineers, Department of the Pacific. By process of deduction we place the drawing of this map soon after the Battle of Table Rock (August 24, 1853) as a trail to the battle site is on the map. The only populated sites shown are Fort Lane and Jacksonville although there was a post office and small settlement at Dardenells not far from the fort.

Present Bear Creek originally named Stuart Creek is shown as "Stewart" as the creek was named for Captain James Stuart, who died from wounds after a battle with nearby Indians in 1851. In the Abbot Report (1857) of his survey through this area in 1855, Abbot spelled "Stewart" obviously after Cram. Did Lt. Abbot have a copy of this map with him?

driving. All lay dead in the roadway. The Indians paid in kind however, when a platoon of dragoons from Fort Lane overtook a scouting party and killed several of them.

On November 3, after a 25-mile forced march, stopping only long enough to make required scientific observations and notes, the party arrived at Fort Lane. The combined group crossed the Rogue River at Evans Ferry which was about three miles west of the river's confluence with Evans Creek. (Evans Creek passes under Interstate-5 at the western edge of the city of Rogue River.)

At Fort Lane, the party rested themselves as well as allowing their animals to freely eat all they wanted for the first time in days. Lt. Abbot recorded:

> We were treated with every possible kindness and attention.... Fort Lane is pleasantly situated on the side of a low hill, near the junction of Stuart [Bear] Creek with Rogue River. The barracks and the officer's quarters are built of logs plastered with clay. Much of the surrounding country is fertile and settled, but destructive Indian outbreaks are not unfrequent [*sic.*]. On the opposite bank... are peculiar basaltic hills with flat tops and precipitous sides.... The principal one, about 500 feet high [above the terrain], is called Table Rock. We took good observations at Fort Lane, by which the altitude above sea level was found to be 1,202 and latitude 42 25' 56". [In 1997, there are no remnants of Fort Lane to be found and even the historical marker is difficult to locate.]

During the northward trek earlier in the season, Lieutenants Williamson and Abbot took many side trips in a great effort to explore all possibilities for railroad routes. Now, late autumn, with Lt. Williamson departed and Lt. Abbot commanding the small force of scientists and helpers, with unrest among the Indians and no dependable military escort, he marched his group as quickly as possible with no side trips. The troupe stopped along the way only long enough to make basic observations.

With this in mind, one might want to look very closely at their next trek after leaving Fort Lane. The course took them south following Stuart (Bear) Creek toward the Siskiyou Mountains. Now known as the Bear Creek Valley, though commonly called the "Rogue River Valley," modern highways (and the railroad) pass through cities Central Point, Medford, Phoenix, Talent and Ashland, the latter being in the foothills of the Siskiyou Mountains.

During the last one hundred years, there have been all kinds of stories as to why the railroad, when finally built, did not go through Jacksonville? At the time of the Topographic Engineers' survey, Jacksonville was the largest town in Southern Oregon and was the county seat. Medford, five miles east of Jacksonville, had not yet been established.

On November 5, Lt. Abbot and his engineering party, without military escort, left Fort Lane and headed up Stuart Creek. Being fearful of an attack by Indians without notice, Lt. Abbot's object was to get through the Indian-troubled Rogue Valley as quickly as he could therefore they marched a "bee-line" for the Siskiyous – straight for the mountains – and did not stop for lunch. There would be no side trips – not even to Jacksonville. That night, camped, Lt. Abbot wrote:

> We found many homes deserted…and great alarm prevailing among settlers. We passed, on the way, a hot spring, the temperature of which was about 100 Fahr. A continual escape of gas through the water gave it the appearance of boiling. *

They camped that night 26 miles from Fort Lane, on Stuart Creek, near the base of the mountains. The following day the men crossed the mountains and the notes aptly describe their way:

> …the ascent was gradual but the road began to wind up a steep slope…very slippery by clay and rain, until at length [we reached] the summit 2,385 [feet] above [our last] camp. The descent for a short distance was very abrupt…. A pile of stones marked the boundary between Oregon and California. **

Lt. Abbot continued south by way of Yreka, Fort Jones then to Fort Redding. Here he was surprised to be met by Lt. Williamson who had traveled there from San Francisco to deliver new orders. The orders revealed it was the official opinion that the winter season was too close at hand to survey in the Sierra Nevadas before spring and anyway, some surveys there had already been done by the new State of California.

Lt. Williamson's orders from Washington, D. C. were for him to dispose of the field outfit, pay off his men and return to Washington as soon as possible. For these expert field surveyors to be bogged down in an office in Washington writing reports must surely have been a come-down from the excitement of the Oregon wilderness. They had viewed its lofty peaks, walked in serene valleys, were amazed seeing 25-pound salmon in rushing rivers, and were on the receiving end of an Indian war.

Lt. Abbot used great discretion in announcing their arrival in Washington for he merely inscribed: "The party reached the city in the later part of January 1856 and immediately entered upon office work." *** ◇

---

* This became famous Jackson Hot Springs on Highway 99 a few miles north of Ashland.
** The pass in the Siskiyou Mountains here is 4,310 feet elevation for highways 99 and I-5. Mt. Ashland, nearby, peaks at 7,553 feet.
*** The "office work" was to write the official report of the expedition. Find this listed in the bibliography under GOVERNMENT DOCUMENTS.

Chapter 1

Crossing the Siskiyous on a Modern Freight

"ALL ABOARD"! is the call by Conductor Ron Kneebone as his only passenger climbed into the cab – the author. Engineer Tom Moore, already seated at the controls, sounded two short blasts of the engine's horn then the freight train commenced to gently roll.

The engineer and Roseburg Dispatch, as well as Medford Depot, had been trading messages by FM radio for several minutes clearing the train to leave. This train, except engines, is 1,360 tons in 11 full cars and 7 empties. It is pulled by 6 diesel-electric units. This train is nearly one-third mile in length. Five of the engines are GP40's and there is one GP-38. The GP40's are rated at 3,000 horse power and the GP-38 is at 2,500 hp. It takes five units to be certain to clear the "hill," as the Siskiyou Mountains are called. However, these trains carry an operating sixth locomotive as insurance.

The summit of the Siskiyou Range is 7,533 feet elevation but the train takes a short cut to the other side using a tunnel at the 4,125 foot level.

This train is cleared to go as far as Montague, California where it will meet a north-bound train. The two crews will trade trains then the Medford crew will bring the new train to Medford.

The loaded cars are headed for and contain:

2 cars to	Roseville	lumber
1 car	Roseville	plywood
2 cars	Roseville	particle board
2 cars	West Colton	particle board
1 car	West Colton	lumber
1 car	West Colton	plywood
1 car	West Colton	laminated lumber
1 car	Klamath Falls	plywood

Track limit through Medford, Phoenix, Talent and Ashland, the four nearly abutting cities that stretched about 17 miles, is 10 mph. With many street and road crossings, Tom Moore is constantly on the horn. He admonished that a train's horn is for everyone's protection.

The railroad crosses Interstate-5 at MP 416.02 on 3.40% grade.

Stopping Distance

A train's stopping distance depends on speed and load. At about 15 miles an hour, with the load on this train, stopping distance was estimated to be about 200 yards.

At MP437, near Medford's south end, the train passed Associated Fruit Company siding. The engine swayed gently as it moved along. An extra tug on the horn handle for the benefit of a boy on a bicycle, who was slowly making his way across the track, brought

Six units of power pull train up the north side of the Siskiyou Mountains on 3.40% grade in this section.

the boy to attention. As we went by, he waved. We waved back.

People love trains and the majority of them wave to the trainmen and most trainmen wave back. It's sort of a friendly fraternity – waving onlookers and waving trainmen.

Ashland sits several hundred feet higher elevation than does Medford (elev. 1,382), Phoenix (1,543), Talent (1,635), Ashland (1,951 - 2,020). The track gently climbs into Ashland along the town's back side, west of highway 99, until crossing over the highway the track swings along Ashland's north edge.

When riding a train one's view of entering a town is from a different perspective, compared to the view from the street where there is seen all sorts of activity, attractive businesses, cars, people. On trains one views the backsides of buildings often shabby, little activity and often heaps of junk.

The once great Ashland railroad yards and active roundhouse in the days of steam, and magnificent depot with its linen-covered tables and napkins in the dining room, are now all historic memories. Our California-bound freight makes no stop in Ashland – merely jogs along at about 10-12 mph with frequent bells and whistles.

On the way through town the train passes a number of retirement complexes, one with a sign that seems aimed at train crews admonishing

GRACIOUS RETIREMENT LIVING

"Yeah," sounds engineer Tom, "Gracious"! Right! It's next to a track" with a whistle signal not 50 feet away. And nearly all south trains passing here are during the night.

There are stray dogs that race toward trains barking ferociously then turn abruptly and roar off the other way. On this sun shining spring Saturday, there is no shortage of sun-lovers. A number of young women, mostly in Bikini's, sun themselves in yards separated from the track only by a see-through (cyclone) fence. (Saturday trains are unexpected.) Some wave. We wave back. Some turn their heads away we suppose trying not to be seen, as an ostrich sticks its head in the sand? Other Ashland women, some in the buff on roofs, are not seen from the street level, but the cab on engines is frequently equal or higher than the roofs. Anyway, even at 10-12 miles an hour, the sights are merely fleeting if indeed seen at all for train crews, of course, keep their eyes glued to the track ahead.

Some autos, with stupid drivers, race across the track in spite of horn warnings. A dog, in a certain yard, always races in circles as the train approaches, observed the engineer.

Taking on diesel fuel in Medford yard before trip. Fuel contractor fills tanks with spill-proof nozzle.

Daily Operating Bulletin
Central Oregon & Pacific Railroad

CENTRAL OREGON & PACIFIC RAILROAD
DAILY OPERATING BULLETIN NO.550
EFFECTIVE AT 00:01 MAY 08,1997

OPERATING RULE OF THE WEEK:
GCOR 3.2 - Watch Requirement

SAFE WORK PRACTICE OF THE WEEK
SWP # 7 - When detraining from equipment which is standing or moving (no matter how slowly)

Where Form "A" is shown, do not exceed the speed indicated. "Flags at" column is used when flags are displayed less than distance prescribed by Rule 5.4.2 to indicate location.
Where Form "B" is shown be governed by Rules 15.2, 15.2.1, and 15.2.2 within the limits shown.
Where Form "C" is shown be governed by the instructions contained herein.

All Subdivisions:

VOID	ITEM	FORM	LIMITS	SPEED	FROM-UNTIL / FOREMAN / FLAGS AT / STOP

Roseburg Subdivision:

ITEM	FORM	MILEAGE/LIMITS	SPEED	FROM-UNTIL / FOREMAN / FLAGS AT / STOP
1	A	643.0 - 642.0	10 MPH	Springfield Jct. and Creswell
2	C	642.0 - 575.0		Uneven footing conditions
3	A	639.5 - 638.5	10 MPH	Springfield Jct. And Creswell
4	C	630.7		Uneven footing at South Switch Walker
5	A	623.8 - 623.6	10 MPH	Cottage Grove and Divide
6	A	621.0 - 619.0	10 MPH	Divide and Safley
7	A	618.0 - 609.0	20 MPH	
8	C	613.2		Safley siding south switch is out of service. None
9	A	612.4 - 612.2	10 MPH	Track 5980 Drain Emerald lead at crossing
10	A	609.0	5 MPH	Yoncalla siding, tk T5994, is out of service.
11	C	603.7		Be prepared to stop short of men and equipment working near tracks during Daylight hours.
12	C	603.3		
13	A	599.0 - 598.0	10 MPH	None
14	C	597.5		Rice Hill siding is out of service
15	C	595.0		Uneven footing on both sides of bridge
16	A	588.0 - 587.5	10 MPH	
17	C	Track 6203		Champion Spur out of service.
18	A	573.0 - 571.0	10 MPH	
19	C	573.0 - 571.0		Uneven footing on West side of main line and Roseburg yard Track 6107
20	C	572.65		Uneven footing both sides MT at Oak St.
21	C	572.3		Uneven footing between North Switch T6105 & South Switch T6120
22	C	571.0 - 507.9		Watch for uneven footing conditions
23	A	567.8	10 MPH	None
24	A	566.8	10 MPH	None
25	C	562.8		Switch 6418 is out of service
26	A	553.0 - 552.0	10 MPH	
27	A	546.0 - 544.0	10 MPH	
28	C	543.8		Uneven footing East side of crossing and materials in toe path.
29	C	538.0 - 536.0		Be on the lookout for men and equipment on or near tracks due to logging
30	A	533.0 - 533.1	10 MPH	
31	A	528.0	10 MPH	
32	C	524.0 - 522.0		Be prepared to stop. Slide conditions.
33	C	522.5		Hot box detector out of service
34	A	519.4 - 511.0	20 MPH	
35	A	516.0	10 MPH	Through tunnel # 4
36	A	502.0 - 466.0	10 MPH	
37	C	490.58		Switch is spiked & Out of service
38	A	462.5 - 458.5	10 MPH	
39	A	451.4	5 MPH	White City Branch
40	A	445.8 - 445.0	10 MPH	
41	C	444.8		Do not occupy Beall lane crossing unless signals are known to be working properly.
42	A	443.8	10MPH	Over switch track 7203

Siskiyou Subdivision:

VOID	ITEM	FORM	LIMITS	SPEED	FROM-UNTIL / FOREMAN / FLAGS AT / STOP
	43	C	441.3		Switch 7109 is out of service
	44	C	441.0 - 400.0		Uneven footing due to fibre optic cable trains
	45	A	440.5	10 MPH	Medford and Ashland
	46	A	435.0 - 433.0	10 MPH	Medford and Ashland
	47	A	422.0 - 421.3	10 MPH	
	48	A	416.25	5 MPH	
	49	C	412.2		Track 7518, Spiked and Locked due to MOW equipment.
	50	C	411.89 - 411.3		Tunnel #13. North and South ends of tunnel. Be prepared to stop short of falling rocks.
	51	A	411.0 - 406.7	10 MPH	
	52	A	406.7	5 MPH	
	53	A	406.7 - 403.0	10 MPH	
	54	A	401.0 - 400.0	10 MPH	
	55	C	398.1		Dragger out of service
	56	A	398.1 - 397.9	10 MPH	
	57	A	391.5 - 381.5	10 MPH	
	58	C	375.5		
	59	A	363.0	10 M	

CENTRAL OREGON AND PACIFIC RAILROAD
Track Bulletin Form C

NO. **340**   ON **SISKIYOU SUBDIVISION**   **May 8** 19**97**

TO: **ALL TRAINS SISKIYOU SUBDIVISION**   AT **ROSEBURG**

Main track out of service between MP 435.5 & MP 430. per Bruce Pfleiger.

Southern Pacific Transportation Company

TRAIN ORDER No. **1212**
To C&I

WESTWARD TRAINS   DATE JAN 2 1982
ENGS WORKING IN YARD LIMITS

Station **ROSEBURG**

DO NOT EXCEED 10 MPH
BETWEEN MP 492.9 AND MP 493.05
EAST OF HUGO BETWEEN MP 514.5
AND MP 514.7 EAST OF GLENDALE
AND BETWEEN MP 563.85 AND MP 563.90
EAST OF DILLARD

DES

Complete Time 147 P
JAN 4 1982 M   FREADMAN

Railroads have traditionally published train orders about track conditions with a separate sheet (LOWER RIGHT) **for each situation. CORP publishes the "Daily Operating Bulletin"** (TOP) **at the Roseburg headquarters. This is distributed to sub-stations by fax daily. "Track Bulletin C"** (LOWER LEFT) **is issued any time during the 24-hour period when a new order is needed. These Form C remarks are correlated at Roseburg and become the next day's "DOB."**

(FROM TOP) View of front of Medford Depot from Conductor's seat in locomotive as train leaves station. The right-of-way through Medford yard. (CENTER LEFT AND LOWER) Boys on bikes watch engine as it passes.

Example of abandoned, dangling, trackside telephone lines. Railroads often issue contracts to remove old pole lines for there is salvage value in the copper wire and glass insulators. In many instances where track runs through heavily forested areas, timber falling contracts are awarded to keep the right-of-way clear, for during winter storms, trees often fall across a track. These clear areas also provide a firebreak in event of forest fire.

Of five CORP dispatchers, Jan Leath is shown. Lisa Clark was on the desk when the call came:

3084 WHERE AAARRRRRRRRRRRRE YOU?

Trains With Radios

Historically, railroads operated their own telephone systems and had miles of wire hung on poles alongside the tracks. Some of these wires operated the signals and in some places commercial telephone lines were also there.

Traditionally, many businesses have used short-wave radio for communications with field forces, but this AM radio method can be noisy at times due to atmospheric interference. In recent years, in many instances, the radio has given way to cellular telephones however, when a great many cell phones are used in a given operation, the cost can become prohibitive. And there are still black-out areas where cellular telephones will not work.

CORP used cell phones for some time after getting started on the Siskiyou Line, but since November 1996, has used Mototola FM radio. The sound is sharp and clear of interference. With repeaters, Roseburg Central Dispatch can reach all geographic areas of its operations .

The train crew is busy every minute. Conductor Ron, with the Daily Operating Bulletin issued by CORP Dispatch, keeps engineer Tom appraised of "slow" and other orders that are pertinent to a safe trip. Example:

Tunnel #13   North and South ends of tunnel
    "be prepared to stop short of falling rock."
MP401.6   Hi-Wide detector is out of service
MP 398.1   Dragger is out of service.

Today our train has been cleared from Medford on Track Warrant #20 only as far as MP416 due to a work crew in the area. At MP416 our train stops as if to allow three deer time to scamper into the forest. Then, conductor Ron seeks clearance, by radio, to proceed. Track Warrant #25 is issued at 12:17 p.m. to proceed to Montague. While stopped, we walk ahead for pictures.

Radios in all trains are a great improvement over having to stop every few miles for the conductor to get off, go to the trackside telephone shed to call in for track conditions and orders. Every one of those sheds had a name and every name was on the railroad map.

On today's trip, several times the radio barked with a question, "3084 where *arrrrr*e you"? Engineer Tom would answer with the number of the nearest mile post to which came a quick reply: "OK – Roseburg Dispatch – out."

The train passes many ranches where in the nearby yards along the trees, are beautiful horses. Many Ashland old-timers live alongside old Highway 99, a grapevine of a road over the summit. It was the main route until Interstate-5 came along.

We rounded Dollarhide Curve where long ago the track was atop a giant trestle. In 1918, this was filled. The train has its own "grapevine" to follow as it swings around graceful curves and enters Tunnel #15.

Concrete movable telephone booths replaced original wood shacks along the track. Booth shown, with equipment removed, is at Siskiyou. Another is exhibited in Medford Railroad Park.

(LEFT) **Steinman Siding and old highway 99 parallel main line.** (RIGHT) **Engineer reads only signal on right of track. Viewed is "Yellow" Block signal – clear. OK to proceed.**

This is a short tunnel (258 feet) with a slight curve. Lo! In the middle, a young deer was caught in the headlights. The gross growl of the engine and its three brilliant headlights spook the deer which froze, then it turned and loped ahead of the train into the sunlight. But the deer ran along the track wavering as if not knowing which way to turn. We were fearful it might turn into the track where it would meet a sudden messy end when suddenly, the deer did a quick turn away from the track and disappeared into the woods. Whew!

Engineer Tom Moore said he has seen deer, a few elk, bobcats, cougars (one with two cubs), porcupines and in the Shasta River Valley, an occasional antelope. When asked, he said he had never seen a bear.

Along the way we passed what was left of trees that had fallen across the track. Gary Michener, a track supervisor, who patrols the line between Medford and Montague in his "high-railer," – a pickup truck with flange wheels – carries a chain saw and clears fallen trees. We passed several examples of Gary's work. In the winter, it is common for trains to carry a chain saw for the same purpose.

On January 2, 1997, in the midst of a disastrous storm that caused major havoc in Southern Oregon for a

Track Supervisor Gary Michener and his High-Railer truck. He, and other track people, has carefully trained eyes to look closely for anything out of the ordinary while cruising around 10 mph. Inspectors often walk the curves. They communicate emergencies to dispatcher by FM radio.

week,* Michener was "tooling long" at his usual 10 miles an hour. He arrived at MP416 and lo! A landslide had obliterated the track for about 200 yards. He radioed Medford and held a train that was about to depart. He said it took a week to get the mess cleared and the track train-ready once again.

The ride from Tunnel #15 to Tunnel #14 is on a great loop that clings to the side of the mountain. The two tunnels are more-or-less nearly on top of each other. It is said that the location of Tunnel #15 – 258 feet long – could not be just a "cut" in the side of the mountain, but a tunnel was required for a cut would have removed the stability of the earth to support Tunnel #14. No. 14 is longer – 1,258 feet – and also curved at 14 degrees. This degree of curvature pushes near the limit of ability of standard cars to keep their footing. Surveyors, in preparing for a railroad, try to keep curves not generally more than 15 degrees, but most cars can handle 22 degrees in a pinch. One degree more, and the whole train jumps the track.** Our train's wheels screech around the curves in spite of frequent automatic wheel oilers in the track.

Not only did the surveyors determine that tunnels needed to be constructed for this line, but trestles as well. There are two trestles that cross Wall Creek. The lower crossing is before Tunnel #15. But it's the big, higher trestle between Tunnels #13 and #14 that is the goal of photographers and artists. This steel girder trestle is higher on the mountain and higher from base to rail – 180 feet. It is also 581 feet long, is curved, and on 3.38 percent grade – MP 413.94 - 413.80. Our train crosses at a steady 10 mph.

We recently walked it and determined that although there is a sturdy steel mesh floor, one may lose his balance if walking and looking down at the same time. We walk with one hand on the guard rail noting we are eyeball-level with the tops of the trees.

Seth Trimpey is probably Southern Oregon's greatest train buff. This 13-year, seen along the way on today's trip, with his dad, Tye, were at the crossings and other access points where they could view the rumbling train and wave to the crew. Seth is special to train-folks and nearly every train person in the region knows about young Seth.

The boy, who lives to know about trains, was born with a heart defect, has cerebral palsy, and other maladies. Railroaders arranged for Seth to have his own

(TOP) **Conductor's view of his train** (CENTER) **Interstate-5 passed under railroad at MP 416.02** (LOWER) **View of freeway from the railroad bridge.**

---

* The damage, particularly in downtown Ashland's historic district, ran into the millions. For details, refer to *FLOOD! Ashland Devastated – New Year's Day 1997 – An Oregon Documentary* in bibliography.

** Crooked logging railroads, for which Shay, Willamette, Climax and Heisler geared engines were designed, can handle up to 30 degrees but, for a safety measure, with few exceptions, track was not put down tighter than 25 degrees. For details, see chapter "Railroading in the Woods" in *This is Logging and Sawmilling* in bibliography.

What's a railroad without tunnels, high trestles and bridges? (FROM TOP) After negotiating Dollarhide curve, southbound train about to enter south portal of Tunnel 15. Train about to emerge from Tunnel 15. Train, climbing a 3.40% grade, about to enter north portal of Tunnel 14.

(TOP) **Curved, Wall Creek High Trestle MP413.80, 581-feet long on 3.38% grade. Research companion, Norm VanManen peers over the side 180-feet above the creek.**
(lower) **Main line highway (I-5) and main line CORP railroad track (the track at 3.38% grade). View from perch on side of cliff is generally southeast.**

Norm VanManen, with stout walking stick who stands 6 feet 4 inches, is miniaturized alongside immense rocks along right-of-way of steep track about mid-way between Tunnels 13 and 14.

genuine full-size caboose in his yard.

Seth and his dad were waving near trackside at Siskiyou as the train rattled along and disappeared one car at a time into the mouth of Tunnel #13.

These railroad tunnels are not lighted and train crews do not usually turn on cab lights (dim as they are) for tunnels, most tunnels being relatively short.

As your cameraman-reporter was at the end of a long roll of film, to be ready when daylight again was met, the Olympus OM-1 camera was unloaded and reloaded in the dark.

Engineer Tom Moore recalled that he "drove" the first Central Oregon & Pacific Railroad train over the "hill" after CORP took over from SP. Southern Pacific had abandoned the line through these mountains for two-and-a-half years. With no maintenance, the track was in poor shape and required much cleanup before it could be used.*

Tunnel #13 is the scene of an infamous affair that has been called "The Last Great Train Holdup in the West." In October 1923, the three DeAutremont Brothers, who were certain that The San Francisco Express Train #13, was carrying a large amount of cash in the Railway Post Office (RPO) Car, boarded the train as the engineer checked his brakes at Siskiyou and entered the tunnel. The brothers, when the train reached the opposite end of the tunnel, forced the train

---

* When CORP announced its first run for June 5, 1995, employees posted bright red posters on all crossings advising locals that trains would start on that date. There was general wailing in some neighborhoods by people who claimed they had moved to the mountains especially to Cottonwood Creek Valley to be "away from noise," etc. They protested the rail line's reopening. But the deed was done and trains rolled on schedule. Tom Moore, as has been pointed out, was engineer on that first train. He reported that people complained about the train's horn which must be sounded at all crossings. His admonition: "This track was put down in 1887 and has, for the most part, run ever since. If people don't like the sound of trains, they should not choose to live near a train track."

32

to stop, murdered the train crew and dynamited the mail car. The blast killed the mail clerk, a federal employee. This brought in the FBI.

After all this disaster, the bandits did not get even one thin dime but had murdered four men. The search for them was long and detailed but eventually, all three were caught and sentenced to life in the Oregon State Pen.*

Starting at the north end of Tunnel #13, the grade is the steepest of all grades on the former Southern Pacific system (now Central Oregon & Pacific Railroad) – 3.67 percent. This grade is nearly constant for 5 miles. The site of the former siding at White Point can no longer be identified. There has never been a siding at Colestin, where the famous Colestin Hotel and mineral springs was located, but SP had a station at trackside there. We passed at 10 mph, with horn shrieking for the crossing at Colestin Road, and viewed the lush green grounds of the hotel's site as we rolled along.**

Seth and his dad had stopped at the crossing where Seth waved and we waved back.

The Siskiyou Line crosses Interstate-5 two times on the Oregon side and once on the California side.

About here there was another squawk on the radio just as before:

3084 where arrrre you?

Conductor Ron answered with the number of the nearest milepost to which came a friendly reply:

OK – Roseburg dispatch – out.

This freight train was winding its way down the track that started as 3.67 percent at the north end of Tunnel #13, as has been mentioned, then eased a little at 3.30 percent around immense Gregory Curve. In this neighborhood, the train passes from Oregon into California, back into Oregon and finally into California as the track zigzags it way south. The route takes so much real estate on Gregory Curve, that no satisfactory photograph of it has ever been seen made from the ground or from a train. The California line is officially crossed at MP 403.157.

Seth and his Dad drive along the road parallel to the track, Seth looking at the locomotive and waving all the while. When the road makes a quick S turn away from the track, the engineer gives Seth a quick "toot" on the horn.

At Cole's Stage Station, some black birds are perched on the trackside wires and deer race across the

---

* For the full story and many original pictures, see *Oregon's Great Train Holdup Bandit's Murder 4 – Didn't Get A Dime* in bibliography
** For an account, and pictures, of the excursions to the Colestin Hotel, see chapter "Rogue River Valley Railroad."

Tunnel 13, 4,125 elevation. (TOP) **Train is about to enter north portal. Dot in center is south portal at end of 3,107 foot bore. (LOWER) Emerging at the south portal. The steep downhill ride at 3.67% started at the north portal and extends for five miles.**
It was at this south portal when Train No. 13, The San Francisco Express, emerged on October 11, 1923, that the DeAutremont Brothers blew up the Railway Post Office car and murdered the train crew and the postal clerk.

Winter Storms Keep Siskiyou Railroaders Busy

Snow plows in the Siskiyous
(TOP) **Picture at Siskiyou about 1900.**
(CENTER) **Antique plow exhibited with antique** (LOWER) **flanger (for removing light snow) at Dunsmuir Railroad Park. Note chimney in roof of flanger for coal stove to try to keep attendant warm. Another flanger is exhibited at Medford Railroad Park.**
When CORP took over operation of the Siskiyou Line, It did so with no snow plow or flanger, but could charter such from SP if needed. Spokesman said CORP's ballast spreader will work "just fine" if needed for clearing snow – *if* the snow is not too thick.

(TOP) **Automatic wheel lubrication device (wheel oiler) installed on rails near curves helps wheels roll easier, also cuts down on screeching of wheels on the curves.** (CENTER) **Worn spot on rail. Mostly caused by slipping drivers on engines sometimes by engineers trying to start a heavy train too fast.** (LOWER) **Rail grinder is a self-propelled "grindstone" used to restore rail surface and preserve life of rails. Keeping track smooth is CORP aim for its 190 miles of 113-pound rail with balance in 136-pound on main lines and on key sidings. Maintenance-of-way crews with CORP grind about 90 miles of track a year. Grinder is based at Roseburg.**

(TOP) Continuous surface (welded) rail makes for safer, quieter travel as there are no "clicks" as wheels bump across usual gap between rails. (CENTER) "Date-nail." The "31" means that the tie into which this nail was driven was installed in 1931. Date-nails are instant record of when a tie was installed, helps determine age of the tie on later inspections. Tie shown in on siding at Siskiyou. There is reason to believe this siding was the main line track at that time. (LOWER) Signal has been removed, all that remains is the base. The Siskiyou summit right-of-way is in the "dark," as all signals have been removed. The same is true for Cow Creek Canyon. Railroads today depend on radio for close contact with trains.

Cottonwood Creek Valley is Scenic Wonderland

The grade in this area is mostly 3.30% - 2.30%. It was a wonderful sightseeing trip on the passenger trains. In days of yore, there were stops made at Colestin Mineral Springs Resort in this area. Note unpaved Colestin Road.

The great Gregory Curve (loop) sprawls around scenic hills in grades at 3.30% on the northern end (Oregon) to 1.80% near the "ONE LANE BRIDGE" sign a few yards into California. (LOWER) Climbing Bailey Hill at 346-foot long Interstate-5 overpass (MP399.27).

track. A little later we get a wave and we wave back to a fellow riding a D-8 cat who is clearing his land near the track as we start up Bailey Hill at MP 399. The weather has turned warm compared to the crispness in the mountains. One could become sleepy here if there was not so much activity.

The train passes a corral full of steers and with the roar of the giant, they turn tail and head, *enmasse*, toward the far fence.

The matter of water tankers came up. Months ago, two had been side-tracked in the Medford yard and we wondered what became of them. Tom points out that the 100,000 gallon converted tank cars, are inserted into trains immediately behind the engines in fire season. On an outrigger of pipes that run the length of the car, are sprinklers that can spray an area to as wide as about 20 feet from the track soaking the weeds near the rails to put out any spark-caused fires.

On top of one water car is a car length platform and a large coiled hose. A man can stand here to fight forest fires if needed.

Sparks can flash from wheels on tight curves, or there may be sparks emitted by the exhaust stacks. The latter is not major with diesel-electrics, but in the old days of wood-fired steamers, for train men to be in a shower of sparks was "the name of the game." Many magnificent wood trestles burned to the ground because of locomotive-caused fires.

The water car season is from mid to late May into the fall. Usually, water cars are required to be carried between 8 a.m. and 8 p.m. As the trains through the Siskiyou Mountains are night trains, they seldom haul water cars.

100,000 gallon water car. Note reel of hose near end of platform. Hose can be used in fighting forest fires.

Which Way ?

Southern Pacific had a language all of its own when talking about directions. All trains operating between 0 degrees and 180 degrees were said to be "east" trains. All others were "west." At Tunnel #13, where the DeAutremonts held up the train, these bandits boarded at the "east" end of the tunnel and the mail car was dynamited at the "west" end of the tunnel according to SP lingo. Yet everybody familiar with the tunnel knows that the men jumped aboard at the "north" portal and did their deeds at the "south" portal.

For Central Oregon & Pacific Railroad, it's just plain "north," "south, "east," "west."

Life seems simpler that way.

Our train was now out of the mountains and had only Bailey Hill to conquer. The train was now moving at about 20 mph. Engineer Tom Moore pointed out a bald eagle's nest atop a power pole – there was an eagle in it – then we were alongside the Klamath River for a way. A big bird, an eagle or an osprey, dives into the river, did his fishing and was sky-bound in what seemed only an instant.

Tom mentioned that an engineer should never rely on his sight alone when following the rails to control his train. "Maintain speed within half a mile per hour, watch instruments and visualize your surroundings for train handling is a finesse."

The bell is clanged on the quarter-mile markers and the horn is sounded with "vigor" with the traditional 2 longs, a short and a lo*nnnn*g. The final blast carries all the way through a crossing.

Engineers must have excellent skills to maintain the posted schedule and operate a train with safety. A trained ear is essential, Tom admonished as the engineer must recognize every sound his train emits.

Tom emphasized that people in cars who "test" trains at crossings usually lose and there is little an engineer can do about it because a train cannot be "stopped on a dime" as many people seem to expect.

By now we were opposite Hornbrook, a near-deserted hamlet on the railroad. There is a yard here and some parked empty box cars, but we do not stop. Six more miles to go and the train is now "flying" at 25 mph. We slow for the stop at Montague. Here the crew and the engines are positioned for return to Medford and the cars are side-tracked. A switcher and crew with northbound cars will arrive from Black Butte Junction. The crews "swap" trains to take the cars from Medford further south, and the incoming

39

Crossing the Klamath River MP 390.94

**Hornbrook yard(MP393.1). Girls scrutinize the sight –
one with hands on hips, the other with hands over ears
as the horns were sounding for next crossing.**

train will be hooked to our 6-engine consist for a trip back over the "hill" into Oregon.

It will be a long day for the Medford crew. We step off, shake hands around, and declare "Thanks. It was an exciting trip."

We go back to Medford on the freeway at considerably more than the 10 mph freight train speed we enjoyed while climbing and descending the mountain. Of the train:

"What an amazing trip"!

◇

Central Oregon & Pacific Railroad Runs Logging Trains Every Day

Freshly cut logs are loaded at Roseburg Forest Products yard at Weed, California then transported on a Central Oregon & Pacific Railroad logging train to the Dillard, Oregon mill. (TOP) **Modern-day log train as it nears Dillard** —Keith J. Johnson photo)
(CENTER) **Each railroad car holds equivalent of three highway logging trucks.**
(LOWER) **Unloading logs at Dillard mill.** —Bert Webber photos

(TOP) **Montague, California. For the photography trip over the Siskiyou Mountains, May 8, 1997, are Bert Webber, Research Photo-journalist, Tom Moore, Engineer, Ron Kneebone, Conductor.**
—Margie Webber photo (LOWER) **Three power units await a train on the Weed wye.** —Bert Webber photo

(TOP AND CENTER LEFT) **Mt. Shasta (14,162 feet elev.), snow-covered all year, is wonderful sight anytime**. —Bert Webber photo. **Black Butte (3,912 feet elev.) holds snow only in winter** —author collection.
(RIGHT CENTER) **Black Butte railroad junction is in shadow of Black Butte. Of the two railroad pictures, top was made in 1957** (author collection) **, lower in 1996.** —Keith J. Johnson photo
(LOWER LEFT) **SP freight pulls into Black Butte Jct.** —Keith J. Johnson photo

George W. Norman
Reminiscences of a Railroad Engineer 1939 – 1979

THE MOST VALUABLE TOOL a railroad man has is his watch. Here is a picture of mine. I purchased this watch shortly after I went to work for the Southern Pacific. For the next forty years this watch was my constant companion. Whenever I went to work, the watch went to work with me.

Over the years I wore out several winding stems that had to be replaced. Regular cleaning and oiling, replacing broken main spring or a cracked jewel was the only attention my friend every required.

The original purchase price was $60 - a lot of money then. But he was responsible for earning all of my pay checks. The safety of myself, my crew and the train was his assignment. If the train was late it was not his fault.

It is with gratitude and respect I have taken this picture and I would like to say, "Thank you Mr. Watch for a job well done."

—GWN

WHEN I STARTED my railroad career, my headquarters was at Dunsmuir, California. The superintendent and all his people were located there.

The people who manned the trains over the Siskiyou Mountains all lived in Dunsmuir. I knew all of them and their families. I came to Dunsmuir in 1925 and went through school there. This is where I studied and became a railroad engineer.

Everything north of Ashland was called the Portland Division. Everything south of Red Bluff, California, was called the Sacramento Division.

All of that has now been changed.

For awhile, men that manned the trains for the Siskiyou Mountain run came from Dunsmuir but they go to Ashland, Oregon and go off duty there. For a long time this was called the Shasta Division.

My seniority district covered from Crescent Lake in Oregon to Gerber, California on the Cascade line and on the Siskiyou Line I ran from Ashland to Black Butte.

At Klamath Falls, I worked the Modoc Line from Klamath Falls to Wendel, California.

I believe I worked on every type locomotive the SP owned and a number on the Union Pacific. I worked in road service, yard service, passenger service and I enjoyed every day of it. Time has changed everything but I still have a lot of fond memories of the old Shasta Division.

—George W. Norman
Klamath Falls, Oregon May 3, 1997

Chapter 2

Oregon & California Rail Road Company

Portland, Oregon   Sept. 5, 1870 - Jan. 3, 1927
Sold to Southern Pacific Company on Jan. 3, 1927
(Springfield Junction - Black Butte Junction sold to RailTex (Central Oregon & Pacific Railroad) 1994—)

WE RECALL there were two routes suggested by the Secretary of War as potentials for north-south railroads in Oregon. One was through the Deschutes Valley and the other through the Willamette Valley. Of the two, which would be decided?

First: Which of the two might best serve shippers?

Second: Which route might best serve the people?

A railroad can only succeed if there is revenue producing freight to be hauled. While the fares paid for carrying passengers is significant, presuming there are many persons who need or want to ride a train, the money maker has always been the freight.

It did not take railroaders very long to decide that the Deschutes route was not feasible at the time: very little freight, very few passengers. A route through the Willamette Valley would serve established and growing settlements, many farms – some quite large as were orchards – and burgeoning timber businesses in the Willamette-Umpqua-Rogue Valleys route.

The western valleys route won.

Enter politics and big money.*

There was a threat in Portland that powerful California interests did not want the track running south of Eugene to pass through Douglas, Josephine and Jackson Counties – the towns of Roseburg, Grants Pass, Medford, Ashland – because they had bigger ideas. The thrust of their plan was to tap into the transcontinental line at Winnemucca, Nevada, cross into Oregon and on into the Willamette Valley, which the rails would cross, then terminate at Newport on the Pacific Coast.

Yaquina Bay, on which Newport was situated, was an excellent port. If freight from California and from the Orient came into Newport (totally skipping the Columbia River and Portland), a load of freight would save hundreds of extra sea and river miles as well as save rail miles by being loaded on trains at Newport with hot-shot destination of Omaha. In the Omaha yards, it would be a simple matter to switch through cars for Chicago, New York and other points. This was called the "Winnemucca-to-the-Sea route.* (Today, highway 140 somewhat mimics the plan starting at Winnemucca then proceeds westerly through Lakeview, Klamath Falls, Medford; then on Interstate-5 to Grants Pass then finally to the coast on highway 199, ending at Crescent City, California.)

---

* Another railroad venture called the "Humboldt Line" envisioned by B. J. Pengra of Eugene in 1867, sought to lay rails for a connection to the transcontinental route (then building east from Sacramento to Utah) from Eugene to the Humboldt River in Nevada. His route would go up the Middle Fork of the Willamette River into the Cascade Mountains to the Deschutes then Sprague Rivers north of Goose Lake near present Lakeview, Oregon then southeast through Surprise Valley and Black Rock Canyon to Lassen Meadows on the Humboldt River. A part of this route, through Nevada's Black Rock Canyon, was first explored then used as the Applegate Trail in 1846. Refer to *Over the Applegate Trail to Oregon in 1846* in bibliography.

(THIS PAGE) **Driving the first spike to begin building the Oregon Central Railroad which later became the Oregon & California Railroad. The excitement of the event was centered around the Portland corner of Southeast First and Washington Streets in 1869. This was Ben Holladay's company at this time. The carpenter's tool chest in foreground took two men to lift it.**

Oregon & California Rail Road locomotive reaches Clackamas River after first 25 miles of track completed from Portland in December 1869. Man in foreground is Hans Thielsen with one of his sons. Thielsen, a noted railroad surveyor-engineer, was brought to Oregon at age 56 by Ben Holladay to build the O&C. He then continued with Henry Villard to complete the line into the Siskiyous but was relieved when Central Pacific took over construction. Thielsen was the power behind decision to drill Buck Rock Tunnel, which successors canceled in favor of present, less favorable route. Mt. Thielsen, elevation 9,173 foot spire in Southern Oregon near Crater Lake, honors him.

The promotion of that scheme was not well liked by influential Portlanders, so it was quietly dropped.

But another direction was pushed. This would skip all the Southern Oregon towns and follow Lt. Williamson's route easterly up the Middle Fork of the Willamette River to the highland east of the Cascade Mountains, then run south to Klamath Falls and into California. The argument went that while there was less revenue to be generated along this route – very few people lived there – the mountains to be crossed were much easier and less expensive in which to lay rails, compared with the Siskiyou route and, operating the trains would be at considerably lower cost.

But the politicians did not reckon with the people who sought the closeness of a train for getting them to and fro. Besides, the people argued, having a train come through existing towns would guarantee steady growth. People in Southern Oregon exerted assertiveness, aggressiveness and brashness absolutely bellowing their demand for the route to California be built through their area. There were businesses already operating along the length of the Willamette Valley and in Jackson County's Rogue Valley. Roseburg was well established and there was business there to be had. The railroad chiefs listened. The arguments for the Willamette-Umpqua-Rogue Valleys route won.

Once the trains started, it was quickly discovered that the steep grade in the Siskiyous always required helper locomotives. Extra engines cost extra money to operate. On all up-hill-bound trains, the speed was

Route of O&C from Portland to California line. Where track crosses name "Canyonville" in its letter "n," is the Cow Creek Canyon. Woodville is now Rogue River. "Old Fort Lane" (now gone), Jacksonville, Ashland shown however Medford was not yet established. Proposed "Humboldt" line shown at arrow.

WASH
OREGON
PACIFIC OCEAN
COLUMBIA RIVER
CASCADE
OREGON AND CALIFORNIA RAIL ROAD
C. Disappointment
Pt. Adams
Astoria
Clifton
Westport
Clatskanie
Quincy
Jewell
Vesper
Saddle Mt.
Rainier
St. Helens
Nehalem R.
Nehalem
Veronia
Garibaldi
Wilson R.
Kilchis
Tillamook B.
Tillamook
C. Lookout
Gaston
Hillsboro
Portland
Milwaukee
Oregon C.
Sandy
Damascus
Eagle C.
Viola
Springwater
Clackamas
Mt. Hood
Prattville
Wapinitia
Kingsley
15 Mile
Mill C.
Cross V.
Deschutes
Baker
Cross Hollow
Ante
The Dalles
Celilo
E. Yamhill
La Fayette
Mc. Minnville
Sheridan
Dayton
Canby
Molalla
Glad Tidings
Silverton
Amity
Dallas
SALEM
Stipp
Turner
Santiam R.
Molalla R.
Salmon R.
Devils L.
Independence
Lewisville
Morgan
Mt. Pleasant
Mt. Jefferson
Cross Keys
Willoughby Creek
Newport
Oneatle
Corvallis
Albany
Tangent
Sodaville
Sweet Home
Black Butte
Metolius C.
Yaquina B.
Newton
Enterprise
Halsey
Blue R.
Squaw
Collins
Alsea R.
Alsea
Monroe
Harrisburg
McKenzie R.
Belknap
McKenzie Br.
Three Sisters
Camp Polk
Pineville
Loon L.
Gate C.
C. Perpetua
Siuslaw R.
Eugene C.
Springfield
Jay
Leaburg
Mohawk
Florence
Chillicoose
Cartwright
Pleasant Hill
Cottage Grove
Paulina Mts.
East L.
Takenitch
Smith R.
Sulphur Sp.
Gardner
Umpqua R.
Elk C.
Drain
Paulina L.
Diamond Pk.
Odell L.
Yoncalla
Kellogg
Oakland
Crescent L.
Butte
Summit L.
Coos B.
Empire C.
Coose R.
Umpqua
Wilbur
North Fork Umpqua R.
Catching
Sumner
Cleveland
Roseburg
Diamond L.
Randolph
Coquille R.
Civil Bend
Otello
Round Prairie
Myrtle C.
Camas Val.
Bear C.
Klamath Marsh
Bandon
Parkersburg
Middle Fk.
N. Canyonville
Elk C.
Pauline
Thor
Silver
Flores L.
Holland
Crater L.
South Fk.
C. Blanco
Sixes R.
Newcastle
Elk R.
Port Orford
Whelpley
Rogue R.
Mt. Pitt
Upper Klomath L.
Pai.
Euchre C.
Lucky Queen
Grant Pass
Woodville
Brownsboro
Naylor
Swan L.
Spring Riv.
E. Ellensburg
Illinois R.
Wilderville
Murphy
Old Ft. Lane
Table Rock
Jacksonville
L. of Woods
Aspen L.
Linkville
Dairy
Bonanza
Williams C.
Applegate
Sterling
Ashland
Lakeport
Pistol R.
Kerby
Uniontown
Baron
Langell Val.
Tule Lake
Brownerton
Althouse
Walde
Steamboat
Wright
Lower Klomath L.
Rhett L.

125 123 121
45
43

48

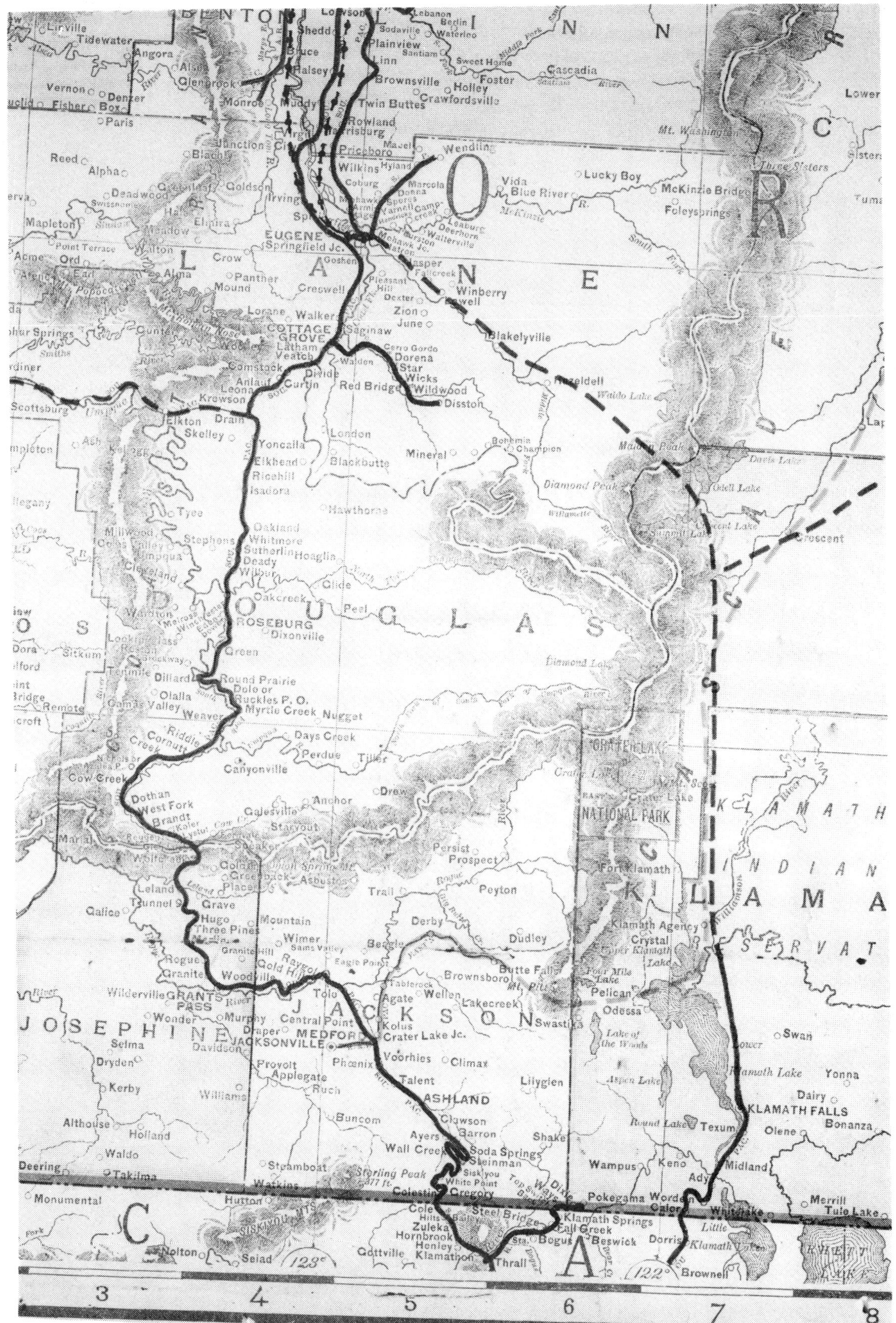

Oregon & California Rail Road Siskiyou Line (bold line) and proposed Central Oregon route (broken line) of Portland promoters. Both routes approximate original Corps of Topographical Engineers 1855 survey. The Siskiyou route was completed in 1877. The Central Oregon "Natron" cutoff, Cascade Line was achieved in 1926. —Ben Truwe collection

"HISTORIC PLACE" reads the Douglas County highway marker seen on the county road along Cow Creek Canyon. Indeed, for across the creek is O&C Tunnel No. 1. Long Ago by-passed, a northbound SP train passed outside the runnel. (LOWER) Train has just emerged from Tunnel No. 2 and crosses the 1905 model bridge at West Fork.
—Keith J. Johnson photos
—(inset by Bert Webber)

very slow, then there was lost time at the summit for dropping the helpers and for brake checking before going down the other side. The accountants kept close watch on expenses. *

ooOOOoo

Henry Villard had come into control of the Oregon and California Railroad through a succession of deals and personages that included Ben Holladay.

> **Ben Holladay is important in Oregon rail history because it was he who got construction going on the railroad in 1868 to link California with Portland.**

By 1873, his trains were rolling into Roseburg but there they ground to a stop for nearly ten years. This "end-of-track" situation is attributed by historians to the national financial panic of that year and by what some term mishandling by Holladay. Three years later, Villard came on the scene. In super-colossal deals, which included taking over where Ben Holladay left off, and involving other railroads and steamship interests that gave Wall Street financiers the "willies," Villard put together his package to push out of Roseburg to the California line.

Villard hired surveyors and ordered them into the field. But owing to the extraordinary challenge of trying to get through the Calapooya Mountains in winter, he had only sixty miles graded during 1881-82. He would not have his route finalized to the California border until the summer of 1883, primarily due to extreme conditions encountered in conquering the Siskiyous. By then he had exhausted his resources. He said in one of his addresses to the Portland Board of Trade:

> The Oregon and California Company gave me more trouble than any other of my enterprises. This continued throughout my connection of nearly twelve years with that ill-fated concern…. The proceeds from new bonds remaining after paying off a mortgage lien [elsewhere] proved upon the final location of the Siskiyou line to fall short by nearly $2,000,000 of the total required to … the junction with the Central Pacific [in California]. This was dreadful … threatening the company with the fatal calamity of having to stop work and consequent dead waste of millions [already] spent on grading, bridging and tunnels. [Our funds] were exhausted in January 1883 but we managed to continue work until spring.

Finally, a scheme evolved for a firm, the Oregon & Transcontinental Company, to work with the O&C whereby O&T would finish the construction then lease the finished road back to O&C.

Intrigue in Southern Oregon

When the Oregon & California Rail Road pushed south of Eugene, folks in Jacksonville began to count the weeks before the track would be at their doorsteps. But, as we have seen, politics and finances stopped construction at Roseburg where the trains terminated for a decade. When work resumed, rumors flew through Southern Oregon that the rails would follow straight up the Bear Creek Valley and *miss Jacksonville* completely. This was unthinkable – if you lived in Jacksonville!

Some sources claim railroad officials met with Jacksonville businessmen offering to bring the track into their city if the town put up money – $25,000. Others claim when it was realized that their town was to be skipped, folks, on their own, assembled with a plan to make "donations." They believed the railroad was running low on money and the railroad would exchange the cash handout for a track into town.

There seems to be as many opinions why Jacksonville was not included in the rail laying plans of the construction engineers as there are speakers and writers on the subject.

Should one claim the ultimate decision as to where to lay track was based on Lt. Abbot's survey, then one might make a case that skipping Jacksonville was because of the Rogue Indian War. 2nd Lt. Abbot had decided there would be no "side trips," as had been the custom, until they were away from the areas of Indian troubles. In his judgment, any route other than straight along Bear Creek to get out of the Indians' way would constitute a "side trip."

Jacksonville is nestled in the foothills of the Siskiyou Mountains. Getting there on the road from Fort Lane by way of Central Point, or on another road later to become known as Stage Road, would entail a rambling route through tree-covered foothills. If there were Indians planning to ambush passersby, most anywhere along this route would have been satisfactory. Lt. Abbot, a seasoned observer of terrain and not yearning for any risks, fails to note his thinking on the matter of these routes in his diary – if he even knew of them. He merely marched up Bear Creek missing Jacksonville by at least five miles as if the town did not exist.

---

* Business in the Portland area was developing at a pace that required construction of a more economical route to California. Accordingly, what became known as the Cascade Line (Natron cutoff) – Eugene to Black Butte in California by way of Klamath Falls – was opened to mainline traffic in 1926. Previous promoters, looking at Lt. Williamson's route, had suggested crossing the Cascades east of Eugene but work progressed only as far as Natron. This route over the Cascades by way of Klamath Falls, would replace the impractical and often troublesome (delays) on the Siskiyou Mountains line. When Southern Pacific completed work, the Cascade Line had 19 tunnels but is 23.7 miles shorter than the Siskiyou route, and saves 2.867 feet of elevation gain and has a maximum grade of 2.2 percent compared with the steep 3.67 percent grade on the Siskiyou.

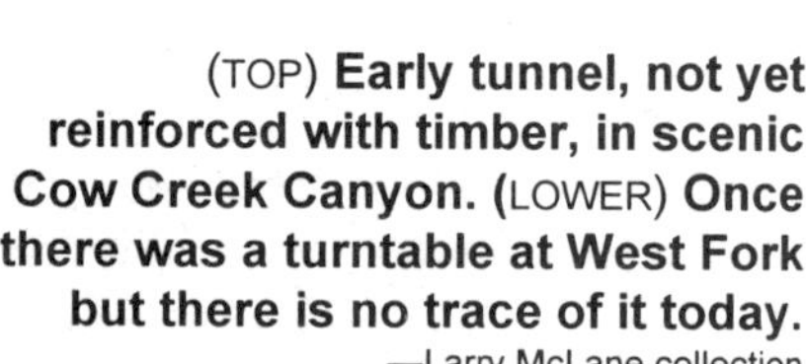

(TOP) **Early tunnel, not yet reinforced with timber, in scenic Cow Creek Canyon.** (LOWER) **Once there was a turntable at West Fork but there is no trace of it today.**
—Larry McLane collection

(TOP LEFT) **SP locomotive emerges from Tunnel No. 4** (TOP RIGHT) **Same tunnel soon after being bored. Note height warning device where man stands — warns anyone on roofs of box cars to get down quickly.** (LOWER LEFT) **Emerging from tunnel with 1905 bridge ahead. View from within the tunnel toward the bridge.** (LOWER RIGHT) **Scene of Cow Creek from bridge deck. Prospectors have been successful in Cow Creek.**

(TOP LEFT) **Railroad at Saginaw where Willamette Industries operates a large mill.** (TOP RIGHT) **Speed on trains can be increased from the 10 mph of Cow Creek Canyon on this straight-away near Riddle.** (LOWER LEFT) **Late afternoon view westerly into Cow Creek Canyon.** (LOWER RIGHT) **Cow Creek , peaceful in summer, can be a raging torrent in winter.**

(TOP) **A close look at the picture shown now gone Wolf Creek Depot on left, a northbound train pulling hard as it disappears into the forest at the beginning of famous Wolf Creek Loop. Train will soon emerge going uphill on trestle in rear. The trestle was replaced by gigantic earth fill** (LOWER) **viewed as passenger train crawls over it.** (CENTER) **Turn-of-century view of double-headers emerging from tunnel will pass under "high" detector. Detector dragged across top of box cars warning anyone riding there to get down – tunnel ahead!** —Larry McLane collection.

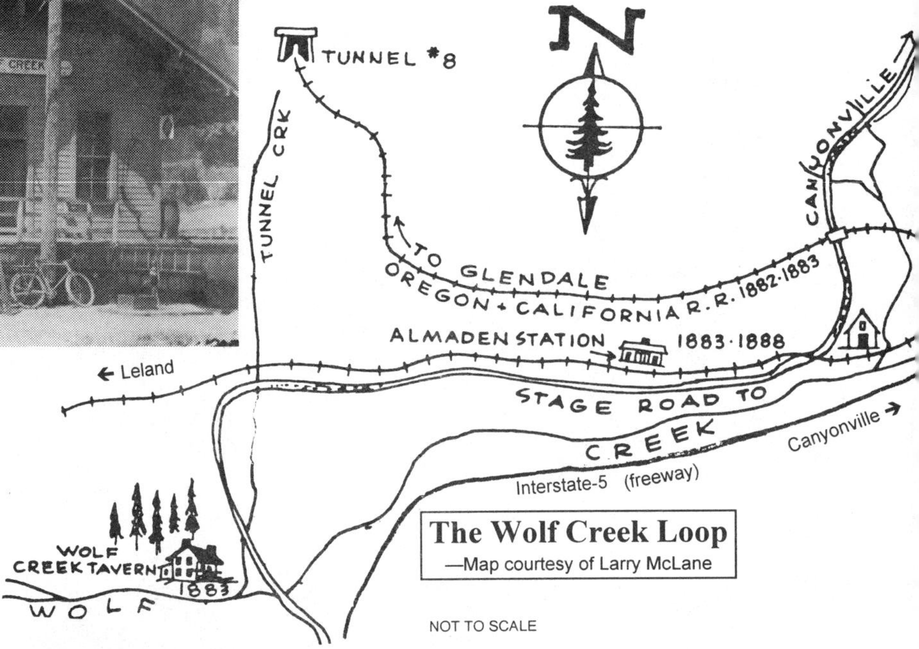

The Wolf Creek Loop
—Map courtesy of Larry McLane

(TOP TO BOTTOM) **Wolf Creek Depot.
Old post card of famous Wolf Creek
Loop. View cannot be duplicated
today due to tall trees.**
—Larry McLane collection.
**Northbound diesel power on modern
train pulls grade along the loop.**
—Keith J. Johnson photo.

Was there any notice on the part of the public, or of official Jacksonville, or of the county court – Jacksonville was the county seat – of this important expedition passing through, and did anyone question why the explorers did not stop if only to say hello and have a cup of tea?

The authors chose what they believe to be the best two documents of the time for looking into that question.

1.) The diary of Welborn Beeson
2.) The local newspaper, *The Table Rock Sentinel*.

<u>First</u>: Welborn Beeson was a young farmer who lived with his father (John Beeson) and his mother on the family farm near today's city of Talent. He had kept a diary since his 16th birthday and would do so until his dying day. His diary is considered unique by researchers because his daily entries cover several decades. On the days Lt. Abbot's command was striding up Bear Creek, Beeson, who prided himself in knowing what was going on, confided to his diary:

> Monday. Mr. Nailor is very sick. Sam Robinson and I sat up with him all night. Father and I went to Jacksonville. I got one pr of pants, 1 pr boots, 1 short. Been a cool day.

Had there been reports of the surveyors passing near the Beeson place, which was not very far distant from the creek, it would seem someone would have mentioned it to Welborn and he would have included it in his diary. On the following day he entered:

> Tuesday. It rained. Went hunting. Nailor is some better.

<u>Second</u>: A search was made on the microfilm of *The Table Rock Sentinel* to see if editor T'Vault mentioned the survey party or its mission. We note first, that when the party went up the valley, the newspaper was yet to be born. Its first issue was November 14, just over a week after the railroad surveyors passed five miles to the east. With such an unusual event as a railroad survey party moving through the valley, and the potential business to be generated in a town with a railroad, this would seem to be front page news. But T'Vault's paper made no mention of topographical engineers being in the area.

ooOOOoo

The singlemost thought in many minds of Jackson County's people was to convince the Oregon and California Railroad to lay its tracks through Jacksonville on its way into California.

There were a number of schemes afoot for getting railroads to build into a certain town. Among them was the federal land grant to railroads where every other piece of land handed to the railroads to "encourage" them to build, the railroads could sell and keep the proceeds as an offset for the expense of construction. Another was for some railroad officials to allegedly accept donations (payoffs) which in turn caused the track to go in a certain direction.

Cornelius C. Beekman had been in Jacksonville since 1853 and at age 29, opened the Beekman Bank. He bought gold dust at discount from miners and hauled it for them making big profits. In short order his bank was one of the richest in the Pacific Northwest. Beekman had many interests and was civic-minded to the extent that he spent nine years on the school board. He ran for Governor and lost by a mere 49 votes statewide. One of Beckman's money-making schemes was to never loan the bank's money but to make personal loans, at good interest, from his personal funds.

When there was talk about a railroad coming to the county and missing Jacksonville, and money was allegedly needed to "convince" the railroad engineers to include Jacksonville, could the citizens get "good old Beek" to loan the money?

Whether Banker Beekman avoided the issue with excuses or merely said "no," does not appear to be recorded. Nevertheless, Beekman did not provide any money to bring the O&C Railroad to Jacksonville.

Some would later claim that "good old Beek" wouldn't put up money because he knew things about the railroad others did not. Although he headquartered his banking business in Jacksonville, and lived there, as a banker he certainly was aware of the world around him. One might say his "horizons" may have been broader than many of his local companions. He seemed to be a nice fellow but often stern, was married, was a family man and he surely was a pillar of the community. And he had investments. One of these investments was in a piece of worthless land, so everybody thought – bare Agate Desert land occupied primarily by field mice, rabbits, grasshoppers, and lots of rattlesnakes, a few miles east of town near Bear Creek. This land was noted more for its ragged desert-like vegetation than as potentially good farm land. But, abutting was a small wheat acreage owned by Ira J. Phipps. Mr. Phipps was successful to the point that local mills would buy all he could grow. Then there was Conrad Mingus and another gentleman named Broback. All four of these men's land abutted with Phipps holding the largest. Phipps and J. W. Broback held land on both sides of Bear Creek.

When the O&C construction reached east of Gold Hill, in the vicinity of the abandoned Fort Lane, the final decision had to be made as to exactly where the track would go through the valley. Some think "good old Beek" was not about to put up any money to run

57

the rails through Jacksonville when he had property in the middle of the valley, *right where Lt. Henry Larcom Abbot's survey of nearly thirty years earlier indicated a railroad might go.*

Did Cornelius Beekman know about the Pacific Railroad Survey and that little part of it that referred to Oregon's Rogue River valley? The survey was published in a large edition in 1857 by the government. It was available to anyone who wanted to buy a copy.

Was Beekman in contact with the railroad engineers long before the line entered the valley?

What about Phipps? Was he really a land speculator with interest in selling out to the railroad?

And Mingus?

J. W. Broback?

What did railroad experts say about a choice of routes?

In the June 1906 issue of the *Oregon Historical Quarterly*, Joseph Gaston provided an essay he titled, "The Genesis of the Oregon Railroad System."

He wrote:

> In seeking the best line for a railway between two distant points. all other inducements being equal, the line of location, like all other forward movements of human effort, will proceed along the line of least resistance. Two facts determined the location of the Oregon & California Rail Road. First, the line of least resistance. The physical features of the region to be developed offered a series of beautiful valleys, rich in all the resources to support a railroad, and so located as to form nearly the shortest line between the termini of the road, and through which it could be constructed centrally through the greatest length of these valleys, and at the lowest cost, and serving the majority of population and interests. Second, here on this line had settled the population of the two States, and made the then existing development of their resources, and upon which the road must rely for its support.

Did Gaston's essay apply to the short segment of line in the Bear Creek Valley?

There could be arguments that Jacksonville, being on the far west side of the valley, did not have a location central enough to attract freight, and the town itself was not an industrial site. There were no factory products produced in Jacksonville on which freight charges would be paid to a railroad.

Then there was the matter of costs of stoking wood into the fire box on a steam locomotive for hauling a train up hill. We recall when Lt. Abbot stopped at Fort Lane, he determined the elevation there was 1,202 feet. To Jacksonville, as the crow flies, is about twelve miles where altitude is registered as 1,567 feet = 367 feet higher / 12 miles (30.5 ft/mile). The Medford benchmark reads 1,383 feet elevation, an increase of only 181 feet for close to the same distance (15 ft/mile), half as steep = less fuel = lower operating costs.

Question: Why go through Jacksonville where that route would have twists and a steeper grade where a centrally placed route away from Jacksonville would have less grade and be straight as an arrow?

Were any or all of these factors used to determine that the bands of steel would be laid in the valley's center and not through Jacksonville?

When it was decided the route would bisect the valley, what determined exactly where in mid-valley would the track be laid?

Mary Phipps, a daughter of landowner-farmer Ira J. Phipps, used a pencil on sheets of tablet paper to write:

> The surveyors first ran out probably a mile west of the present R. R. The next line ran about parallel with Central Ave. but it ran right thru [*sic*] the cemetery at Phoenix so they shifted it to the present location.
>
> The land owners of Central Point immediately began to raise objections to giving right-of-way and the R. R. had to force the right-of-way.
>
> The R. R. officials came to my father, I. J. Phipps, and asked what he was going to charge for a right-of-way. He answered, 'Whatever you think it is worth.' They took 120 feet a mile long and paid him less than $100.
>
> The next move was to locate the town. The man who had that in charge told my father that he wanted to locate the town and he said all he would ask was every other block. He also assured him that the town would prosper because of the fair treatment of the R. R.
>
> The Phipps acreage was north of Main [Street] extending one mile and containing 120 acres. South side was owned by J. W. Broback. The west portion by Banker Beekman from Jacksonville.

Mary Phipps' statement, which she titled,
"Locating of Medford"
stops abruptly and is here faithfully transcribed. There is no mention of the fourth landowner, Mingus.

ooOOOoo

In her essay, Mary Phipps mentions Central Point and some challenges with the people there to lay the track through that hamlet. In the author's book *Single Track to Jacksonville; The Rogue River Valley Railway,* is this passage:

> One night the railroad engineers roomed and ate in the village of Central Point, which is about six miles northeast of Jacksonville. It was probably not happenstance that the railroaders put up in Central Point for they had a plan. The plan was to convince the local folks to hand over lots of money as well as property to be used for a rail yard. With the main line station in Central Point, the planners hawked, Central Point would become the largest town in the valley. The town was near the planned right-of-way already.

It was pointed out that if Central Point had a goal for becoming a successful city, going along with the railroaders' plans was the way to achieve it.

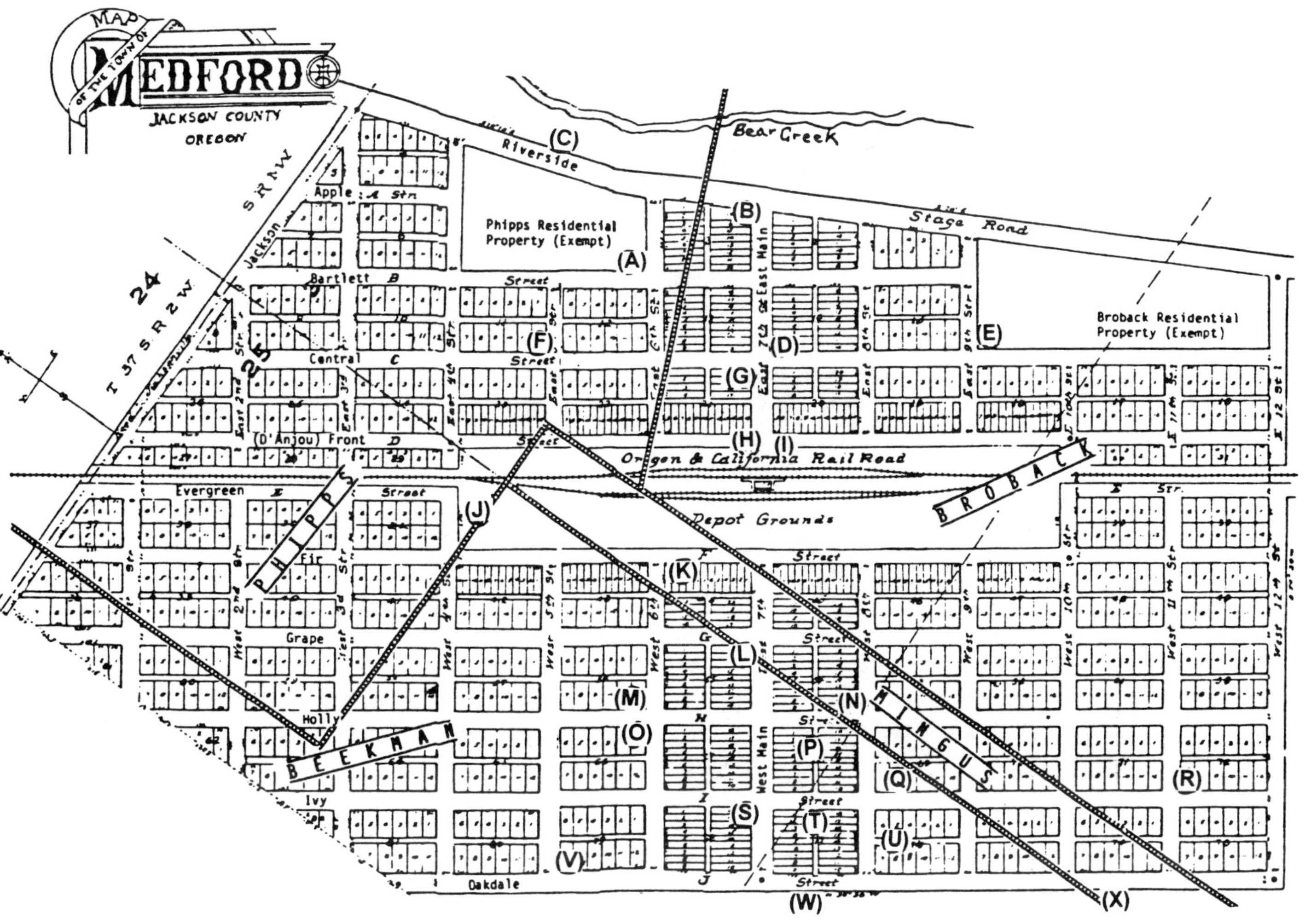

Original plat of Medford, Oregon showing the four property holders' original land overlaid on city blocks and streets. Each man held considerably more land that extended beyond the limits of the city. Original streets east-to-west were letters "A" "B" "C" etc. renamed later as shown. 7th Street became Main Street and was originally blocked by the railroad station as shown. Evergreen Street, alongside the railroad right-of-way, was never developed.

Some of today's prominent sites shown in bold face letters

A	Greyhound Depot	M	Holly Theater Bldg.
B	Hubbard's Hardware	N	Presbyterian Church
C	Red Lion Motel	O	Federal Bldg.
D	Vogel Park	P	Alba Park
E	Vacant (Rogue Comm Col ?)	Q	Post Office
F	Elk's Lodge	R	Catholic School
G	U.S. National Bank	S	Medford Hotel
H	1st Interstate Bank	T	Public Library
I	Key Bank	U	City Hall
J	Goodwill Industries	V	Episcopal Church
H	*Mail Tribune*	W	County Court House
L	Pacific Light & Power Co.	X	Catholic Church

Base Map - Jackson County Court. Overlays Copyright Bert Webber Feb. 1985 / July 1996

For some unrecorded reason, the proposition was not well received by the listeners. Folklore tells us that these locals told the money-juggling railroad men to "buzz-off." In retaliation, the railroad engineers decided to build a new town a few miles south thus drawing trade and development away from Central Point. It's plausible. And it happened.

Four miles south, Medford was built amid those field mice, rabbits, grasshoppers, and rattlesnakes in the Agate Desert.

A few years later, the handful of businessmen and a few farmers around Central Point, now seeking a railroad station, moved their town a little over a mile to the southwest to be alongside the track. The O&C set up a station, installed a switch and a short siding.*

When Ruby Hiatt wrote a paper for a class in history at Southern Oregon College in 1957, her paper was to show property affected by an agreement made October 27, 1883. The agreement was between P. P. Prim, Trustee, and the Oregon & California Rail Road Company as to how the property was distributed and how the results of the transaction became the basis for the founding of the City of Medford.

The four men, Phipps, Broback, Mingus, and Beekman, with Prim as their trustee, drew agreement wherein they deeded two hundred forty (240) acres to a trustee designated by the O&C. This trustee was David Loring. Prim and Loring worked out a comprehensive property agreement.

Loring would receive a free and clear title to two hundred forty (240) acres as designated in the contract providing he met certain requirements. His responsibility was, as a professional engineer for the O&C, as well as trustee for the deal, to survey, lay out and establish a townsite. When the work was completed, he would deed the acreage back to Prim who in turn would deed it, according to the previous agreement, to the four original property owners, O&C and the Oregon and Transcontinental Railroad Company (O&T) leasee of O&C.

On December 22, 1883, when Loring had completed all the work and with papers in hand, he filed a deed showing change of ownership to Prim. The townsite agreement stipulated that O&C would be deeded not less than twenty (20) acres of its own selection for a depot and for other railroad needs, and

that O&C was to receive alternate blocks throughout the townsite. This latter was to be held in trust for the company's sole use and benefit.

The agreement further stated that the remaining blocks in the townsite would be conveyed back to the original property owners in such proportions as they would agree. Every transaction was duly recorded in the Jackson County Courthouse, then in Jacksonville. The transactions between the four principals and the railroad companies took place and were filed in 1883, but the patents for the original donation land claims in the names of R. B. Packard and B. B. Evans, of which the land was a part, were not filed until October 20, 1887.

On December 20, 1883, Prim, in the Plat and Dedication filed at the County Courthouse that day, dedicated all the streets and alleys to the public. With this, the City of Medford was founded. No record has been found as to what the people of Central Point thought about it, but many businessmen in Jacksonville were openly upset.

Just two days later, Mr. P. P. Prim, Trustee for the Oregon & California Rail Road, appeared at the courthouse to file additional deeds:

1. O&C RR. received 19.86 acres for depot and railroad purposes
2. O&C RR. received forty-one (41) blocks of property and certain selected lots
3. The balance of the blocks and lots were divided between Beekman, Phipps, Mingus, Broback in proportion to the extent of their previous holdings within the townsite

During the winter of dedication, 1883-84, the railroad was built as far as Phoenix, five miles southeast of Medford. By April, 1884, there were about forty buildings in Medford and many tents. Quite a number of merchants in Jacksonville put up buildings in Medford which they claimed were merely "warehouses" conveniently near the railroad. Some just made a clean break, closed their places in Jacksonville and moved to where the action was.

Who Started Medford?

A committee. The members were the four land owners, Beekman, Broback, Mingus, Phipps; two trustees, Prim and Loring and the Oregon & California Rail Road .

By May 17, 1892, O&T had sold most of its property to the City of Medford. What remained was on that day sold in a package to George H. Andrews, Portland, in a transaction that bought all O&T properties in Grants Pass, Dardenells, Gold Hill, Central Point and Ashland. Andrews was the secretary-trea-

---

* The railroad, commonly said to run "north and south" through the valley, is actually on an angle. When Central Point reestablished at trackside, the city streets were aligned with the track and cross streets at 90 degrees with the track. (The same is true of Medford.) The corner of North 9th Street and Laurel Street is Lot 1 Block 1 of the new addition to Central Point 1910, and that corner is North-South / East-West TRUE. The original village was near the intersection of Table Rock Road and Vilas Road, called "Midway," which is 2 miles by present roads northeast of Central Point Exit 33 on the freeway.

Oregon & California Railroad Company Abandons Section of Original Track

On June 8, 1891, a Resolution was passed by the Board of Directors of the Oregon & California Railroad Company to abandon a stretch of track in the Cow Creek Canyon of Douglas County, Oregon.

After experiencing numerous delays to its trains, and some wrecks, because of land slides and washouts, some track, 3.541 miles long was abandoned, then replaced by new track on the other side of Cow Creek.

The abandoned portion was between Survey Stations 2710+70.3 to 2897+26 between West Fork and Glendale. The Survey Stations and distance were certified by William Hood, Chief Engineer of the Oregon & California Railroad Company. Filed: United States Land Office, Roseburg, Oregon June 26, 1891.

By 1882, the Oregon & California line had progressed as far south as Myrtle Creek where the picture (TOP LEFT) shows No. 8 with sufficient fuel piled on the tender to reach the nest "wooding up" stop perhaps 20 miles away. (RIGHT) Today's line at Wolf Creek. The depot is gone but a siding remains. (LOWER) An O&C passenger train ready to leave Wolf Creek.

—top and lower photos Larry McLane collection. Center photo by Bert Webber

surer of the Southern Pacific Company that took over the management and operations of the Oregon & California Rail Road on July 1, 1887. In addition, Andrews was a director of several other companies active in transportation. He was reported to be a close associate of Henry Villard.

The land, city blocks and lots acquired by the Southern Pacific were largely sold a little at a time but after 1955, when passenger service through the Rogue River Valley was terminated, many lots were sold to major Medford businesses after the passenger station and ramps were demolished.

The Jackson County Federal Savings & Loan Association and the First Interstate Bank were on some of this former SP property. But all the switching facilities including parking tracks, the freight station and the rights-of-way through the city are still owned by SP. Later the Savings and Loan was bought by Key Bank of Oregon and First Interstate became a part of Wells Fargo Bank. In 1994, SP sold (and leased other parts of) its railroad between Springfield Junction near Eugene to Black Butte Junction in California to RailTex, which operates the Central Oregon & Pacific Railroad (CORP) over these former SP tracks. (CORP also now operates the former Southern Pacific Coos Bay - Eugene line.)

Medford's historic freight station is presently being converted into a restaurant and mini-brewery. Medford's Evergreen Street, which the early map shows running parallel along the west side of the track, was never developed.

Conquering the Siskiyou Mountains

The Oregon & California Rail Road was barely able to scrape together enough money to push its rails through Medford and south to Phoenix another five miles. Here, the work stopped and the construction crews were sent home. Simply stated, the O&C was out of money.

In the meantime, Southern Pacific had been growing slowly and surely first from the Gulf of Mexico into California. It reorganized to control and operate the trains of the Central Pacific over the Sierra Nevada Mountains from Oakland to Ogden, Utah. SP was looking for a way to get into Oregon and with the O&C in a moneyless condition, negotiations began.

In the fall of 1885, crews of the Central Pacific, thousands of men – mostly Chinese – working for one dollar a day plus room and board, were pushed to lay a track to the Oregon border.

On May 12, 1887, Southern Pacific took a forty-year lease on the Oregon & California Rail Road .

On the Oregon side, substantial work had been done by the O&C. These were primarily drawings and surveys plus digging and blasting of tunnels such as at Buck Rock and at the summit. But neither was completed.

When, in 1887, SP engineers re-studied the route planned by the O&C four years earlier, they were not convinced that part of the route was the best. The new engineers took no shots at the plans for the Ashland yards or for the start up the mountain, or for the track plan at the summit, but they wanted to eliminate the long loop and the Buck Rock Tunnel near the top. The proposed O&C route was not overly steep, and track here would be exposed to the warming rays of the sun which would melt snow. But the route was longer and this meant more fuel and longer travel time, so the SP engineers declared.

Southern Pacific, in all its wisdom, decided to construct the line on a much steeper and troublesome to build route, the latter being considerably shorter. They believed it would be less costly to operate. The plans for the O&C long loop were dropped even though the Buck Rock Tunnel drilling had been started. The more expensive to build steeper route started and SP had trouble with every mile.

From the summit, the single track descends to the floor of the Rogue Valley some 2,234 feet in 17 miles. Tunnel 13, at Siskiyou, is on an incline toward the south but it is straight – one can see daylight from end-to-end.

As the work progressed toward joining the track from the south to track already installed near Ashland, officials from both ends, Portland and San Francisco, went aboard special trains and headed for Ashland to celebrate. The "northern" party, which included Henry Villard, made its timely appearance at end-of-track near the Ashland yards. The "southern" party's train was delayed in the mountains. Finally, the mid-day planned ceremony to drive the final spike commenced at 4:45 in the afternoon. It was already dark on this December 17, 1887. And it was cold. Nevertheless, the program, with special speakers, including installing the traditional golden spike, went forward.

It was a great day for the nation and for the Pacific Northwest and especially for Oregonians who could now ship their products by rail directly to Oakland for the first time.

(TOP) **Carpenters at Siskiyou Village prepare heavy timbers to shore up the walls and ceilings of Tunnels 13, 14 15.** (LOWER) **Portals of Tunnel 15 in center of view and Tunnel 14 at arrow very close together yet separated by huge loop in track. It is claimed that Tunnel 15 "had to be" for if a mere cut in the side of the hill to allow the right-of-way, would have collapsed the hill and track above after first heavy rain. Picture probably made in 1887. View is not possible today due to heavy forest. Dotted line represents location of track. Building X believed to be cookhouse-dining room for workers. Abandoned track attendant's shed remains.**

First passenger train to operate on Siskiyou Line after "last spike: was driven at Ashland December 7, 1887. Picture made at Dollarhide Trestle, 11 miles south of Ashland. In 1918, trestle was dismantled and replaced with giant earth fill.

The Dollarhide Trestle was site that attracted many photographers. (TOP) with freight going down grade toward Ashland. (LOWER) Two engines on point and a "pusher" chug to get passenger train to the top of the Siskiyou Mountains. Lower picture appeared on thousands of post cards sold by Southern Pacific. SP2507 Class C-15, 2-8-0 with 50-inch drive wheels was Baldwin constr. No. 17398. It worked until scrapped on September 25, 1950

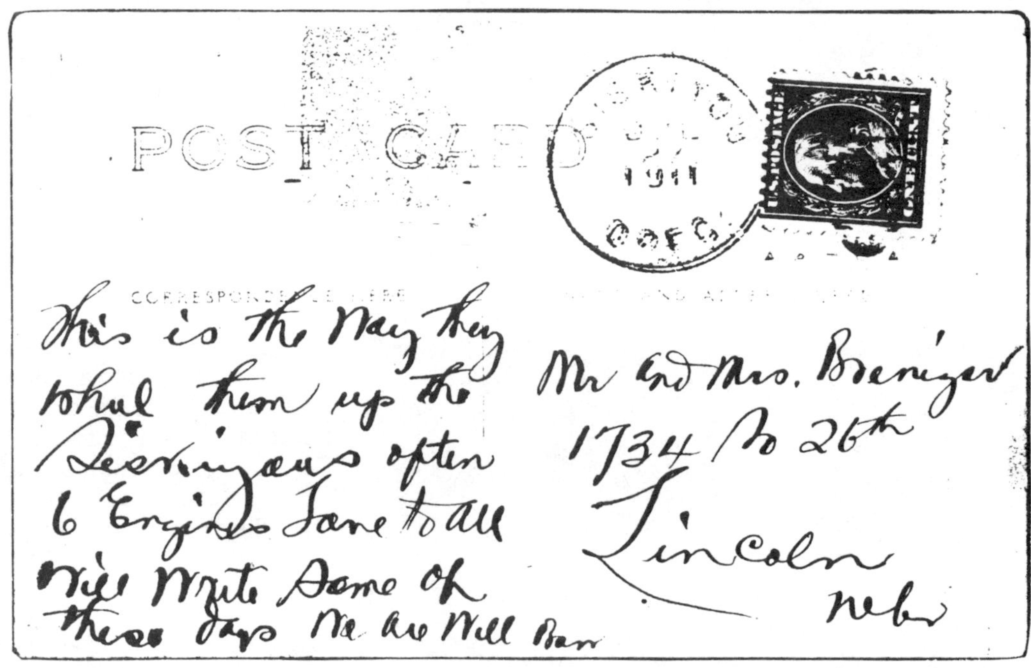

Triple-header freight with fourth engine in middle of train. Train appears to have stopped for benefit on a cameraman otherwise why would engineers be leaning out of their cabs and man standing on front tender? Engine on point is 2-8-0 but number unclear. Could be No. 2622 Schenectady of 1901 rebuilt June 1907 or No. 2822 Brooks built 1908. (LOWER) Post card reads *"This is the way they haul them up the Siskiyous often 6 engines."* Postmarked at Siskiyou, Oregon July 22, 1911 in the days when a 1¢ stamp would carry a post card anywhere in the United States.

Upper Wall Creek Trestle, 180 feet from platform to creek, tallest trestle in Siskiyou Mountains, is 581-feet long, curved, and 3.38% grade. Safety rail was installed many years later.

Work train and men at Siskiyou during construction in 1887. Note long gold watch chains on three men, indicates they are "operating" crew.
—George W. Norman collection.

(RIGHT) **Signal control station at Siskiyou. The generator was in adjoining shed.** —Author collection

Old No. 50 (?) shown as 2-6-0 ran from Hornbrook to Ashland in 1889. *Bulletin 94* (locomotive directory) lists No. 50 as an 0-6-0 Schen. built 1900. But early numbers are often hard to track. —George W. Norman collection

Statistics of the Railroad Between Redding and Ashland

- **Maximum elevation: 4,135 feet above sea level**
- **Tunnel 13 at Siskiyou Summit: 3,108 feet, longest of 16 tunnels**
- **Maximum grade 3.67 percent, the steepest on the SP system**
- **In 171 miles, there are 100 miles of curves totaling 31,700 degrees of curvature. This is equal to each train doing 88 complete circles**
- **The track crosses the Sacramento River 18 times**
- **From Ashland to Siskiyou Summit is about 9½ straight-line miles but 17 miles by track**
- **About 2,178 feet elevation gained from Ashland to Siskiyou Summit**

Southern Pacific highly publicized its trains. The trip over the Siskiyou Mountains from the viewpoint of a passenger car window must have been spectacular. On the north side of the mountain, one could see far below into the Rogue Valley and at one place, could see the track below and around a bend they would soon be passing over. The southern view down the steep Cottonwood Creek Valley and around the gentle Gregory Loop was equally delightful.

Today Interstate-5 crosses the Siskiyou Summit within a short distance of Tunnel 13, the highest elevation tunnel on the Siskiyou line. From the Mt. Ashland turnoff, one can hike* about ¼ mile up a very steep access to the site of the former village and post-office of Siskiyou. Railroad sidings there are still used.

* Permission needs to be obtained from the railroad before one walks on its right-of-way. Due to compound risks, one should never walk in tunnels or on trestles.

ooOOOoo

In the face of "insufficient volume" of business to keep the line open, so said Southern Pacific, SP closed the 80-mile section across the Siskiyous in 1992 and diverted all its trains via the Natron Cutoff. In short order, SP moved its handful of employees out of Medford after 110 years of service. This left the Rogue Valley with no through rail service and such action caused much havoc among the local shippers.

Southern Pacific continued to serve shippers along the line from Eugene but only as far as Ashland, then turned around. Freight originating with the valley's lumber mills, orchards and other shippers, now had to go north to Springfield Junction then south over the Natron Cutoff by way of Klamath Falls – over 300 miles extra travel and delay – to get to California.

The shippers were *not* pleased.

Classic 3/4 front view of GP-40 on point of six-units of power just out of Tunnel 14 on May 8,1997.

RailTex
Central Oregon & Pacific Railroad

RailTex, a Texas organization that specializes in acquiring small railroads in light-density areas, completed a deal in December 1994 to acquire more than 400 miles of track from SP. Most of the track was purchased, but about 100 miles (20 miles on the Oregon Coast, the rest over the Siskiyou Mountains), was leased with a buy-option.

The entire length of the Siskiyou Line was involved. RailTex will operate freight trains with its Central Oregon & Pacific Railroad (CORP), announced Bruce Flohr, RailTex president, in Medford on December 6, 1994.

A number of SP people signed with RailTex.

CORP is a non-union operation with a profit-sharing plan for its employees.

Flohr said although the company does not expect to run passenger service, it will work with organizations that might want to develop commuter or tourist trains on the CORP system. RailTex seeks to be profitable and realizes that running excursion and commute trains would be a potential source of revenue. RailTex has been made aware that some business and political leaders in the Medford and Grants Pass area have been proposing commuter service by rail between Ashland and Grants Pass for some time.

RailTex owned 145 diesel-electric locomotives at the time of the deal and transferred 28 to its new Oregon operations. In spring of 1997, additional engines were sent to Medford as that sub-headquarters makes up trains going both north and south. (Trains going over the Siskiyou Mountains require six engines due to steep grades.) It also owned 700 box cars and announced it would lease 100 wood chip cars.

In addition to the Siskiyou Line, CORP now runs on the former SP line between Eugene and Coos Bay where there is a lot of wood chip hauling presently mostly by truck that the railroad hopes to capture, said Robert W. Libby, General Manager of CORP.

An executive in the RailTex organization called the Siskiyou Line a "jewell."

The Central Oregon & Pacific Railroad uses 4-axel GP-38 and GP-40 engines. These are lower cost to acquire, to operate, and they are easier on the rails compared with more powerful 6-axel units. In the Siskiyous, with tight curves, the big engines tend to jump the track and rip out rail.

Siskiyou, Oregon in the early days. There was a post office, hotel, eateries, boarding houses, "sporting house," in addition to railroad buildings and turntable. The village a "glorious" place to live in summer but was "desperately cold" in winter. There is no trace of the village today. (LOWER) Railroad shacks at Siskiyou used by Maintenance-of-way men today photographed in July 1996 by author. The turntable is long-gone but there is a siding and a go-around track. The date-nail "31" pictured on page 36 is on the go-around track believed to have been the main line at that time.

There are two factors that are a challenge to CORP. One is the high cost of maintenance especially in the Siskiyou Mountains and in Cow Creek Canyon. The other is the traditional shortage of cars. While there may be idle box cars in a given week, that's the week the need is for other cars such as center-beam flat cars – always in demand for shipping lumber. Fitting the particular design cars to the particular customers is an ongoing challenge, General Manager Libby related.

Now that raw logs are being carried, arrangements had to be made for bulk head flat cars modified with bunks. These special cars are required for regular shipments from Weed, California to Roseburg Forest Products Company at Dillard, Oregon. CORP presently owns 51 of these cars and currently runs 8 loads of logs a day, as part of a mixed train, five days a week. (Each of these flatcars hold the equivalent of three highway logging trucks.)

A part of the deal with Southern Pacific was for CORP to have use of the SP yard in Eugene, and joint use of the SP track between Eugene and Springfield Junction.

With the exception of the Glenbrook Metals Company operating out of Cornutt switchyard, most of the products hauled by CORP are timber related.

Since December 1887, trains have been running over the Siskiyou Mountains. Although Southern Pacific closed the route in 1992, RailTex and its Central Oregon & Pacific Railroad reopened this line in June 1995 running between Springfield Junction and Black Butte Junction in the shadows of Mt. McLoughlin, Mt. Ashland and Mt. Shasta. ◇

Central Oregon & Pacific Railroad Hauls Forest Products Every Day

Of the dozens of timber operations along the Siskiyou Line, the five shown are a mere representation. From a modest stud mill, Central Point Lumber Company (UPPER RIGHT)**, to the "biggies": Roseburg Forest Products, Superior Lumber, Willamette, Boise-Cascade – CORP hauls them all.**

Old Ashland Depot in its heyday (TOP), contained wonderful restaurant with linen tablecloths and napkins. Dining was "elegant" and the prices were reasonable. The dining room did not cater to the townsfolk as it was heavily crowded when passenger trains made the scheduled "meal stop." (CENTER) Thousands of Ashlanders turn out to greet train of First World War troops on way to "win the war." (LOWER) Ashland yard in 1996 with 1986 track diagram from SP. Yard once was had a 10-bay roundhouse plus two outside parking spurs also served by the turntable. Now all gone.

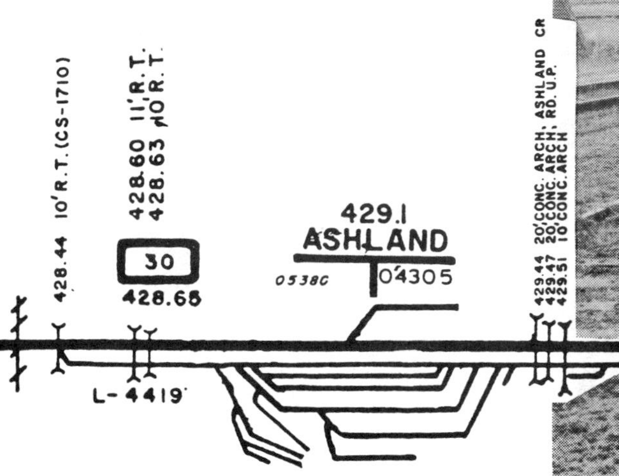

(TOP) **Long 12-coach troop train carrying soldiers for Spanish-American War stop for lunch in Ashland. Men stood to eat. Train was a "special" and carried a caboose. It was a hot day to be in the scorched Agate Desert (upon which all Bear Creek Valley towns were built) under a mid-day sweltering sun. Note umbrellas serving as parasols.** —Author collection

(LOWER) **Central Oregon & Pacific Railroad earns extra revenue by hauling special excursion tritons. This one rear Riddle.** —Keith J. Johnson photo

Gold Hill, Oregon

(top) (l to r) Old covered bridge and early railroad bridge crosses Rogue River.
—Gold Hill Historical Society

(CENTER AND LOWER) **The 1906 railroad bridge and modern arched highway 99 bridge. In summer, the inviting river has many swimmers who used to jump from both bridges until officials had to "get tough" about it.** —Bert Webber photos

(OPPOSITE PAGE - TOP) **Building the Brimstone Trestle over Grave Creek. View faces south.** (LOWER) **The Grave Creek trestle and old flume.** —Larry McLane collection
(THIS PAGE - TOP) **The trestle with train in classic post card view.** —Author collection
(LOWER) **SP 6-axel power on point on southbound freight on modern trestle.** —Keith J. Johnson photo

(TOP) **Maintaining driveways over private crossings is responsibility of the owner of the crossing, say railroad officials. Some, as shown, are "poor" and can be dangerous.** (LOWER) **Railroads have on-going program for replacing worn out ties, rails. Loose spikes in old ties are constant chore of Maintenance-of-way workers.** (LEFT) **New spike shown full size.**

(LEFT) **Signal at MP4514 near Gold Ray Dam on Rogue River. Short freight running from Medford to Grants Pass has just passed.**
—Bert Webber photo (RIGHT) **High-railer carrying track inspector makes rounds at track-limit speed. Inspector identifies places in need of repair, posts small flag with daily inspection report number on the flag. Maintenance-of-way crew locates "trouble" spot by reading report and looking for flag.** —Keith J. Johnson photo
(LOWER INSETS) **"FRED" (Flashing Red Electric Device) marks last car of train. On car shown, flasher quit during run so trainman hung a lantern on poor "FRED."** —Keith J. Johnson photos

(TOP) **Mounted on flange wheels, self-propelled BUCYRUS steam-shovel was monstrous thing, is clearing way preparing for grading of right-of-way near Gold Hill. Year was about 1882-83.** (LOWER) **Boswell Springs Resort and Hotel on Elk Creek was between Drain and Yoncalla. It was so close to the track there was seldom a need to hire a porter to carry the suitcases.**

Springfield Junction
The Springfield Wye

SOUTHERN PACIFIC'S trains enter the Eugene-Springfield megalopolis from the north through the SP's Eugene Division Yards. Here trains are split. Cars for points in California and beyond are separated from those destined for points along the Siskiyou Line. California-bound trains will take the Cascade Route (Natron Cutoff) heading east from the Springfield wye, and those for Roseburg, Grants Pass, Medford, and way-points, go south from the wye.

The wye is in the Eugene city limits on the edge of the Glenwood District cradled within a 90 degree turn in the Willamette River. It took the name "Springfield Wye" at some undetermined time in the past. The city of Springfield is across the river to the north and east of the wye.

Springfield Junction (wye) is the northernmost point on the Siskiyou Line, the line presently operated by Central Oregon & Pacific Railroad (CORP). Southern Pacific and RailTex, owners of CORP, concluded a sale of 220 miles of track with an additional 80 miles leased in late 1994. The leased portion includes the line through the Siskiyou Mountains and the high flatland to Black Butte Junction (wye) south of Weed (wye) in California. In this 300.3 miles, there is also a wye at Grants Pass and one at Tolo Junction a few miles north of the Medford yard. From Tolo wye, CORP operates switchers that delivers and picks up cars from the Medford Industrial Park which is served by White City Terminal & Utility Railroad (WCTU).

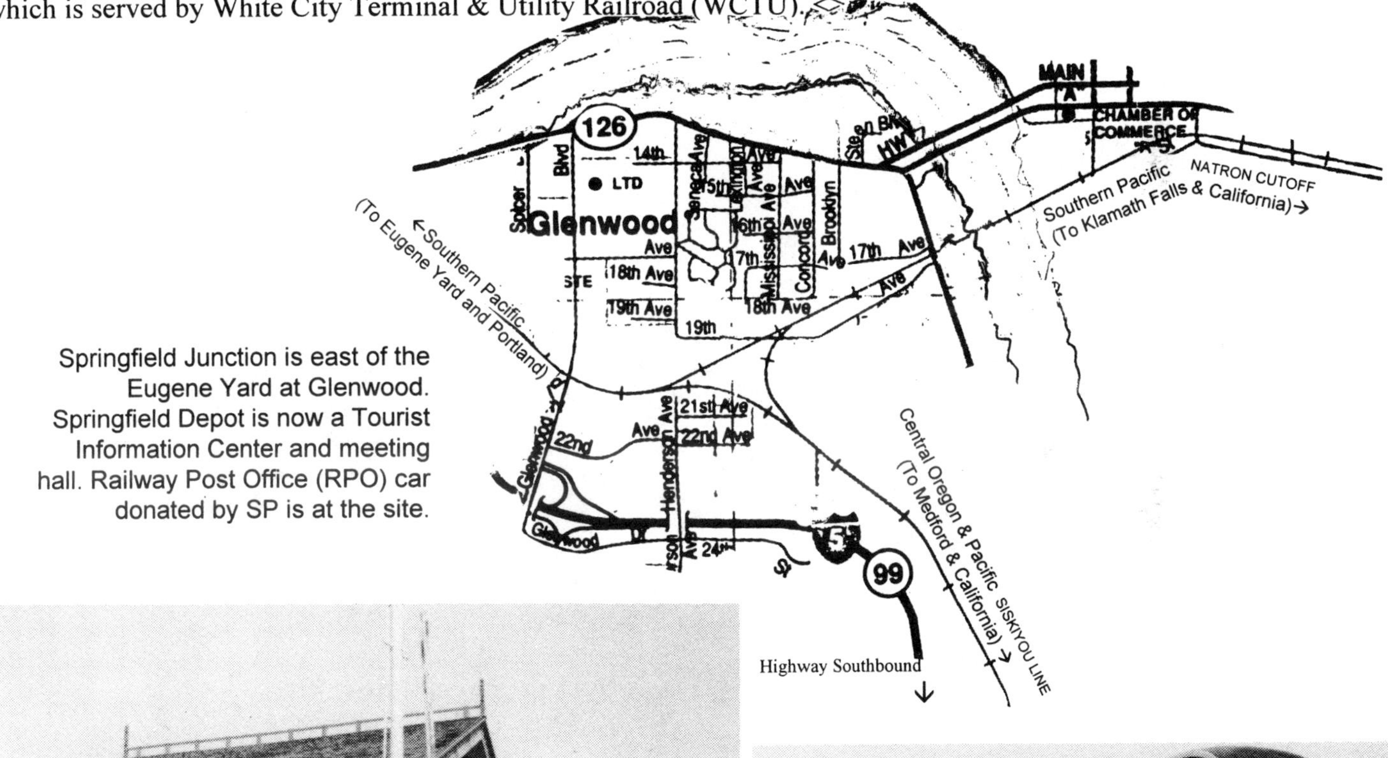

Springfield Junction is east of the Eugene Yard at Glenwood. Springfield Depot is now a Tourist Information Center and meeting hall. Railway Post Office (RPO) car donated by SP is at the site.

(TOP) **Cottage Grove has one of many antique bridges along the CORP route.** (CENTER) **This might be called a "Roundhouse" but without a turntable more simply stated, it is an engine maintenance shop.** (lower) **Yard at Cottage Grove.**

Chapter 3

Oregon & Southeastern Railroad Company

Operated: August 4, 1902 - December 31, 1913
Became: Oregon, Pacific & Eastern Railway Company

Operated: Jan 1, 1914 - ? 1990 (Abandoned November 22, 1993)

THE ORIGINAL line, the Oregon & Southeastern Railroad, with headquarters in Cottage Grove, laid track from Cottage Grove to Disston, a distance of 19.8 miles. Disston was a logging town and was named for that famous brand of saws. The town had a post office from October 1906 until the fall of 1974.

The railroad switched into the Southern Pacific track at Cottage Grove. The purpose of the line was to haul logs from the mill, as well as produce from nearby farms, and passengers. In September of 1903, the train made two round trips a day from Cottage Grove as far as Wildwood, on the Row River, as the track did not reach Disston until 1906.

During the period of its operation, the road owned nine locomotives all built before 1886 except for the 4-spot 4-4-0 Cooke of 1896. Most were probably acquired starting in 1909. When an inventory was made in 1905, it had only two locomotives along with two passenger cars and 33 freight cars.

The line to Disston was a steady uphill drag with a rise in elevation of 360 feet for the distance. It would seem that the return downhill trip would be easier, but such was not the case due to severely sharp curves between Cottage Grove and Dorena.

On January 1, 1914, the railroad was sold to Oregon, Pacific & Eastern Railway Company which had been incorporated in 1912 as the J. H. Chambers Lumber Company. Six of those locomotives were still around but in the next 76 years of operation, an assortment of steamers, including a Shay, then a Plymouth and six diesels were added. The business managers of many of these shortline outfits were always on the prowl for good used equipment. The Plymouth (see the WCTU and the Yreka Railroad) took a lot of jokes for the company gave it a spot number "14½."

At the start of 1918, the company was running three locomotives, 3 passenger coaches and rostered 45 freight cars.

Spot No. 19, a Baldwin 2-8-2 (constr. No. 42000) built in 1915, was from Yreka Western as its No. 19. It was acquired in 1971. Years later it would return to Yreka Western, still No. 19, to pull the seasonal "Blue Goose" excursion train between Yreka and Montague.

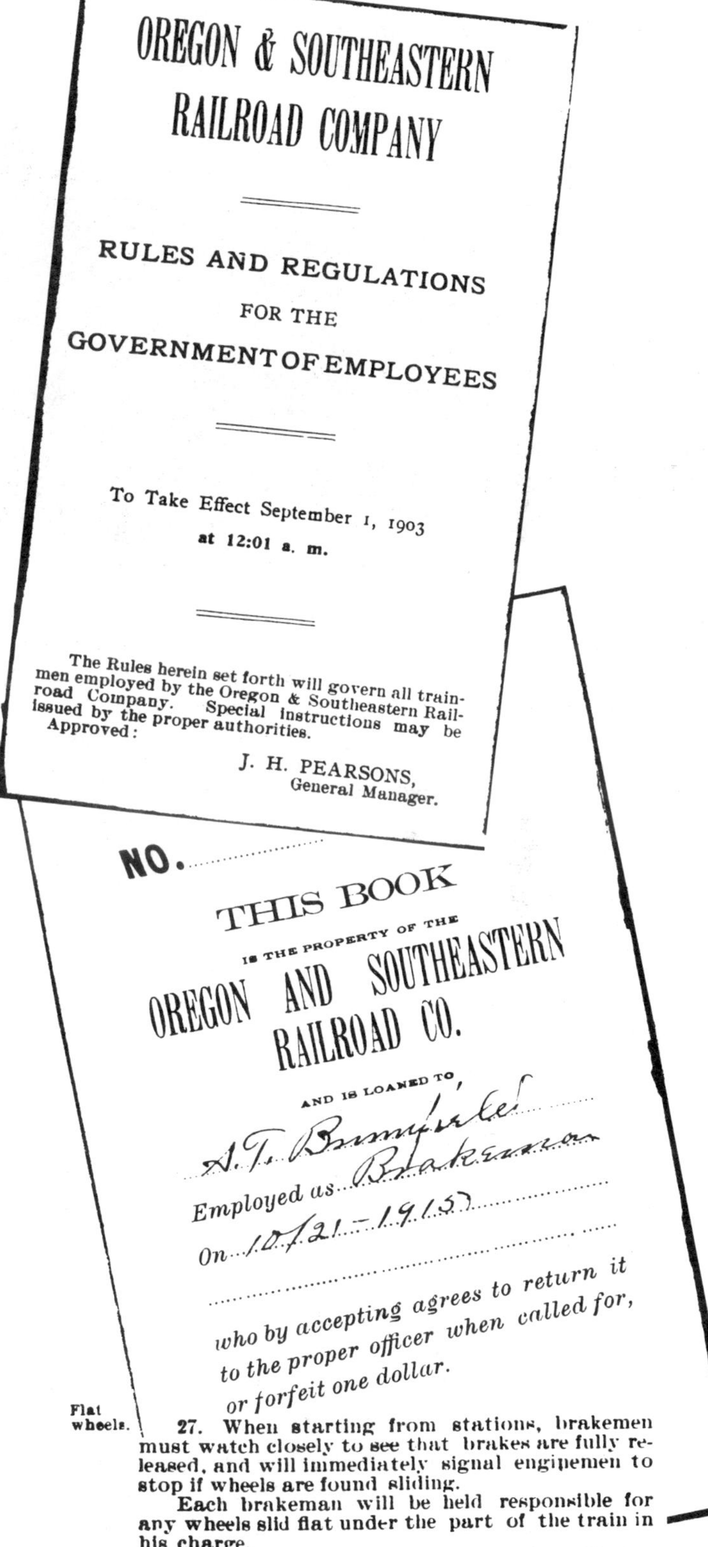

The Oregon, Pacific & Eastern extended its track to Rujada, 21 miles in 1952, then to 24 miles as far as Herman station in 1953. (McArthur, writing in his *Oregon Geographic Names* says that "RUJADA" was a telegraph company code word meaning "a considerable body of standing timber is available.")

There were enough people living along the line that from April 1, 1917 until March 1929, a Railway Post Office (RPO) car was in a daily train from Cottage Grove to Rujada.

Handling United States Mail

Whenever the duties of employees require them to handle United States mail, care must be used to see that it is safely and promptly handled and correctly delivered in sacks or pouches. When the latter are without marks, or improperly marked, to show destination, they must not be received. If, however, they are in this Company's charge before the error is discovered, they must be turned over to the nearest postmaster, and the facts reported to the Superintendent by wire.

—Rule 37. Oregon & Southeastern R. R. Co.
Rules and Regulations. Sept. 1, 1903

In 1924, ownership changed from Chambers to Anderson & Middleton Lumber Company and a 5-mile long branch line to Upton was discontinued. The rails were pulled up and moved to extend the line to end-of-line station named Herman.

By March of 1929, passenger service had to be curtailed due to lack of business. By now just a three-times-a-week train ran as far as Rujada, 21 miles from Cottage Grove. All passenger service stopped in 1930, then the Herman extension was abandoned in 1938. Little by little, the various extensions were shut down until in 1990, the total line was abandoned.

The town of Dorena had to be relocated when backwaters from Dorena Dam on the Row River flooded the site in 1949, forming Dorena Lake. What was left of the railroad became a seasonal tourist attraction running from Cottage Grove to the lake with Baldwin No. 19 puffing ahead of the tourist train. This scene lasted until final abandonment in 1993 and No. 19 went back to the Yreka Western. ◇

Chambers Covered Bridge

The Chambers mill burned in 1943. In 1925, a very tall Howe Truss covered bridge was built for the logging trains but use of the bridge ceased after the fire. The bridge remains in Cottage Grove as an historic attraction.

—Details about the famous bridge are in *Oregon Covered Bridges* Refer to bibliography.

Chapter 4

Glenbrook Nickel Company (Short Line)

Operated as Hanna Nickel Company 1953 – 1987; Glenbrook Nickel Company April 1989–

THE SHORT LINE of the Glenbrook Nickel Company is only about 1½ miles in length but hauls one hundred percent of the nickel smelted in the United States.

Nickel ore was discovered in 3,546 foot high Nickel Mountain, Douglas County, in 1865 by sheep herders. A mine was not opened until 1891 and not mined commercially until in 1954. This was by the M. A. Hanna Company which built the rail line to connect with Southern Pacific at Cornutt siding MP 540.3. The mining firm owns the siding which, with the track to the smelter, is 110-112 pound steel due to very heavy loads entering and leaving the plant on the steep, curved track.

The grade between the siding and the mill is 2 percent and all traffic is moved by either a 50 ton or 65 ton GE switcher owned by the company. The firm also owns three flatcars.

Hanna discontinued its business in 1987 and the facilities were sold to Nickel Mountain Resources. Apparently the plan was to dismantle and sell the equipment. However, Glenbrook purchased the closed business and presently operates the works.

In recent years, nickel deposits were discovered on an island in the South Pacific Ocean. Ore from this source is now shipped to the Port of Coos Bay then hauled to Glenbrook for smelting.

While it is true that nickel for the United States 5¢ coin is an Oregon product from this smelter, the majority of the product goes into stainless steel. The firm ships about $1 million in ferro-nickel every four days in covered hopper cars weighing about 200,000 pounds and some lighter loads by truck.

Occasionally a car might loose its footing on the siding but to date, no cars have been upset or damaged. ◇

(TOP) **Glenbrook's two switchers.**
(LOWER) **Switcher moves cars to siding at Cornutt. Mainline track on left.**
—Keith J. Johnson photos

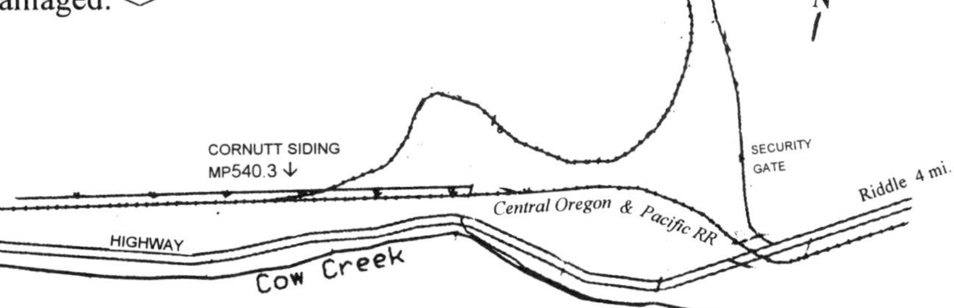

(RIGHT) **It might be said that Riddle is the major source for people employed at the Glenbrook Smelter west of town.**
Bert Webber photo

Operations at Glenbrook Nickel Company. (LEFT CENTER) **Ferro-nickel "shot" (50/50 iron/nickel) and** (RIGHT) **nickel "pig" ingot, weighs about 40 pounds.**

—Keith J. Johnson photos. (LOWER) **Nickel for all 5¢ coins in U.S. A. is smelted here.**   —Bert Webber photo

Chapter 5

Superior Lumber Company (Short Line)

Glendale Lumber Company Glendale, Ore. 1902 (Operated railroad March 1910 - 1932)
Ingham Lumber Company 1932 - April 1946
Robert Dollar Company April 1946 - 1981
Gregory Timber Company 1981 - 1985
Superior Lumber Company 1985 –

THE GLENDALE LUMBER COMPANY railroad hauled logs from the forest on its approximately 12 miles of standard gauge track along Windy Creek to its mill at Glendale. After milling, lumber was transferred from the mill yard to the mainline interchange by whichever locomotive was available.

(LOWER) **Old Glendale Depot now long gone, was at side of switchyard.**
(TOP) **Model of gear-driven logging engine (Shay) was presented to former General Manager Tom Mell when he retired.**

For power, there was an Heisler (builder No. 1197) and a Shay (builder No. 2559). The latter had twice the weight (38,000/64,000 pounds). The company purchased two used rod engines then another Shay, 100,000 pounds (No. 2978).

In 1910, the rolling stock amounted to 1 Heisler locomotive, 3 logging cars, 3 flatcars. Sometime later, an unknown number of disconnected trucks were added.

Tom Mell, who retired after 50 years in the timber business, arrived at the Glendale mill in 1946 at age 34 and stayed until he retired as General Manager in 1979. He told the authors that while the Heisler had "power to spare," that engine "rattled and clanked and vibrated so badly someone had to almost live with it to keep all the nuts and bolts tight or the locomotive would shake itself apart. On the other hand," he related, "the Shay was an all-around dandy in every way – dependable." Earlier, Mell was an engineer on both models thus he spoke from experience.

As to the original trackage, "This was pulled up before I got there, I believe in the early 1940's, for we opened a road for trucks about 1948."

Mell recalled in 1951 he bought the present Model B-B/90 switcher from the government as it had been declared war surplus and "it didn't cost much." This 90,000-lb. General Electric diesel (serial 17730) was built in December 1942. It has twin Cummins engines and develops 300 horse power. Dennis Carlton, the mechanic, said the old engine was growing "tired" and the company hoped to replace it with another about twice its power. The present switcher will easily pull 3 fully loaded lumber carriers.

The switcher moves cars from the Central Oregon & Pacific Railroad's large Glendale yard to the mill's two spurs for a combined run of about one mile. The spur that crosses Cow Creek to the mill has occasional trouble when the creek floods. Mell recalled one winter when the trestle was washed away, and others when trestles were weakened.

The mill's so-called mainline track was upgraded in the early 1970's and a new steel trestle (RIGHT) was built. Some of the parking spurs (OPPOSITE PAGE) are believed to be Glendale Lumber Company original lightweight rail.

(ABOVE) Manufacturer's plate for switcher, the locomotive now in 55th year of service.

(LEFT) Engineer Kim Alexander, Grants Pass, moved switcher to pick up string of cars then hauls cars (LOWER OPPOSITE PAGE) to pickup point in Central Oregon & Pacific RR switch-yard.

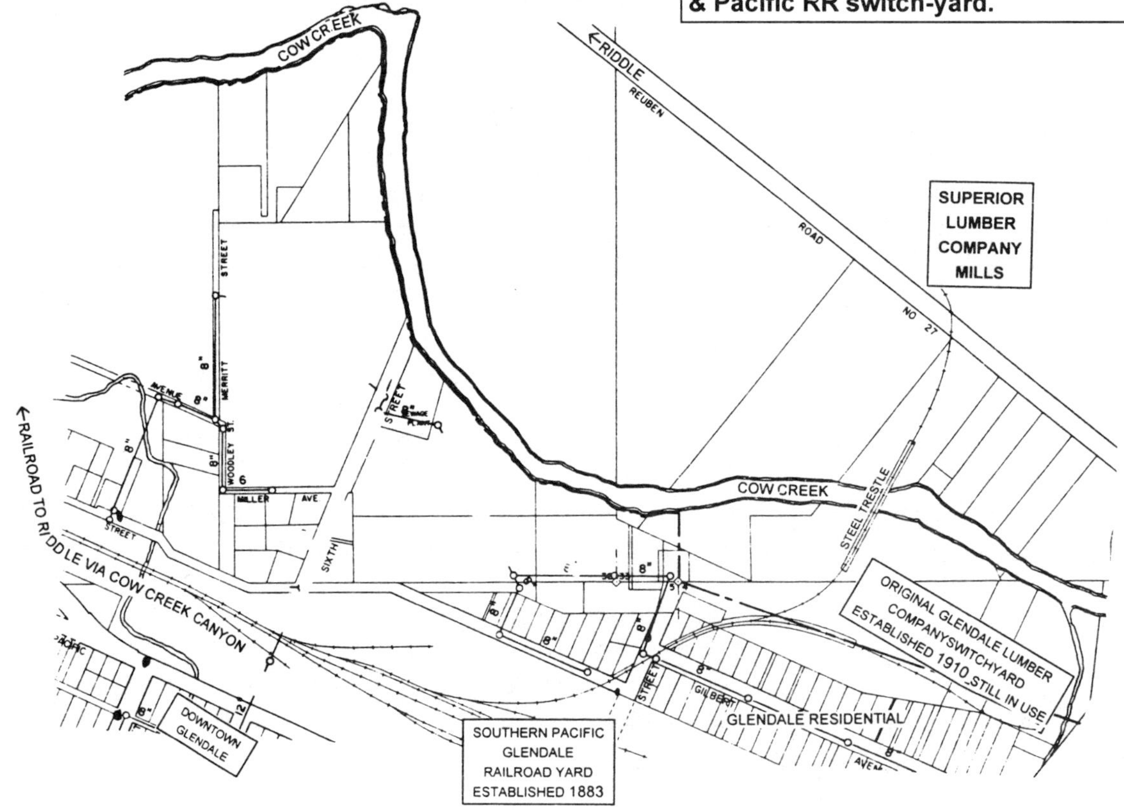

Blocking switch with rocks (ABOVE) to prevent switch being changed, is old custom on logging railroads.
(LEFT) Mechanic Dennis Carlton, 25 year employee, moves switcher during test.

Drain

The village was founded by Charles Drain and his son, John C. Drain, when the father realized the O&C railroad was coming that way. The Drains conveyed 60 acres to James Hughes, a real estate agent for $1 in February 1872 with a stipulation that the land be made available to the O&C railroad and a station and townsite be established which would be named "Drain." The town Platt was filed April 9, 1873. The United States Post Office Department opened a post office at Drain April,25, 1872. The postoffice changed the name to "Butler," for reasons apparently known only to the Department, but was renamed Drain on March 18, 1873. The town is about 5 miles from Yoncalla.

Drain became the end-of-track terminal for the O&C on May 17, 1872 where a stage line met trains to forward passengers on to Oakland. The O&C expected to have track to Oakland in about two more weeks.

On June 21, 1872, a newspaper reported there had been a an accident at "Drain's Station." For awhile the village was called "Drain's Station," but the shorter version, "Drain" prevailed. An attractive covered bridge built in 1925 (rebuilt in 1986) crosses Pass Creek in the city park. Refer to *Oregon Covered Bridges* in bibliography.

Chapter 6

California and Oregon Coast Railroad

Incorporated December 3, 1913 - Abandoned November 26, 1956
Operated: September 7, 1914 - October 31, 1954

IF LUMBER, ORE, AND OTHER PRODUCTS from Southern Josephine County were to be shipped by rail, the first part of the trip was by slow mule teams to Grants Pass where the O&C stopped on its route between Portland and San Francisco. To speed things up, promoters decided to open a shortline. The road would go at least to Kerbyville (today's Kerby) as that village was the former county seat, was sufficintly well populated and, they believed, there should be quite a lot of passenger business. But loftier schemes were also in the wind.

County Seat Moved On Account of the Railroad

The site of Grants Pass was originally in Jackson County. When the O&C put down its track with a water tank and planned a station at the village of Grants Pass, people in Josephine County petitioned Jackson County to slice off that corner of Jackson County and donate it to Josephine County so Josephine County could claim a stop on the railroad. The Jackson County Commissioners agreed.

The orchard business around Medford was growing every year. If a line could be built between Grants Pass and Crescent City on the northern California coast, tons of fruit from these orchards, as well as lumber, could reach the seaport much faster and for less freight cost than by any other route.

The first survey was done in 1902 by Colonel T. Waln-Morgan Draper. He was from San Francisco. He called the project the "California Oregon Coast Railway." During a period of about ten years, there were at least three routes surveyed. By 1911, the people of the area had become excited about this newly proposed line to the coast and willingly subscribed about $70,000. This particular venture carried the name "Grants Pass Rogue River Railroad."

Meanwhile, in Crescent City, which was fighting for survival as an ocean port in competition with San Francisco and Portland, personages wanted to build a railroad to Grants Pass. Of interest, there already existed a logging railroad, with a bridge over the Smith River, extending about twelve miles from that port city. This could be a starter for a long, hard route through rugged mountains to Grants Pass.

C&OC 2-8-2 was ex-Hetch-Hetchy #3 built by BLW became engine No. 301. It was received in 1927, used awhile then rusted beside cement plant for years, was scrapped in 1950.

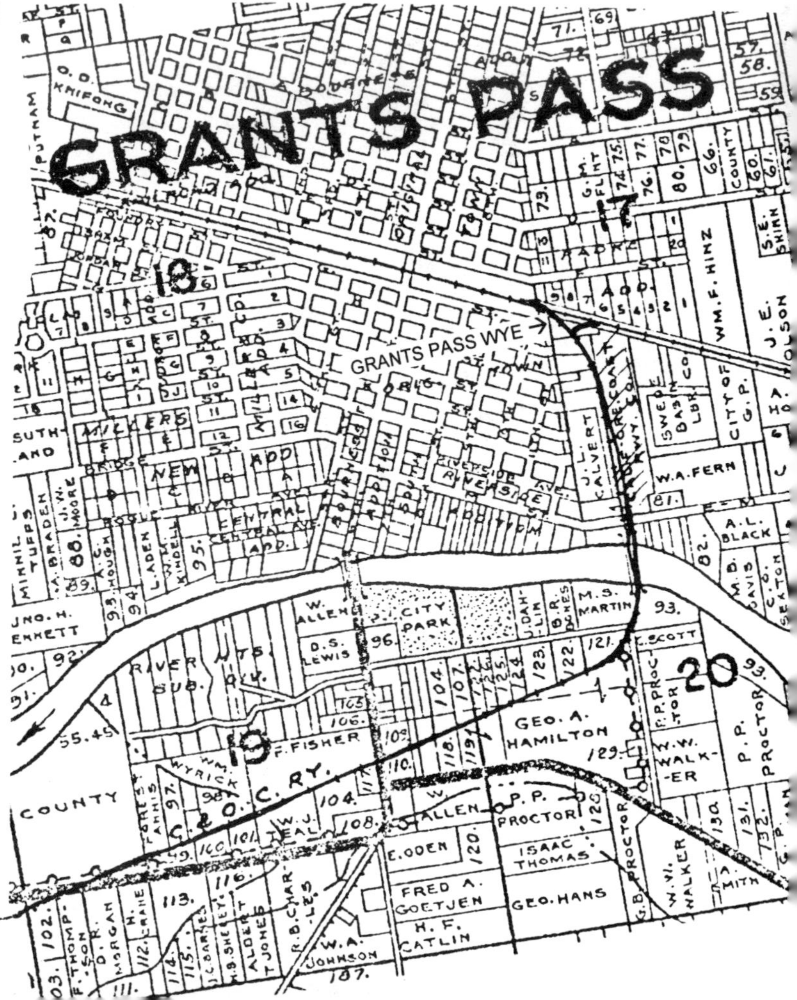

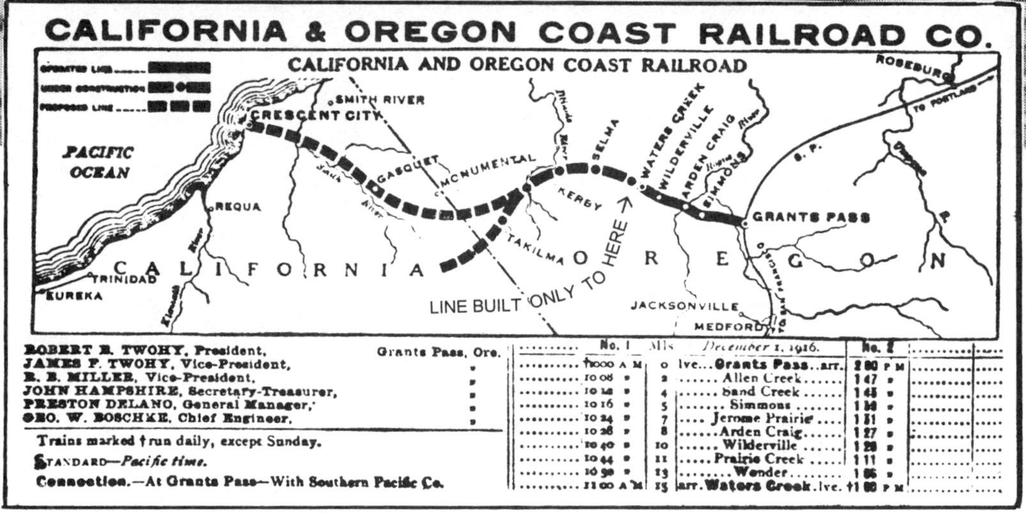

CALIFORNIA & OREGON COAST RAILROAD CO.

CALIFORNIA AND OREGON COAST RAILROAD

ROBERT B. TWOHY, President,
JAMES F. TWOHY, Vice-President,
B. B. MILLER, Vice-President,
JOHN HAMPSHIRE, Secretary-Treasurer,
PRESTON DELANO, General Manager,
GEO. W. BOSCHKE, Chief Engineer.

Trains marked † run daily, except Sunday.

STANDARD—*Pacific time.*

Connection.—At Grants Pass—With Southern Pacific Co.

Grants Pass, Ore.

No. 1		Mls	December 1, 1916.	No. 2		
†10 00 A M		0	lve...Grants Pass..arr.	2 00	P M	
10 08	»	2	.... Allen Creek	1 47	»	
10 12	»	4	.... Sand Creek	1 45	»	
10 16	»	5	.... Simmons	1 34	»	
10 24	»	7	.... Jerome Prairie	1 31	»	
10 28	»	8	.......Arden Craig.......	1 27	»	
10 40	»	10	.... Wilderville	1 20	»	
10 44	»	11	......Prairie Creek	1 11	»	
10 50	»	13	.... Wonder	1 05	»	
11 00 A M		15	arr.Waters Creek.lve.	†1 00	P M	

(UPPER PICTURE) **Oregon and California Rail Road track reached Grants Pass on December 2, 1883 but the first passenger train did not arrive until Christmas Eve 1883. Area was once solid forest until trees were felled for the town and for railroad right-of-way. There was not yet a depot built when this photo was made in 1884.** –Author collection

(ABOVE) **C&OC 2-8-0 #201 (Ex O&C#47 - Ex CP-2501) Built 1888 sold to Twohy Bros, Grants Pass on Sept.19, 1910.** (RIGHT) **"All Aboard." The consist of this train was one engine, one tender, one passenger car. The big question: Had the railroad been able to build to Crescent City, would there have been enough revenue (freight) to make the venture worthwhile?** —Author collection

For Grants Pass, March 2, 1911 was an important date. It was on that day when promoters drove the silver spike into a tie as a kickoff of the railroad building venture. As one writer described the scene:

The Commercial (Chamber of Commerce) Club's band provided stirring music and a great many speeches were made.

Within about six weeks, the track bridged the Rogue River and a locomotive crossed the bridge to track's end. The Commercial Club again brought out the band and people cheered as they watched the engine puff steam and smoke and listen to the whistle's blast. The track was only about one mile in length. But it was a start. Regrettably, that was as far as the track would go for some time and dreams of taking the train for a ride to the beach would have to wait.

The next effort was to lay rails to Wilderville eleven miles to the south. The work was the project of

Locomotives of the C&OC. (TOP) **Built by Rogers, this 4-4-0 engine sported 56-inch wheels, was ex-CP #180 then SP #1524 built in 1872. Sold to Grants Pass as Spot No. 1 March 13, 1911.** (LOWER) **Passing view of No. 201, 2-8-0 formerly used on Central Pacific was ex-SP #2508 build by Baldwin in 1900. It was obtained on April 21, 1911 and was finally scrapped on June 28, 1939.**

The C&OC's bridge over the annually turbulent Rogue River was a gangly appearing affair some say was as an accident waiting to happen. Winter high-water often weakened the structure, once tore out a section. A later washout forced the line to shut down.
—Gold Hill Historical Society

TIME TABLE JAN. 20, 1916 DAILY			
RETURN TRIP READ UP RIGHT COLUMN			
2:00 pm	Lv Grants Pass		6:00
2:16	Simmons	5	5:39
2:40	Wilderville	10	5:20
2:44	Prairie Creek	11	5:11
3:00	Waters Creek	15	5:00 pm
One daily round trip each morning leave Grants Pass 8:30 except Sunday			

the Grants Pass Municipal Railway which then controlled the line. On completion, it was time for another celebration so the people of Wilderville and Grants Pass put on a great excursion and picnic over the Labor Day weekend of 1914. As the rolling stock was limited to one locomotive and some work cars, passenger cars were rented from Southern Pacific. To get back home, everyone rode backwards as there was no way to turn the train at Wilderville.

Money was always short so the city made a deal with the Twohy Brothers in 1915. The sale carried with it the condition that track had to be laid to Waldo within three and one-half years. With the First World War already started in Europe, there was some leeway allowed with the time limit should the United States get into the fight, which it did in April 1917. With enthusiasm running high, rails were laid to a point south-west of the Water Creek Crossing. Here our tale could close for no more track was ever put down to meet the end of that 12-mile stretch of logging track that ran east from Crescent City. This railroad, what there was of it, reached 14.507 miles from end-to-end. Had that gap been filled – through 54 miles of rugged mountains – the line might have had at least a chance for success as it would have established rail connections from Grants Pass to the sea. But it never happened.

In the meantime, taking a cue from the Rogue River Valley Railroad, the 6-mile long "Jacksonville line," the C&OC bought a little gasoline engine powered dinky "scooter." It would haul a few passengers at a time quicker and for less cost of operation than the steam train which required several employees. But the line remained without a turn-around at the end of the track. The scooter took the name the

"Yellow Streak" as it was painted yellow and was quite fast. Because this little car rattled and jerked over the second-hand rails, a newspaper dubbed the car "The Yellow Peril."

By mid-1917, any activity for continuing the project was only on paper. The nation was at war in Europe, there was a shortage of available rails to buy – even second-hand rail – and there wasn't any money any where. Passenger service, as well as freight hauling, had slumped so badly that the daily runs were cut to three times a week.

Of importance to the lack of vitality for the railroad, was the opening of a suitable highway between Grants Pass and Crescent City. This is Highway US 199, which continues to the present time as the only public thoroughfare between the two towns. For much of the way, it still follows the original hairpin 20-mph twists along the cliffs overlooking the amazingly exciting Smith River.

(In the 1980's some of the super-sharp turns were straightened and widened and one of several supernarrow bridges was eliminated. But today's speeds are still limited to 25 mph on many sections.)

In the early days, a six passenger jitney, with hard rubber tires, took people and small parcels to Crescent City in a back-aching and jerky trip many hours long between the towns.

The shed (terminal) at the end of the track near Water Creek was in the middle of nowhere and seemed seldom used except by tramps as a place to get in out of the rain.

For all of 1924, passenger tickets amounted to only $24. Therefore, on this sad note, all passenger service was abandoned. In the years following, there was only occasional freight traffic and very little of that. There was no money for repairs. What trains ran were frequently late when steel wheels slipped from the rails and crunched through decaying ties. There

was great concern for the safety of the bridges, especially the major bridge over the Rogue River. Often, in spring runoffs, logs jammed the bridge supports and weakened the bridge. One winter, a section of the bridge was washed away.

A proposal was made to the Reconstruction Finance Corporation in 1933 for a loan to complete the railroad to Crescent City. After about five years hassle, the effort died and with it the death of all ideas for connecting Grants Pass with the Pacific Ocean by rail.

ooOOOoo

Back in 1923, a cement manufacturer took over the line from the City of Grants Pass after ownership by the Twohy's was lost. The Beaver Portland Cement Company laid track about four miles to the base of Marble Mountain which is south of Wilderville. The firm engineered a unique sequence of operations for moving rock from the mountain to its plant in Gold Hill on the Rogue River. The system included what became known as "The Marble Mountain Incline Railway."

Near the top of the mountain, on a bench, a small four-wheel "saddle" switcher moved limestone in several small dump cars. How far these small cars were moved by the 0-4-0 switcher has not been established. But it took the rock to the edge of the mountain where it was processed in a crusher then lowered down the side on the Marble Mountain Incline Railway. This was intended to haul just rock but workmen snitched rides up and down the incline when going to and coming from work. At the bottom of the incline was a large hopper into which the rock was dumped.

The firm apparently rented cars from Southern Pacific to haul limestone from the bottom of the mountain to Gold Hill. A locomotive pulled this train of cars on its spur from the mountain to the old C&OC track into Grants Pass then over SP track, by special

(TOP) **No one seems to know why "San Diego" is lettered on side of this 0-4-0 saddle-tank "mule" used at top of famous Marble Mountain Incline Railway** (RIGHT) **unless it came from San Diego and was never renamed.** (LOWER) **Abandoned C&OC box car was used as power company transformer shed for many years.**

permit, to a siding at the cement works.

In time, Beaver Portland Cement Company became Ideal Cement Company. In 1941, Ideal bought a more powerful but second-hand locomotive which could haul a heavier load faster, at least on the short-line to the mountain and over the old C&OC track. The" faster" was somewhat academic for the original road bed had received no maintenance other than a little extra ballast. During this period, a train derailed. Some if its cars of crushed limestone lost balance, tipped and were spilled. Others remained upright but had to be unloaded before the cars could be re-railed.

The death blow to the railroad was caused by the weather. The bridge over the Applegate River washed out for the last time in 1950 and the company immediately put its resources into a fleet of trucks. To mitigate some of the loss, the firm pulled up the track south of the river then sold the rails to an out-of-state short-line.

An unrelated firm on the north side of the Applegate River used the line for hauling ore from its Redwood Highway Chrome Depot to the S. P. switchyard at Grants Pass. Even with this limited business, the outfit folded on Christmas Day 1955 when the flooded Rogue River took out that bridge. Within two months, approval was received from the Interstate Commerce Commission to dismantle what was left of the bridge. Railroading west of Grants Pass came to an end. ◇

➔Editor's Note. When Southern Pacific operated the commuter service between Grants Pass and Ashland (see Appendix "Interurbans Along the Siskiyou Line," SP installed a wye at the Grants Pass end on which to turn its train-car. When the C&OCR came along, this wye was convenient for it to also turn its train there. This wye exists to the present time and may serve to turn trains when commuter service again runs between Grants Pass and Ashland. But as the saying goes, "Don't hold your breath"!

Chapter 7

Medford & Crater Lake Railroad

December 29, 1904 - May 10, 1907
Became Pacific & Eastern Railway
Became Medford Logging Railroad Company - Abandoned 1962

TURNING OF THE FIRST SOD.

Between 3,000 and 4,000 People Witness the Breaking of Ground for the Medford & Crater Lake Railroad

Apr. 4 - 1905

Tuesday was an occasion long to be remembered by the people of Medford and the Rogue river valley, being the inauguration of an enterprise which will do more to develop the latent resources of the country than anything which has occurred since the building of the Southern Pacific road through the valley.

The event was the turning of the first sod on the Medford & Crater Lake Railroad.

At one o'clock a constant stream of carriages, horsemen and people on foot commenced flowing in the direction of the terminal grounds of the company north of the old distillery building and from that hour until after three, the streets of the city were practically deserted. Very nearly every one went to the celebration. The business houses all closed for two hours, to give the employes a chance to witness the ceremony, and the public school took a vacation. Over 3,000 people were present.

THE VILLAGE OF EAGLE POINT, along with Jacksonville and Ashland, had been on maps for years before Medford was a happy thought. Eagle Point dates from 1853, just two years after Jacksonville. The reason for the activity at Eagle Point was its excellent climate – extra-long growing days in summer – to grow produce for Jacksonville's markets. The Eagle Point folks had fair size gardens and orchards, some 800 acres, and business was prospering. By 1872, the town was recognized for a post office, missionaries from the southern part of the country were developing congregations, and support for public transportation was being considered. Also that year, the Butte Creek Mill opened. Using the creek for turning the stones, the mill ground grain into flour on great mill-stones (buhrstones) for the area residents. (It's still doing it 125 years later.)

Eagle Point is about 11 miles, mostly across then uninteresting Agate Desert, to where Medford would be located 11 years later. At the time, it was the distance between Eagle Point and Jacksonville that needed to be conquered with publicly available transportation. It never materialized, except for a very round-about non-cooperative multi-train method years later.

Length of 56-pound rail made in 1882 was salvaged from Camp White switch yard after the close of World War II.

By the turn of the century, a railroad through the Rogue River Valley had been working for about 17 years. Originally, telegraph and rail lines were proposed between Eagle Point and Medford, but the plan was changed for these facilities to go between Jacksonville and the newly founded Medford. Eagle Point was left out.

In 1904, a group of investors incorporated under the title Medford & Crater Lake Railroad Company with the intention of laying track by way of Eagle Point to Crater Lake, then eventually, hopefully, continue southeasterly and connect to a transcontinental railroad.

Crater Lake became a National Park just two years earlier, 1902, and was quite isolated from the public. Medford, being the largest town in its vicinity, proclaimed itself to be the "Gateway to Crater Lake."

If seasonal tourist trains were established for a run to Crater Lake National Park, it would be a money-maker, especially if the train did a lay-over at Eagle Point, so the promoters believed and hawked.

On April 4, 1905, a robust Mrs. A. A. Davis took a shovel and stepped forward to break ground for the line. According to a newspaper account of the day:

> Between 3,000 and 4,000 people witnessed the breaking of ground for Medford & Crater Lake Railroad near the old distillery. [Medford] business houses closed for two hours and the public school took a vacation. Nearly every one went to the dedication.
>
> Contractor Ewing will move 41,000 cubic yards of earth between here and Eagle Point … not difficult there being no deep cuts or heavy fills.

The newspaper reporter quipped that the main "handicap" to the work would be the moving of the construction camp quite often to keep up with the work.

The major part of the labor gang would be turban-wearing East Indians who had been "imported" for the work. Camps for them would have to be set up along the route. A major need was for water which would be dipped from the Rogue River which the track crossed.

At 3:10 in the afternoon, the speeches over, a bottle of champagne was broken and poured on the ground (to soften it–?) for Mrs. Davis, who was the wife of the road's president, to "lift the sod from its

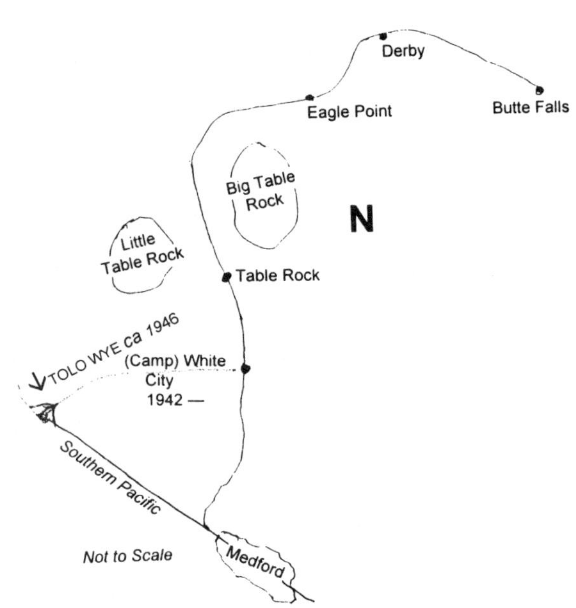

bed [as] the band played, people cheered and camera shutters snapped." Mule teams loitering nearby, and were immediately, on dispersal of the crowd, put to work as the contractor took command.

Plans for the railroad called to extend the line to Butte Falls then on to Crater Lake and, even further in time. Nearing Eagle Point, construction workers encountered rocks which at first hindered the job then halted the work. Shortly thereafter, the line was foreclosed never having rolled a train on the new track.* ◇

---

* A photograph shows a 1-spot on a 2-4-0 locomotive claimed to have been used on the Medford & Crater Lake Railway, but apparently no equipment ever moved on that line. The locomotive was reported to have been taken over by the Pacific & Eastern. However, the *Encyclopedia of Western Railroad History* does not show a 1-spot for either road. Yet the background in the picture clearly shows an end of the Butte Falls station. We observe however, that railroads did not always paint current numbers or names on their equipment. Example: A Climax locomotive lettered with the Sunset Logging Company name, used on that line, was moved to Columbia County for use at the Rock Creek Logging Company. To the confusion of historians, the owner, Anton A. Lausmann, never painted out the Sunset name. For more about this refer to *This is Logging and Sawmilling* in bibliography.

Chapter 8

The Pacific & Eastern Railway
May 27, 1907 - Jan. 30, 1919. Operated until March 1921
Sold to Brownlee-Olds Lumber Company on Aug. 20, 1920 (later MEDCO)

JAMES A. HILL had always wanted to get a line through to California. If he could take control of the Medford & Crater Lake Railroad, and extend it on each end, he believed his dream could materialize.

Under the authority of the Spokane, Portland & Seattle Railroad, Hill's attorneys renamed the Eagle Point line the Pacific & Eastern Railway. Their corporate papers are dated May 27, 1907.

(TOP) **First locomotive into Butte Falls was on November 15, 1910 although the line was not quite ready for business. When this 4-8-0 Rogers engine was parked, steam pipes were run from the engine into the depot's radiators for heat. Locomotive was constr. No. 5404 built in July 1899. It was obtained from Great Northern Ry as its #736. (LOWER) Scenes as this on commercial photo post cards sold very well and are in demand today. No. "1" on tender seems a wild number as the P&E roster does not show such number.**

Sometime later, the firm went to work on the 21 miles to Butte Falls, which the promoters pitched was "just over the mountain" from Crater Lake. The work to Butte Falls was finished by April 1, 1911.

There was no doubt that the engineers had in mind hauling logs, as they put down heavy steel rails – 60 and 77½ pound weight. For rolling stock, there were three locomotives, spot Numbers 101, a Rogers 4-8-0 (Builder No. 5404 from Great Northern); No. 103, another Rogers 4-6-0 (Builder no. 5772 also from Great Northern). There were four passenger coaches and 17 freight cars at the end of 1917. They also had at least one hopper car used for laying ballast. In all, the Pacific & Eastern was operating 34 miles of track. The hopper car is presently exhibited in Medford Railroad Park.

(TOP) **P&E brick depot faced on E. Main Street less than one block from Bear Creek. Service on the P&E started from the SP Depot in town but was changed to this new location when the building was ready.** (CENTER) **Old P&E hopper car is exhibited at Medford Railroad Park, is last remnant of P&E RR.** (LOWER) **First excursion into Butte Falls was on April 9, 1911. Medford newspaper proclaimed event as a "great day."**

PACIFIC & EASTERN TO USE NEW DEPOT

Beginning Saturday, the trains on the Pacific & Eastern railroad will leave and arrive in Medford from the new depot on East Main street, where business will in the future be transacted.

The Snowy Butte Mill (presently known as Butte Creek Mill) on Little Butte Creek in Eagle Point, had been constructed in 1872. It milled flour for local people as well as accepting jobs for out-of-area customers. Shipments to Portland had started on the Pacific & Eastern. The line also carried mail which had been transferred at Medford. Daily passenger trains were on the schedule and there were weekend excursions. The view through the valley between the two Table Rocks, north of Medford, and the scenic woodlands viewed after crossing the bone-dry Agate Desert, were visions to write home about.

Trains from Eagle Point switched to the SP track near the present North Medford freeway interchange and initially used the Southern Pacific depot in Medford. Their own station would not be ready until late December 1910.

The new depot was a converted two-story brick rooming house on East Main Street near the east end of the present Bear Creek bridge. This depot was new,

(TOP) **In effort to cost costs during First World War, Pacific & Eastern Railway bought this Omnicar in Portland, had it equipped with flange wheels and used it on the railroad. It sat six adults but up to four more could squeeze in if everyone was friendly. Driver and conductor rode in front.** (CENTER) **Butte Falls Depot with first arrival of train from Eagle Point.** (LOWER) **Depot at Eagle Point served the railroads well – still stands.**

(TOP) **The way to ruin a perfectly nice day is to wreck your train. Accident on Medford Logging Railroad which took over P&E properties.** (LOWER) **Passenger coach dating from early P&E days abandoned on siding near village of Derby, west of Butte Falls.**

it was brick, it was impressive, and was about where the Statue of Liberty statue is in Hawthorne Park.

The P&E track ran from the switch at North Medford, along approximately where Biddle Road is today, and ended at East Main Street alongside the terminal-depot.

During the First World War, revenue fell as operating costs went up – a familiar story for all railroads. About the only freight was load after load of Douglas fir railroad ties for shipment to France. These came from a small lumbering outfit at the end of the track, Butte Falls. By the time the war was over, the little mill had run out of timber so it closed. With few passengers and no freight revenue, the Pacific & Eastern Railroad also closed. ◇

Central Point "Comes of Age"

The village of Central Point, where local farmers allegedly refused to cough-up money to have the Oregon and California Rail Road locate its switchyard there in the 1880's, saw its town nearly wither away in the dust of inactivity over most of the next 100 years. Four miles south, Medford quickly became a big town. Then Medford and Central Point started to sprawl along the track to where in 1997, one merely steps across a city street that separates the cities.

Central Point, which for decades had only a 2-lane main street with one traffic signal, is now cut in half by four-lane Pine Street, seven stop-and-go lights and within one year added McDonald's, Burger King, Subway, TacoBell, and Pilot, a major interstate truck stop. Coming soon will be a motel and sit-down restaurant near the truck stop.

Central Point has come of age but it took the I-5 freeway to do it.

Central Oregon & Pacific switcher with empties moves from White City (WCTU) yard heading to Medford. Track parallels highway 99 between Central Point and Medford. Shown is crossing at Ehrman Way and the highway.

Chapter 9

Medford Logging Railroad
– MEDCO –
Operated: November 14, 1932 - February 11, 1961
Scrapping started March 21, 1961

FOR SEVERAL YEARS there had been specu-
lation about major timber availability in the mountains
above Butte Falls. In fact, investors had already ac-
cumulated thousands of acres of virgin timber and
some of this was being cut. There were also thousands
of acres of timber in the "O & C" land grant. It took
James N. Brownlee, who had run a timber operation in
the deep south, (Mississippi), and Millard D. Olds of
Wisconsin – both having depleted their earlier holdings – who eventually pooled their resources into the
Brownlee-Olds Lumber Company. In the meantime,
Brownlee bought the Pacific & Eastern Railway and
all of its rolling stock.

Brownlee's idea
was to extend rails in-
to the forest then con-
vert the entire railroad
into a log hauler. The
Brownlee-Olds agree-
ment was short lived
but set the stage for
bigger operations.

About the time
Brownlee bought the
P&E, he started to
build a new mill near
today's North Med-
ford freeway inter-
change. This was close to the switch between P&E
and Southern Pacific's main line.

His mill construction started in the fall of 1920
but mills, timber holdings, and railroads, often change
hands. Three years later, Brownlee sold his interest to
Olds then Brownlee retired to Mississippi.

Next to enter the scene was John S. Owen, who in
May of 1924, purchased all of Old's timber holdings,
the mill and the railroad.

With over one million board feet of timber under
his control, as well as a railroad to haul cut logs to his
new mill in Medford, Owen and his backers formed
the Owen-Oregon Lumber Company. In a separate arrangement, the Medford Logging Railroad Company
was incorporated as a wholly-owned subsidiary.

Of the many railroad logging systems throughout
the greater Pacific Northwest, the Medford Logging

**Typical load of logs out of Butte Falls forested area
headed in to Medford Corporation Mill at Medford.
Engine is in the distance.**

Railroad was a major carrier. Within a short period,
over 20 miles of track was laid deep into the forest
FROM Butte Falls and kept a 5-man crew busy just
maintaining it. Writing in his book, *Medford Corporation, A History of an Oregon Logging and Lumber
Company*, Jeff LaLande reported:

> Owen-Oregon began with about forty flatcars and
> Brownlee-Olds' [60-ton] Porter rod engine, but soon expand-
> ed ... to forty more cars and a 75-ton Baldwin locomotive.
> The Baldwin pulled the loads between Derby Station (a few
> miles west of Butte Falls) and Medford, while the ... Porter
> traveled from Derby to the switch point in the woods. From
> there, hauling was done with two 70-ton Willamette geared
> locomotives. A Lima-Shay of the same weight was employed
> pulling ballast and track steel throughout the woods.

The Willamette "side-winder" engines (construc-

Medford Corporation (MEDCO) Shay (Lima) Spot No. 5 (TOP) and MEDCO No. 7 (Willamette) (CENTER). When the logging line closed, the Shay was scrapped and No., 7 went to exhibit at (LOWER) Dunsmuir Railroad Park where it can be viewed today.

(TOP) **Excursions were popular means of entertainment in decades before high-performance automobiles and TV. There was usually a basket picnic at the end of the line, the traditional baseball game for men and boys while women watched. Then the ride back to town. Train pulled by MEDCO No. 4 probably never went faster than 10 mph largely because of rickety track.** (LOWER) **No. 4, a Willamette, is exhibited today in Medford Railroad Park.**

tion numbers 6 and 18 – MEDCO numbers 2 and 4) – were designed after the famous Lima Shay when the eastern firm's patent expired. Of only 33 Willamettes built, just six remain and one of those, MEDCO No. 4, from the Medford Logging Railroad, is preserved in Oregon. It can be seen in the Medford Railroad Park. MEDCO No. 2 is displayed at a unique Railroad Park 2 miles south of Dunsmuir in California.*

In the 1930's, when there was pressure from orchardists and timber operators to obtain lower freight rates at Southern Pacific, some serious thought was given to extending the old P&E line from Butte Falls over the mountains to join a Weyerhaeuser line out of Klamath Falls. If this was done, observers forecast, Medford would be served by two railroads, not just the SP. But the Great Depression was then running in full force and funds for the extension were estimated up to $50,000 per mile – a fortune! – for 37 miles. The money could not be raised.

Owen-Oregon Lumber Company had its difficulties during the depression and the Medford operation went into receivership. In 1932, a committee of Chicago-based bondholders reorganized as the Medford Corporation (MEDCO).

Although man-power was substantially limited during World War-II, the woods operations continued and the Medford Logging Railroad hauled logs regularly over the old P&E track. But there was some sudden heavy traffic competing for the southern end of its line due to a decision made by the War Department.

---

*The park is actually a "motel" with no rooms – people rent refurbished cabooses in which to sleep. See the chapter "Lonesome Cabooses."

Quite early in the war, the Army announced plans to build a large military training post in the Rogue Valley. In its usual majestic manner for selecting a site, the military took a piece of land largely inhabited by rattlesnakes, field mice, crickets, and rabbits – the Agate Desert. Camp White came into existence. As the P&E track ran through the middle of the site, the government assumed the right to use the track for the prosecution of the war effort. (See chapter on WCTU.)

After the war, the MEDCO management looked closely at its operations. Although gasoline and later diesel fueled logging trucks became popular, the railroad was already there, was working well, so it was further expanded. By the early 1950's, there was about 70 miles of track. With expanded operations, MEDCO bought a second-hand Mallet saddle-tank locomotive. This engine was in poor condition and was later junked in favor of a new 100-ton Baldwin diesel (800 horse-power) in 1952 for use on its line between Medford and Butte Falls. This became Road No. 8.

In 1959 many of the old spurs in the forests were pulled out as trucks took over the job of hauling logs. A depot for reloading from the trucks onto the railroad was established at Butte Falls and the trains kept up schedules on the 40-mile trip to Medford until final phase-out in 1962.

On the last load, there were 19 cars of logs. The right-of-way, after the rails were picked up, was disposed of except for two sections. The track within the former Camp White became part of the WCTU. A 2-mile section from the Medford mill to the cold decks, named "Desert Pond," near the Rogue Valley International-Medford Airport, was used for logging trucks until the day the MEDCO mill was shut down. Soon afterward it was dismantled. Today, one can see the old narrow railroad right-of-way, a pre-stressed concrete bridge over the freeway immediately north of the North Medford interchange.*

The locomotives of the Medford Logging Railroad were dispersed widely. The fairly new Baldwin diesel (No. 8) went to Arizona where for the next 24 years it hauled trains of copper ore. The Lima Shay, worn out, was scrapped. As mentioned, one of the Willamettes went to a railroad museum just south of Dunsmuir, California. The other Willamette, the 4-spot, is on exhibit in Medford Railroad Park. (For a number of years it was in Jackson Park, in West Medford, awaiting the time for its final move.)

The former MEDCO little rod engine built about 1924, operates on the California Western Railroad's "Skunk" tourist line between Fort Bragg and Willets hauling 70,000 passengers and about 500 cars of freight a year.

In 1995, the Southern Oregon Chapter of the National Railway Historical Society, purchased the Baldwin 8-spot diesel from the Arizona owners. It had been put to pasture due to breakdown. But the volunteers of the Medford-based society brought the locomotive through Medford to Albany and to the Willamette Pacific Railroad Company shop where it has been restored. The objective of the society is to obtain right-of-way between Medford and Butte Falls, put down rail, and offer tourist rides. Jerry Hellinga, a volunteer locomotive engineer and President of the Society, declares the goal is within reach. He says all it takes is cooperation and m-o-n-e-y! <>

Gear drive for Willamette logging engine applied power to every axle under the engine and tender.
Gear is on MEDCO No. 4 at Medford Railroad Park.

Editor's Note:
For track map of MEDCO Logging Railroad, refer to Medford & Crater Lake Railroad for basic route to Butte Falls. There seems to have been at least 20 miles of "portable" track used beyond Butte Falls. "Portable" track refers to track used in one location then removed and set down in another place. This occurred frequently in the woods. For an un-scaled sketch of the tracks out of Butte Falls refer to LaLande in bibliography.

---

* On November 15, 1996, the Oregon Department of Transportation announced plans to build major highway extensions near the North Medford interchange of Interstate-5. This is to relieve the grid-lock presently faced by motorists at the interchange, which is also to be rebuilt. The new roads will cut across the land formerly owned by the huge MEDCO mill.

(TOP) **U. S. Army Quartermaster Corps switcher assigned to Camp White in World War II.** (LOWER) **General Electric 500 hp switcher does daily work in 1997.**

Chapter 10

W C T U Railway Company

(White City Terminal Utility Railroad)
Established 1950 —

ONE OF THE FIRST things the U. S. Army did when it decided to build a military training camp in the Agate Desert, about 9 miles north of Medford, was to consider the availability of rail connections to the main line of the Southern Pacific. Nearby was the old Pacific & Eastern track that had been taken over by a logging company whose rails ran straight through the center of the area chosen for the main cantonment. How handy! As quickly as plans were ready, track crews went to work to suit Army specifications.

GE switcher of WCTU on yard duty at Medford Industrial Park White City

To handle local switching, the Army's Quartermaster Corps assigned a small steam switcher to Camp White. Southern Pacific locomotives hauled the freight trains, later passenger cars with troops, that were parked on the "loop" (balloon track) at whatever position would clear the switches. After dropping the cars, the SP locomotive continued on the loop back to the main line. The Army's switcher would hook to then jostle the cars wherever they had to be spotted in the camp's warehouse area.

Troops arriving and departing would usually be handled from a spur that paralleled the mainline but, when there were large movements, especially departures, a second section of a troop train would be made up on a spur off the end of 16th street (see map). It took a little juggling to turn a train from this location as there was no wye for that purpose.

The troop train would leave the spur but proceed only far enough the clear the switch. With a flagman walking, the train backed past two switches. On clearing the second switch, the train would move forward on the balloon track at about 5 miles per hour (allowing a leisurely sighting seeing trip), through the warehouse area then eventually enter the main line.

When the war was over and the camp deactivated, the cantonment area of Camp White became the Medford Industrial Park.* Many of the military buildings were either dismantled and sold as used building material, or were moved intact around the valley having been sold at auction. Very few remain to this day at their old sites. Some of the land was sold for home and trailer (mobile home) sites. The name of the camp was changed to White City, Oregon then the Post Office Department assigned ZIP 97503 to the area. At this writing, White City is the largest unincorporated but populated area in Jackson County. The army hos-

---

* For an exciting treatment of rugged recruit training and life at Camp White, refer to *Camp White Oregon* in bibliography.

(TOP) **Plymouth switcher was badly underpowered.**
(CENTER) **Engine garage and work shed, also trainmen's break room and lockers.** (LOWER) **Part of main switchyard showing antique track.**

pital underwent a major rebuild, and is today the Department of Veterans Affairs Domiciliary.

The development of the Industrial park included the access to the mainline Southern Pacific railroad plus the balloon and spur tracks in the old camp's warehouse area.

During the war, there had been some competition for use of the rail line from the Southern Pacific switch at the north end of Medford to the camp. The logging trains and the military trains often vied for its use. The military had an in-built priority because of the need for the line due to the nation being at war. The logging company had a government priority because of the high requirement for lumber. Which was it to be? This sometimes heated argument was settled when it was decided the Army would use the rails at night and the loggers during the day. The only exception was when the military had troop trains on the track. Then, by mutual agreement, a change in the arrangement would be accommodated.

By 1950, when some heavy industry had taken residence at the new Industrial Park, a short line railroad to handle switching went into business. For locomotives, the operators acquired two gasoline-powered single-truck "engines." These units had standard automobile stick shifts and each was powered with a V8 Plymouth engine.

These were the infamous Plymouth switchers many railroads tried to use but with various levels of success–? According to the men who operated them, the units were "hard to drive, sluggish, and wore a guy out." They were also limited in the number of freight cars they would move as they were grossly underpowered for the task. It became necessary to keep the two identical engines as one could be used for parts in emergencies. The short line took the name White City Terminal and Utility Railroad – WCTU.*

In 1962, the Medford Logging Railroad was shut down and its track, which extended into the timber harvest areas near Butte Falls, was pulled up.

(Logging continued for many years, using diesel trucks until 1995, when all Medford Logging Company operations, including its Medford mill, called MEDCO, shut down and the mill was dismantled.)

Miles of rails of the old logging line were pulled except for the short section at the Industrial Park. This

---

* The initial reaction of many on hearing of the W.C.T.U., the initials also standing for the historic Woman's Christian Temperance Union, is entertaining for some wondered if the anti-liquor ladies had gone into the railroad business.

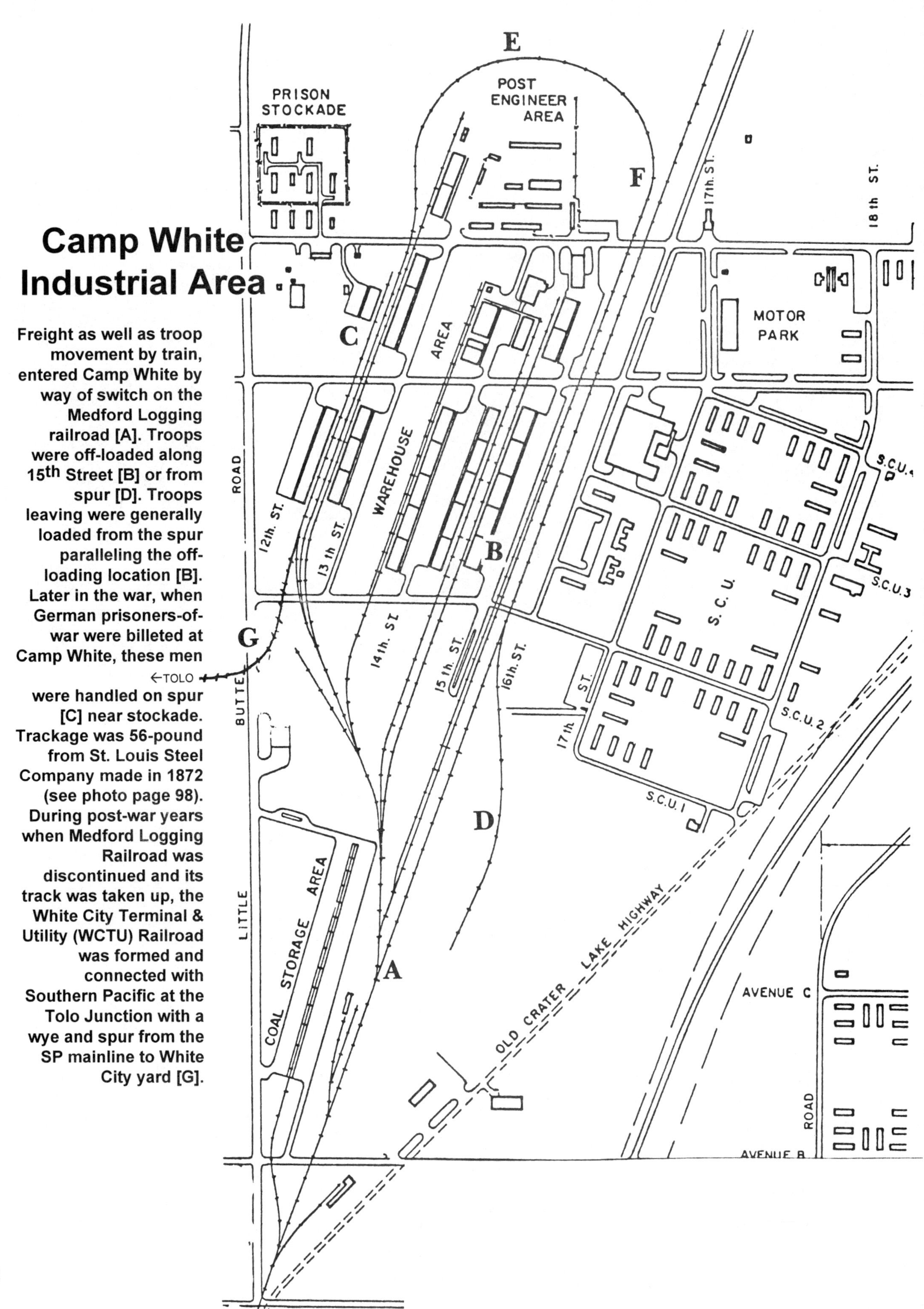

Camp White Industrial Area

Freight as well as troop movement by train, entered Camp White by way of switch on the Medford Logging railroad [A]. Troops were off-loaded along 15th Street [B] or from spur [D]. Troops leaving were generally loaded from the spur paralleling the off-loading location [B]. Later in the war, when German prisoners-of-war were billeted at Camp White, these men were handled on spur [C] near stockade. Trackage was 56-pound from St. Louis Steel Company made in 1872 (see photo page 98). During post-war years when Medford Logging Railroad was discontinued and its track was taken up, the White City Terminal & Utility (WCTU) Railroad was formed and connected with Southern Pacific at the Tolo Junction with a wye and spur from the SP mainline to White City yard [G].

was given to the W.C.T.U. But White City Terminal Railroad had a challenge on its hands. With logging by rail terminated, and the switch to the Southern Pacific track at North Medford about to be pulled, how to switch its cars?

By agreement, SP put in a track from the site of the village of Tolo on its main line, north of Central Point, to an interchange (switchyard) a few yards east of Pacific Avenue at the west end of the Industrial Park in White City. The link to the main line became Tolo Junction. This included a wye at Tolo as well as a switchyard and parking spurs.

Southern Pacific pulls White City destined cars to the Pacific Avenue interchange on which it leaves cars for the WCTU. The WCTU Plymouths putted to the yard, hooked to the cars and spotted them at destinations within the park. Forty-five years later, the WCTU still operates with the same 13 miles of track. Earlier, the balloon track was dismantled as superfluous to the operation.

After the Union Tank Car Company purchased the WCTU in 1974, some of the track was upgraded from 56-pound steel to 75-pound. The worn-out Plymouths were sold to railroad fanciers, and two 600 horsepower General Electric diesel-electric switchers were brought in.

The operational plan was simple. Southern Pacific hauled in cars during the night, then early the next morning, a WCTU switcher picked up the cars and spotted them to the businesses around the park that had ordered them. The work to be done was the same every day whether it was with the former Plymouths or the new GE's. Except with the GE switchers, there was less griping and the work went more smoothly and much more rapidly.

On outgoing trains, WCTU pulled loaded cars to the interchange during the days, and SP picked them up usually during the night. Factory men at White City, as well as elsewhere, love to harangue with railroads over what they call shortage of cars. That gripe continues to the present day, even after Southern Pacific turned over its Siskiyou Line to RailTex, in 1994, now operating in Oregon as Central Oregon & Pacific Railroad – CORP.

In the 1980's, WCTU owned and was a major lessor of modern, double-door box cars, owning some 3,000 of them. By 1996, the railroad had sold its cars and turned to leasing some of them back.

In recent years The Marmon Group of Companies absorbed Union Tank Car Company and with it the WCTU. White City Railroad Company still operates as a Division but its day-to-day work continues on the same 13 miles of track.

Railroad Safety Admonition

It Takes

ONE MINUTE to write a safety rule
ONE HALF-HOUR to hold a safety meeting
ONE WEEK to plan a safety program
ONE MONTH to put the plan into operation
ONE YEAR to win a safety award
ONE SECOND to destroy this with only
ONE ACCIDENT

**The Way to Ruin A Perfectly Nice Day
Is To Wreck Your Train**

**Keep Safety In Mind
At All Times**

Although the WCTU is one of the shortest lines in Oregon, it is responsible for moving all rail freight in and out of Southern Oregon's largest industrial complex, the Medford Industrial Park.

DeAnn R. Carlton, Manager of Operations at the White City Railroad, commented that much rail business has been lost to trucks in part due to the continuing hassle about obtaining cars appropriate for her customers' needs, when her customers need them.*<>

---

* A number of years ago, when KOGAP Manufacturing Company, a major plywood maker in Southern Oregon, was having continuing beefs with SP over the proverbial shortage of appropriate cars, KOGAP management started sending its product by truck over the mountains to Klamath Falls where Great Northern Railway was happy to supply cars knowing it was doing SP out of some business. Once SP got wind of this, the Medford firm got all the cars it needed. "KOGAP" stands for "Keep Oregon Green and Productive" but the firm no longer makes plywood.

Jacksonville Depot and shops at Oregon and "C" Streets. The depot is still there, is now Chamber of Commerce summer office. The track is under the street.

Chapter 11

Rogue River Valley Railway Company

Medford and Jacksonville Railway January 17, 1890 - February 6, 1891
Rogue River Valley Railway Company February 7, 1891 - June 30, 1895
Rogue River Valley Rail*road* Company July 1, 1895 - August 2, 1899
Rogue River Valley Rail*way* Company August 3, 1899 - September 1904. Re-incorporated same name to June 30, 1915
Electrified as part of Southern Oregon Traction Company (founded July 15, 1913) March 27, 1916 - November 5, 1919
Medford Coast Railroad Company November 6. 1919 - Service stopped April 1, 1924 - Discontinued 1925 - Abandoned 1930

EVEN THOUGH the Oregon & California Rail Road would never touch Jacksonville, five miles west of Medford, business interests in Jacksonville wanted a railroad so badly they put possibility thinking together with money and decided to build a railroad of their own.

Expectations were high that with a short line between the two towns, freight and passengers would keep Jacksonville alive. This was a fight for survival in the minds of many Jacksonvillians as the new town of Medford was growing as an unwelcome weed. Ashland, never before of much concern to Jacksonville's people because of the distance, suddenly seemed closer. Ashland, as a division point on the mainline railroad saw its population spurt as railroad folks moved in and soon topped Jacksonville's numbers. In addition, there was the uncomfortable situation just six miles northeast: Central Point. This almost-a-village nearly doubled in size due to the new railroad. Although that hamlet had not been directly in the line-of-sight of the O&C plans, its people promptly moved what they could and quickly straddled the track. About the only advantage "CP" had from the railroad was a switch and a spur for a cattle chute.

In Jacksonville, meetings, often heated, were held by committees trying to determine where to put a railroad right-of-way between their town and Medford. (Some Jacksonville business men are reported to have referred to Medford as "Medfordsville" in an effort to make the new town sound small, instead of acknowledging the reality of the rapidly expanding town Medford was obviously becoming.)

A railroad would hire people for construction as well as for operation. This meant money would flow to Jacksonville. Medford individuals became interested therefore the Minutes of the Town Board of Medford (January 23, 1899) includes names of Medford people who agreed to pay a bonus of $7,500 when a rail line was completed between the two towns. In "J-ville" as the town was often called – but never in official matters – $12,500 was pledged. Part of this came from a bond issue. Accordingly, the Medford and Jacksonville Railway was incorporated January 17, 1890.

William S. Barnum, President, Rogue River Valley Railway. He was an intense gentlemen who set out to make his railroad a success in the face of many obstacles over which he had little or no control.

Its committee set about to determine a route, locate potential depot sites and prepare final surveys. There was a deadline: One year (January 1, 1891) for a train to actually operate on the line for the contractor, Crawford, Howell and Company, Corvallis, Oregon, to collect the $20,000 bonus.

Pressure mounted to get the track put down but it is one thing to envision an operating system on paper and quite another to let the "idea" give birth by placing an order for all the needed goods, receive and install ties and rails, buy an engine and cars and have everything arrive to begin operations.

Time waits for no one! With less than a month before the construction contract expired, rails had not been delivered let alone nailed to ties. The contractor walked off the job.

To believe such a project could have been completed within the allotted time seems, with the advantage of 20-20 hindsight, to have been ill-conceived. There are no records found today for anyone to review as to supply source or the rail specifications. There seems good reason to believe, however, that a hardware store in Portland, Oregon, Honeyman, DeHart and Company, which specialized in heavy metals, received the order. This dealer took delivery on second-hand rail that had originated in England.

Examples of this rail excavated years later range from 36-pound to 51-pound and 56-pound. (Rail is measured by weight of a 36-inch length.)

A new contractor, no less than the firm that supplied the rails that also had large timber holdings in the area, plausibly envisioned using the railroad to haul its timber, was given the job of completing the work. The firm went at it quickly and created a new enthusiasm throughout the area as the work progressed rapidly. What had been noted for delays, now moved ahead with amazing speed. Final grading was completed just as Southern Pacific told the builders that a full train of flat cars carrying rail was due on the morrow.

Rails were nailed to ties in record time.

Fully aware that there was no rolling stock, the contractor leased a locomotive and car from Union Pacific. (As there was still ill-feeling against the mainline firm for not routing its track via Jacksonville, why rent from them? It was now Southern Pacific to be reckoned with as the O&C had gone bankrupt while trying to get over the Siskiyous.)

The deadline of January 1, 1891 was at hand. It was a very cold and rainy Thursday. There was no ballast yet placed to weight the ties in the soft, wet earth but the UP engine made steam and was ready. On sig-

The 10-ton 2-4-0 Porter engine, built in December 1890 was "Jacksonville No. 1" It proved, on the first day, to be too small for the job. After years of idleness, use elsewhere and loss of its front wheels, it was rebuilt and is ready for service in spring 1997. Railroad historians and buffs pray that its California owners will eventually return it to Jacksonville (even for a visit).

Regional Rail Lines
Rogue River Valley Oregon 1891 – 1925

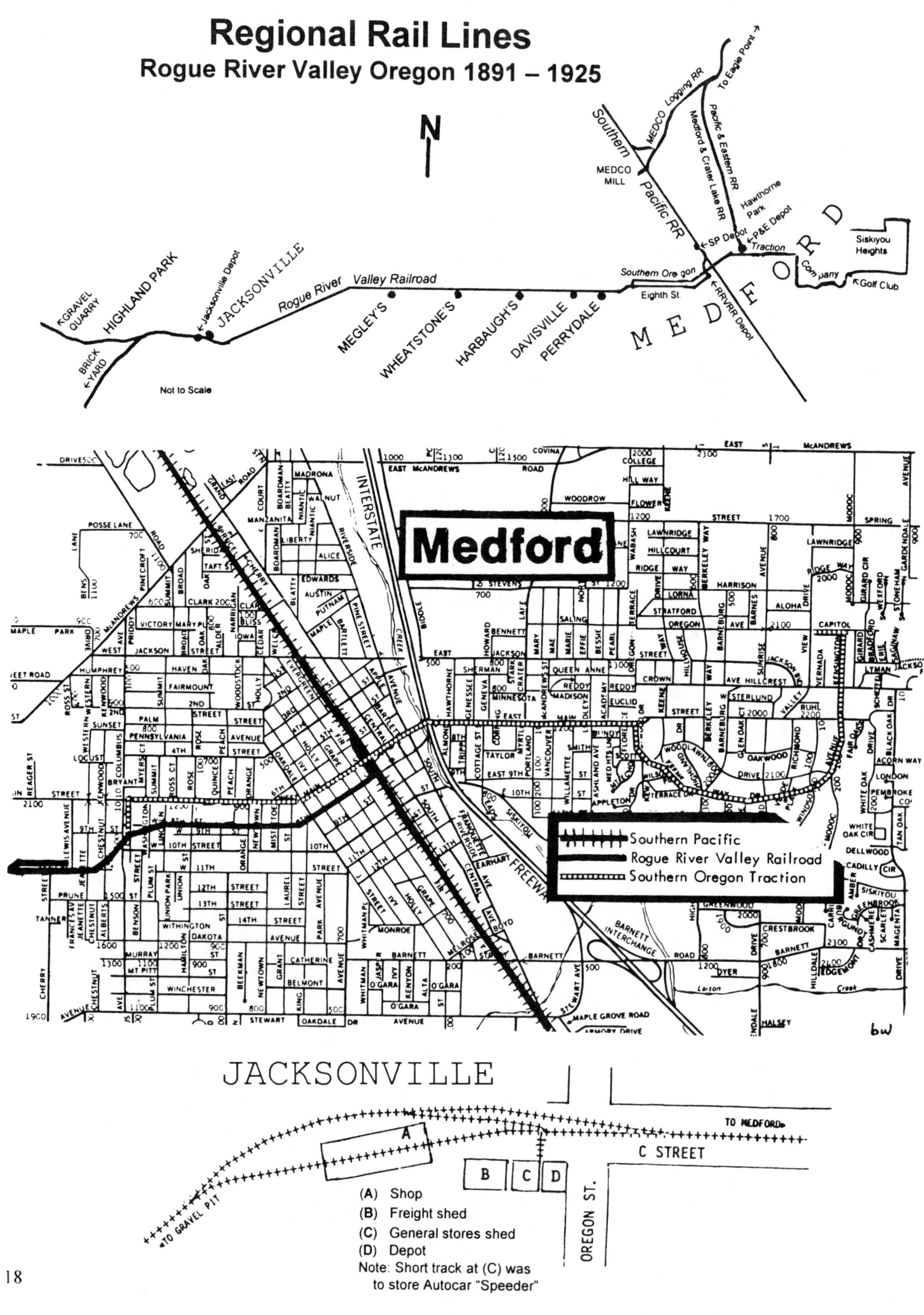

(TOP) **Porter 10-ton engine is dwarfed by its combiantion car. It was too small and had to be replaced.** (LOWER) **James H. Barnum (left) father of W. S. Barnum and John Corbin Barnum, a son of Wm. S. Barnum in business office in the depot in 1913.**

nal, it barely started to roll when the track slipped and the engineer found his mount parked firmly in the mud. The locomotive was far too heavy for 36-pound rail on non-ballasted ties.

Jacksonville's people were not dismayed for long. They were pleased with the progress of their new contractor so they granted an extension.

About two weeks later, folks froze in their activities as a sudden shriek split the air – a locomotive whistle! The first train hissed and chugged its way into town to the site where the depot had not yet been built. It was mid-morning of January 6, 1891. The townspeople caused a spontaneous celebration that rivaled those of the 4th-of-July.

ooOOOoo

Nearly everyone wanted to ride the train. One story is told how two teenage girls in Jacksonville were so caught up with excitement they got on the test train as it was returning to Medford. But they had to walk all the way back home. These girls were the first passengers for the line although regular service had not yet been announced.

All the early trips were with borrowed equipment as the engine and car ordered had still not arrived. Groups chartered the train for special trips which

included a number of Masons in Medford who, one night, boarded the train to Jacksonville for a visit to the Jacksonville Lodge.

It was announced that the ride to Medford lasted only twenty minutes. There was concern, in official circles, about the westbound trip which took longer as it was a steady uphill pull. It was noted that the grade was not overly steep or mountainous nevertheless, Jacksonville is higher. The Medford Bench Mark reads 1,383 feet elevation and Jacksonville is 1,567 feet, a trifling increase on the railroad for the distance. However, it costs more fuel to puff a train up any grade than when a train goes downhill.

As January faded into February, construction on the two depots – one at each end of the line – was moving right along. While many magazine articles about the railroad speak only of the so-called "main line" between the towns, little is said about the western extensions.

From Jacksonville, rails were placed along the north side of Jackson Creek to a gravel pit about two miles upstream. From this quarry it was an easy run downhill to lay ballast from the bottom of an old hopper car all the way to Medford.

Another extended went about one mile southwest to a brick yard and kiln. The brickmen indicated they would use the railroad's freight service if the spur was built. But what about extending the line all the way to the coast?

Extend Railroad to the Coast?

Crescent City, on the northwest corner of California, had been a seaport for decades and it was from there that long, heavy wagon trains had been hauling freight to Jacksonville since the town was founded. The idea, saloon-born talk, was just to extend the gravel pit spur to Crescent City. This seemed like a good idea but the notion never went farther than the saloon.

The contractor, Honeyman, DeHart and Company, formed the Rogue Valley Railway Company on February 7, 1891. Capitol stock was set at $100,000 which was split into 1,000 shares. The stated purpose was to operate the railroad between the two towns plus the two extensions.

The first scheduled service began February 12, 1891 with two trains a day. But there was already money being made with the demand for special charters before regular service began.

If there was disappointment about the project, it had to do with the choice of the company's locomotive which had recently arrived. The Porter engine "No. 1" was a 10-ton 2-4-0 with 30-inch wheels factory number 1236. "The little engine that could" could not. It was too light. The locomotive rented from Union Pacific would have to be kept until a larger engine could be obtained.

During this period, there was some experimental "tinkering" with the Porter to try to increase its power. Limited success was achieved allowing the engine to pull a single passenger car if there were not too many people on board.

Except for the loads of bricks as freight revenue, Jacksonville had no industrial base. In short order, the only income for the railroad came from passengers as the brick yard closed. It had operated for fifty years.

When freight consigned to a merchant in Jacksonville arrived at the SP depot in Medford, it had to be off-loaded, hauled to the "J-ville" track and reloaded. This was costly as well as bothersome for both railroads and caused delays. As a link between the track of the SP and the "R.R.V.R.R" (as painted on the locomotive), would be of mutual interest, Southern Pacific installed a switch and laid rail for about 100 yards to join the end of the Jacksonville track. Upon completion, the occasional freight car destined for Jacksonville could be "humped" to that track. *

The only sure freight between Medford and Jacksonville was the contract with the Post Office to haul mail. As the Post Office Department in Washington, was very friendly toward railroads during this era,

---

* Sometime later when the streets were paved in Medford and the abandoned RRVRR track was covered, a section of track leading to the switch into the SP, north of 6th Street, was kept by SP as a "caboose" parking track. In later years, with the arrival of diesel locomotives, this 56-pound rail was still used to park those engines. Shortly after CORP took over the SP interests here, all excess track was removed including the remaining visible rails of the old Jacksonville line. There still remains however, hundreds of yards of RRVRR rail under pavement on Main and on Eighth Streets.

the transfer of the contract from horse-drawn wagon to rail was swift. While there were literally thousands of Railway Post Offices (RPO) special cars on the nation's railroads, none would be assigned or needed on the line to Jacksonville. The mail would be put on the local train at each end of the line by a contract carrier. This was a job limited to moving mail in closed sacks or locked pouches between a post office and the trains. On an RPO, a Post Office employee, actually a train-riding mail clerk (who always carried a gun on his belt), sorted mail and postmarked mail as the train sped along. While there was no such service

on the Jacksonville-Medford line, and the railroad did not officially accept mail other than in the closed containers, some single pieces were left at the depots for dispatch. As a courtesy, the depot clerks accepted these letters then "hit" each envelope with the railroad's rubber stamp. These "covers" as they are called, are quite rare and are highly sought by postal historians today.

While there does not seem to have been much effort to coordinate schedules with the mainline SP, passengers who had time to spend between trains found plenty to do in Medford.

Jacksonville was the county seat therefore it saw numbers of lawyers, mostly from Medford, traveling between the towns to attend to their unique business in a regular manner. As an incentive to keep regulars using the train, the railroad offered "commute" tickets good for one month. Each trip, on the discount plan,

Barnum earned good money with excursions, had considerably less income from daily commuter runs. This appears to be engine No. 3, built May 1886. It is a 4-4-0 Cooke with 56-inch wheels.

was rated at 20¢. Every cent in fare was important for the operators, in their earlier role as contractors, who had spent $41,160.11 to install and start service on the line. Of this, $8,257.24 was in locomotives and cars. The promoters and the construction people agreed that the job was completed in May 1891 so the promised $20,000 bonus was paid.

A portion of the final work was the finishing of the two depots. On the Medford end, this small building was near the track and across Main Street from the SP Depot. Many years later both the SP and the RRVR depots would come down. The SP's, because the original depot was no longer serviceable as well as it was the city's pain-in-the-neck. This was due to the fact that O&C had built it precisely in the middle of Main Street. This obstructed traffic on the street. The

The citizenry from Jacksonville and Medford seemed pleased with the train service and patronized it steadily. This little short-line railroad was "different" than riding on the SP. Besides, this was a fun trip – almost as going to an amusement park to ride a toy train.*

Jacksonville line's depot had to come down because the State of Oregon, following an inspection, demanded the owner build a new one. After the Jacksonville Railroad ceased business, this second depot was demolished to make room for a business building.

---

* The Southern Oregon Live Steamers, a chapter of the National Railway Historical Society, in cooperation with the Parks and Recreation Department of the City of Medford, operate Railroad Park. The members have a large layout of 7½-inch gauge track where they run model trains on which the public can ride free. The park operates every second Sunday from April through October weather permitting.

The **RRVRY** did not officially postmark any mail but such rarities (TOP RIGHT) will bring top dollar at philatelic auctions. Mail postmarked on trains (see page 121), also choice collectibles. (CENTER) Whenever there was freight, a combination train was made up to handle passengers on the same run. This saved fuel. (LOWER) After electrification, Barnum renamed his operation the Medford Coast Railroad and used his No. 3 for occasional freight hauls.

Locomotives of R.R.V.Ry.

Road Number	Type	Cylinders in inches	Drivers in inches	Boiler Pressure	Builder	Builder's Number	Date Built
1*	2-4-2T	8 x 14	30	150	Porter	1236	Dec 1890
2**	2-4-0	10 x 18	48	#	Cooke	1718	May 1886
3***	4-4-0	15 x 22	56	130	Cooke	1720	May 1886
4	(no details)						
5##	0-4-4T	11 x 16	42	#	Baldwin	6292	Jul 1882
6###	2-4-2T	10 x 16	40	140	Porter	1487	Oct 1887

*Original locomotive sold in 1895 to Albany Street Railway where it became an 0-4-2; sold again 1905 to Skelly Lumber Co, became 0-4-0 where it was badly ruined in 1911 fire then abandoned. Salvaged by J.H. Chambers Company and used until 1946. Helen O'Conner bought this Porter as a gift to her railroad hobbiest husband Chadwell. Engine hauled to O'Conner private track in Alta Loma, California and rebuilt from Porter blueprints which included boiler re-tubing, replacement cab, cowcatcher, stack, instruments, bell and headlight. Moved to Valencia, California where, on private layout, is rented for motion pictures and commercials by Short Line Enterprises who state: "We can move track, locomotive and crew to your location" or it can be rented for use on the grounds.

**Formerly owned by Oregon-Pacific R.R. Disposition unsure.

***Formerly owned by Northern California & Oregon R.R. Later used by Barnum on same track but designated Medford Coast R.R. Disposition unsure.

#Data unknown.

##Formerly used on New York City elevated R.R. Disposition unsure.

###Formerly owned by Port Townsend Southern R.R. Disposition unsure.

NOTE: Fuel for all locomotives was wood.

In Medford, on West Main Street, there is a bronze plaque, on the south side of the street just west of the CORP track, on the building mentioning the little RRVRR depot.

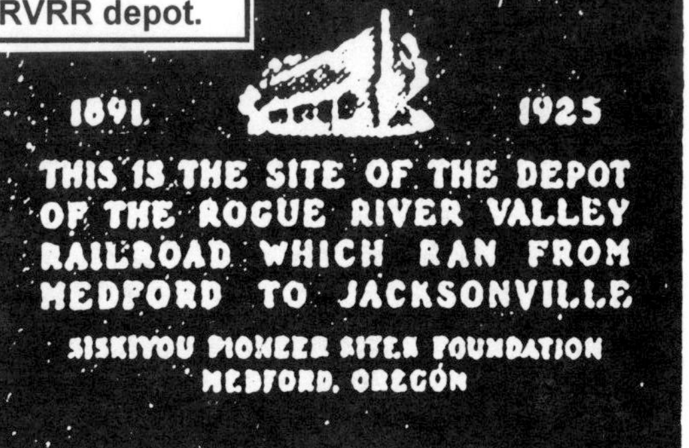

The depot in Jacksonville still stands although it was refurbished about 1989 and turned to face another direction. It presently serves as the Chamber of Commerce Information Office, open every day in summer and limited hours in winter.

ooOOOoo

In 1893, there was talk about extending the line from Medford to Eagle Point as there was a continual need of persons in Eagle Point to go to and from the court house. There was also an obvious seasonal need for hauling fresh produce to Jacksonville markets. The Snowy Butte Flour Mill, established in 1872, had a good business but at this time did not need freight cars to haul its products. Nothing came of the plan.

A new company, incorporated by Honeyman, De Hart and Company, as the Rogue Valley Railway and Improvement Company, capitalized at $500,000, was to raise funds for the track to Eagle Point. It was also an ambitious plan to bring water to Medford by flume for domestic as well as to power an electric plant with the runoff intended for irrigation. It was envisioned in the prospectus that Medford would put up $40,000 so that city would get its much needed water. Although all of these ideas looked good on paper, Medford's officialdom declined.

The periodical, *Railway Age and Northwestern Railroader*, (April 7 and July 28, 1893) carried artic-

John Corbin Barnum at age 12, was reportedly the youngest full-fledged Conductor in American railroading history. He grew up in the business and eventually became Secretary and General Manager.

Letterhead of Rogue River Valley Railway Co. Across top are names, W.S. Barnum, President; W.H. Barnum, Vice President and Treasurer; J.C. Barnum, Secretary and General Manager. The logo at left is: SOUTHERN OREGON SHORT-LINE in top half and monogram: FRUIT BELT. Under the logo is a line: COUNTY SEAT ROUTE. Illustrated are two trainmen's validation punches. A punch manufacturer offers hundreds of different designs in various models. The designs for these two punches is the letter R and a ship's anchor. Punches are from the collection of Dr. Wm. L. Barnum, DMD, and had been used on the railroad.

Special postal history cover issued to celebrate the centennial of the opening of the Rogue River Valley Railway in 1991. Jacksonville Postmaster canceled stamps on outgoing letters with this postmark on January 6, 1991.

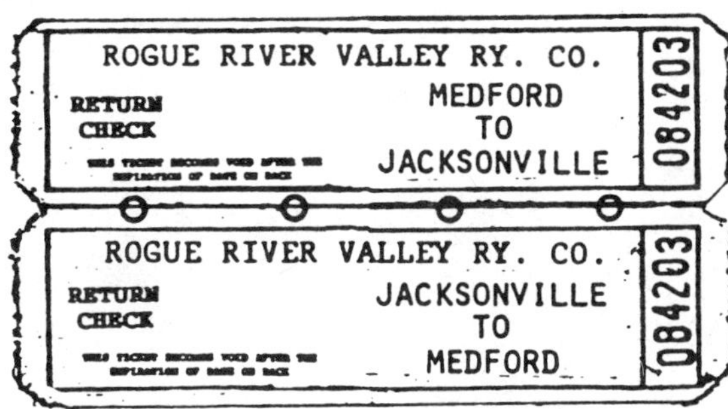

les about the plans. One piece suggested that President C. H. Leadbetter of the Improvement Company, wanted the railroad to run over the mountains to Klamath Falls. The deal included that Southern Pacific would sell some of its "O&C" land, which was loaded with old-growth timber. All of this hoop-la could have been "promotional only" as no way has been found to validate any of it. When Medford said, "No," promoters, who were from Kennewick, Washington, left town after leasing the railroad for the remainder of the year to a local man, William S. Barnum.

With Mr. Barnum at the throttle, an adventure was about to begin.

> **Note:** For the purpose of the narrative of this railroad, the authors do not differentiate between the legal forms rail*road* and rail*way*.

This railroad, commonly called "The Jacksonville Railroad," had few employees and these were let go in favor of Barnum's plan to make the entire operation a family affair. He, his wife and his sons, became the operators for all facets of the system.

In an issue of the *Railway Gazette*, the front cover featured a photograph of John Corbin Barnum, the 12-year old son of the owner. The boy was in his official uniform as Conductor and was declared to be the "youngest conductor in the nation."

The Sr. Barnum took easily to being a railroadman and some suggest his interest was, at least at first, more hobby than business. He held the lease only for a couple of months before it expired. Although his operation didn't make any money, this was nowhere the end of Barnum's railroading on this line. Although he no longer had a lease, the owners, Honeyman, De Hart and Company, who had let the Kennewick men "in," apparently allowed Barnum to keep their railroad running.

During the next two years there were spurts of activity aimed at expansion, but the road itself continued to lose money. Passengers were the main means of income with liitle freight. In addition, the Railway Express Agency (which some call a fore-runner to United Parcel Service which started in 1907), as well as Wells Fargo Express, contracted with the railroad to carry their shipments.

William Honeyman, one of the owners. declared that rumors about his looking to lay a line to Eagle Point by way of Sams Valley, thus missing a piece of the Agate Desert, were true. He declared he had completed his survey. Some Jacksonville merchants, including C. C. Beekman the banker, were interested in business from Eagle Point, as were some farmers in and around Sams Valley.

Had the route from Medford to Eagle Point crossed the desert, there would be no prospects of generating revenue along that way, but the route by way of Sams Valley had potential, Honeyman preached to his prospects. He saw people there with valuable farms whose produce would need to be shipped. If he had a railroad in their neighborhood, he reasoned he would get their freight business.

Everyone who would listen was approached by Honeyman who asked for a handout of $4,000. Even with his speeches and personal pleas, no money was forthcoming. He dropped the plan.

The railroad was beginning to earn some money and became prosperous enough to purchase a 20-ton locomotive in 1895. It went into service that October.

One of the best ways for Barnum to harvest addi-

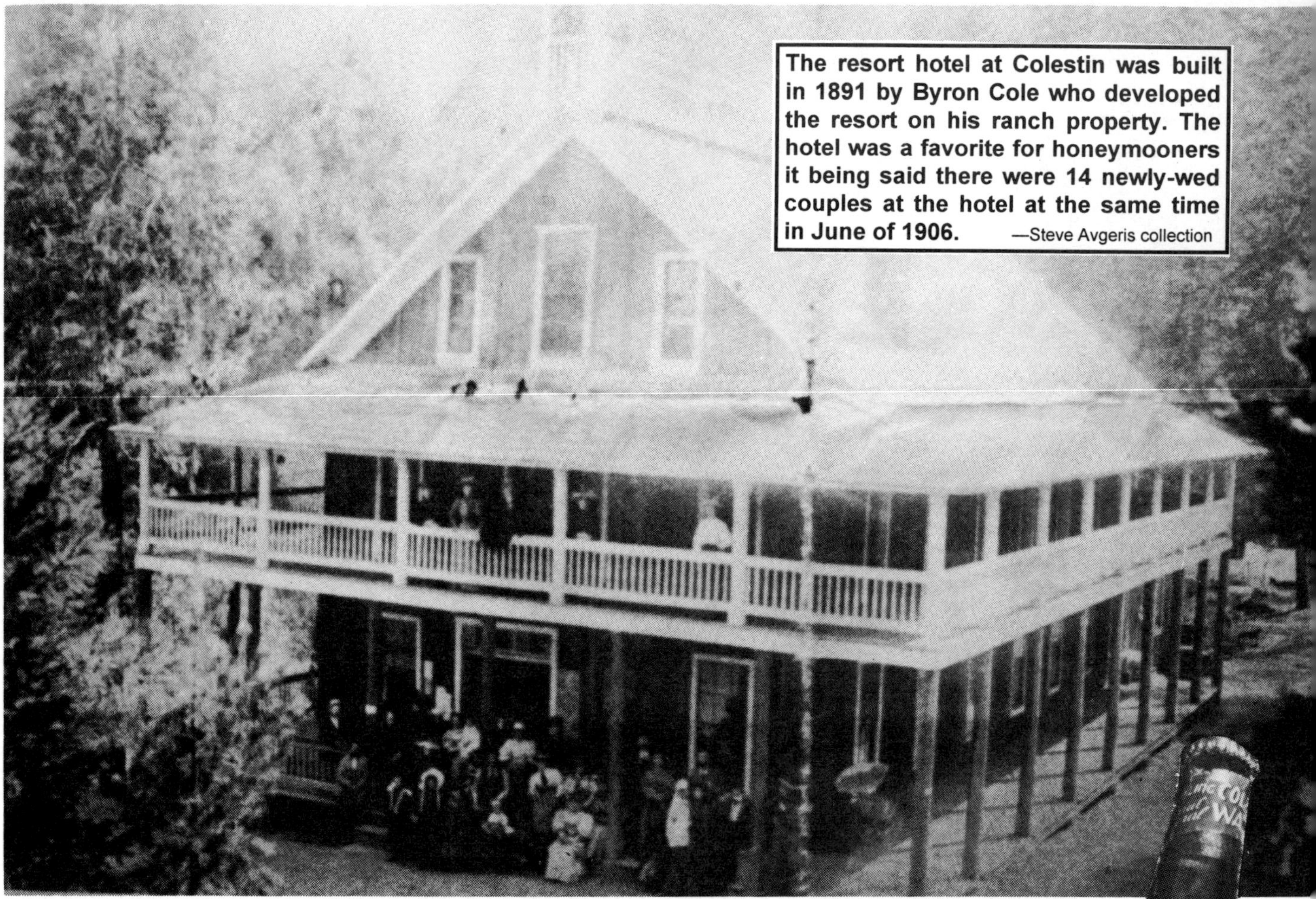

The resort hotel at Colestin was built in 1891 by Byron Cole who developed the resort on his ranch property. The hotel was a favorite for honeymooners it being said there were 14 newly-wed couples at the hotel at the same time in June of 1906. —Steve Avgeris collection

tional fares, was to promote charters and excursions. Probably his most popular excursion was an over-nighter to the mineral springs at Colestin. This was a resort in the Cottonwood Creek Valley on the south side of the Siskiyou Mountains just inside Oregon.

The regular train left Jacksonville for Medford in mid-morning where an excursion car was attached to Southern Pacific's southbound passenger train. The ride passed through the south end of the Bear Creek Valley to Ashland where a stop was made for lunch in the dining room of the SP Depot.

Back on board, the train chugged to the top of the Siskiyous. The ride was steep and slow but was an enjoyment to the passengers. After a brief stop at the summit station, Siskiyou, where mail was thrown off for the postoffice (which operated between 1895 and 1932), the train picked up speed on the down-mountain side. The Colestin resort was just a few minutes away. The train stopped with the excursion car spotted in front on the SP waiting room.

After an evening of dancing, overnight stay then an easy morning relaxing in amazingly clear and crisp weather, among other enjoyments, the excursionists re-boarded their car, now on the northbound train, and were returned to Medford and Jacksonville.

It should be observed that the excursion car was not usually exclusive for Barnum's passengers. Southern Pacific had a regular "deal" with the Colestin resort and ran these junkets on a schedule. Should Barnum completely fill a passenger car for one of these trips, that was fine with SP. If his trip was under-subscribed, his partiers merely took seats in the SP's car.

Another over-nighter promoted by SP was a shopping trip to Eugene. Barnum hawked this and every other deal that came his way in an effort to bring in revenue. But Jacksonville people mainly left the shopping trip for others. When Barnum cut his Jacksonville-Medford trips to once-a-day because he was losing money, the Eugene Shopping Extravaganza was lost in the shuffle.

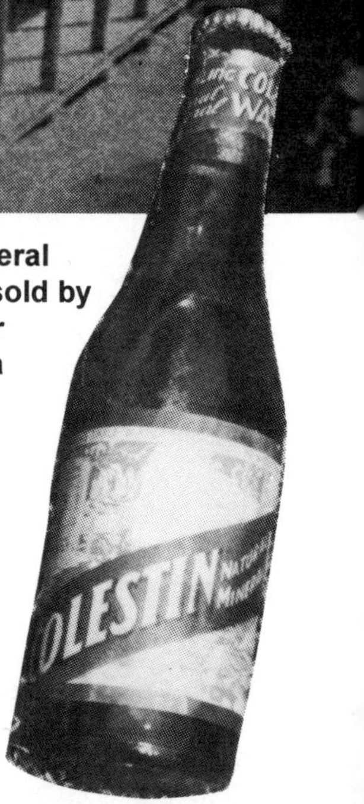

A plant was set up at nearby mineral springs enabling its water to be sold by the bottle. Colestin Mineral Water bottles are rare today and bring a good price. Colestin post office operated until 1943.

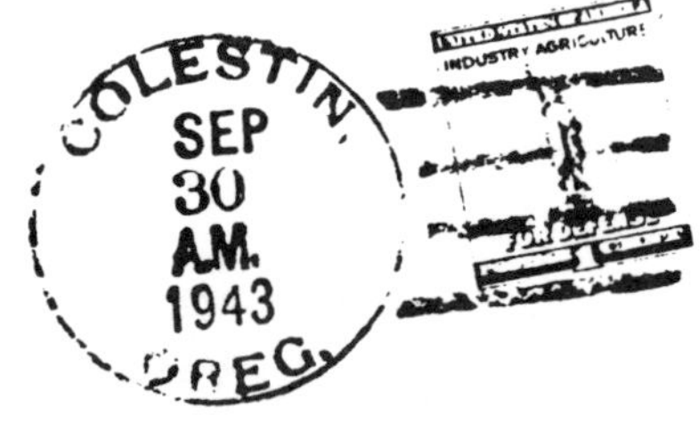

Southern Pacific Station, Colestin, Oregon

Special excursion trains brought people to Colestin resort for many years. The spring of "superior medicinal value" water was just a few hundred feet from the SP station. A promotion in which the hotel engaged was for boys to pass through passenger cars giving paper cups of Colestin Mineral Water as samples, following by a hawker selling bottles of the water.
—Steve Avgeris collection

There were frequent local charters. Politicians often rented the train for outings with loyal supporters. Some candidates mouthed their platforms to people who accepted "Free Ride – Free Lunch in Jacksonville" offers. These "specials" made money for the railroad but the daily commuter trips did not do well.

The Rogue River Valley Railroad was losing revenue for two reasons.

- As the new wore off, people, unless they were business travelers, lost interest.
- As Medford prospered, Jacksonville showed a decline in business houses and in population thus there was less need for the service.

During its lifetime, Barnum's steam engines used cord wood for fuel. There was plenty of wood available along the 2-mile spur to the gravel pit west of Jacksonville as there was on the line to the brick kiln. But in the summer of 1897, Barnum was contacted to demonstrate the use of coal as a fuel. A small coal mine had opened on Evans Creek and the mining company sought to demonstrate its product by advertising that its coal was used to fire the locomotive on the Rogue River Valley Railroad. This sounded pretty good to Barnum if for no other reason he was not expected to pay for the coal.

This trip was made from Medford to Jacksonville – up hill. One can presume that Barnum and the coal people were unable to strike a deal, or perhaps the coal didn't work very well, for Barnum continued to fuel with wood.

Owner-operator Barnum did almost no maintenance and in time his roadbed, engines and its car – there was seldom need for more than one car at a time – began to creak and lurch even though the run between towns was a straight line. Mishaps were inevitable. The car derailed now and then and getting it back on the track was a chore as the RRVRR had no derricks or wrecking equipment. In early 1899, a locomotive lost its footing on the curve entering Medford. A team of heavy draft horses had to be hired to re-rail the engine. The incident also tore up some track. While repair was underway, passengers who could not put off their trips, were taken between the towns, along with the mail sacks, in a buggy.

Much of the acreage along the track was open range therefore cattle often occupied the right-of-way. This could result in the engineer having to jam on the brake. Once, there was an encounter with a steer during which the locomotive lost the argument so the engine had to be sent to a repair shop.

The haul between the towns was too short to generate enough income to keep operating. There was only one recognized stop along the way – Perrydale Avenue. It was about midway between the terminals. There never was any freight for Perrydale, just a quick passenger stop. What freight there was went up the fuel-consuming "hill" to Jacksonville, recalling the west-bound trip was up hill all the way. Jacksonville, as county seat, needed passenger service but the trip to Medford, the money-making (less fuel needed to go down hill), was without freight.

Nature and people played unplanned tricks on the railroad. As we have seen, everything about it was low budget. When the engineer got up a good head of stream in Medford for the run westward, he tried not to pile any more wood into the fire box than was absolutely necessary to get the train through to Jacksonville. If he had to stop at Perrydale – *Mercy!* – this took most of the reserve steam just to get the outfit rolling again.

On making an entrance to Jacksonville over the "trifle" of a grade near the school, the train sometimes met with unscheduled delays and exasperation. Boys would be boys. The rascals sometimes greased the rails then disappeared into the building to watch the engine's wheels spin on slick iron then stop. The engineer would appear shortly with a bucket of sand which he carefully spread on the track so the wheels

(TOP) This picture may well be on the first day the railway gasoline car was ready for service. Cow-catchers have been installed on each end and some folks have been seated. Persons identified are (left to right) Rollie Hines, engineer; Bill Barnum, car's designer and Acting Manager of RRVRR; Bill MacIntyre, Frank Coleman (in front window); Dick Gaskin, Curley Wilson, Bruce Mayfield, Frank Robinson (in window leaning on right arm) ... Dunkin, Lewis Ulrich, Charlie Dunfield. (RIGHT) Engine No. 6 was 0-4-4T (tank) built by BLW in July 1872. It was bought in 1907, had been used to pull New York City elevated trains.

might regain traction.

The "grease-on-the-track" prank in time proved costly to Barnum. With his steam nearly consumed just getting into town, especially if there had been a Perrydale Station stop, more fuel had to be used to get the train the last couple of hundred yards to the depot.

In February of 1890, William Honeyman arrived in Jacksonville presumably on a routine inspection trip, which was not often. But this time there was more to his visit. A month later, an announcement went out that Honeyman, DeHart and Company had sold out to Barnum. The price was reported to be $12,000. By this time, William S. Barnum felt he could make money with the railroad as he had been "practicing" for a couple of years and his business friends believed they now knew what he was doing. In September of 1904, he dissolved the Rogue River Valley Rail*way* Company and started a new corporation under the same name, as a family operation with capitalization at $25,000.

"Barnum's Railroad," as some called it, became a family operation as his wife was named Secretary-treasurer and the business manager for daily operations. The boys worked in the little shop near the Jacksonville station and did the track repairs and ballasting that was needed now and then. The youngest son was the Conductor. "Father" Barnum was the General Manager who handled public relations, promotions and did what wheeling and dealing he felt necessary.

The family attended to business and did their best to make the venture a profitable enterprise, but without substantial freight and with dwindling passengers – automobiles were becoming common – the future was not bright. Jacksonville was definitely not growing. Truly, it was the other way. Medford quickly surpassed Jacksonville in population and in the number of business houses.

The orchard industry, apples, pears, peaches, was centered in the valley and Jacksonville seemed miles from the action. The people of the town silently (but a few were loud), blamed all of Jacksonville's troubles on Southern Pacific for its "shortsightedness" in skipping Jacksonville in the first place. And shame! There was talk of moving the county seat to Medford.

The complaints were growing about the rickety ride on the J-ville line and Barnum was fully aware that some of his track was bad. The 36-pound rail that had been used in the 1891 installation was too light.

His world as a railroadman was never easy but he succeeded in bouncing from one complaint to another without too much visible stress. With some improvement in freight in late summer due to the orchards, he might lease a few freight cars. But his trains frequently tied up traffic in Medford at intersections. He was at times physically arrested by uniformed Medford Police for blocking traffic, and on one occasion was forced to pay a $5 fine.

The Oregon Railroad Commission issued an order that he replace his depot in Medford as the building had been declared unsafe. When word leaked that all he planned on doing was to move his ticket sales to a second-hand wooden shed he planned to move onto the property, the Medford City Council pushed through an emergency amendment to the fire prevention ordnance that outlawed new buildings in that part of town that were built of other than brick or stone.

Barnum really didn't have any cash for a new depot and he was furious at Mayor J. F. Reddy for the mayor's forcing the extended fire ordnance that was pointed right at Barnum.

He seemed to pay little attention to complaints unless some state regulatory agency banged on his door. In January 1909, the Railroad Commission provided Barnum with an order that he must:

> …provide heat and water for drinking on passenger coaches and to provide accommodations [restrooms] in waiting rooms … [and] suitable ventilation at the Medford terminus….

In 1907 the railroad reported to the state that it owned this equipment:

    2 locomotives
    1 car, passenger
    1 car, combination passenger/express
    1 car, box (freight)
    5 cars, flatcars

Two years later, when the pear orchard business picked up, he reported the addition of

    3 cars, box (freight)
    6 vehicles (company cars - automobiles)

With his operating costs continuing to go up, but still seeking to provide adequate service, Barnum made a deal with a San Francisco builder to make a self-propelled car with a truck engine fueled with gasoline. Barnum presumably got his idea from reading about the McKeen self-contained cars that were then making appearances on some of the nation's railroads, including on the Southern Pacific.

Barnum's vehicle was a neat idea, but its hard-truck ride and the poor track proved this to be a passing fancy for he soon took it off his schedules. (For details, refer in Appendix A to "Ferry Garage Company.")

He bought into another idea to handle his few passengers with his home-made "speeder." This was similar to and may have been a Fairbanks-Morse one-speed railroad service car that he fit with seats. The

It has been said that the only difference between a boy and a man's toys are the size of the toys. (TOP) Here may be Bill Barnum's formal portrait with his Ferry Rail Gasoline Car (RGC) ready for service as a scheduled train on the RRVRR. The RGV could do 35 mph but probably never did due to worn out rails and ties that caused the car to creak and sway at about half that speed. It cost lots less to operate than the steam train especially as passenger traffic had dropped due to the arrival of automobiles. Many of Barnum's passengers complained that his rail car "stunk." (LOWER) Barnum came up with another idea. He could cut his costs still further and offer "intermediate" stops in the sparsely settled country between the towns with a "speeder." He bought a basic power unit with a platform then had the body built to his liking. A ride to Medford in the "speeder "was called "fun," but it jerked just as badly as his other vehicles.

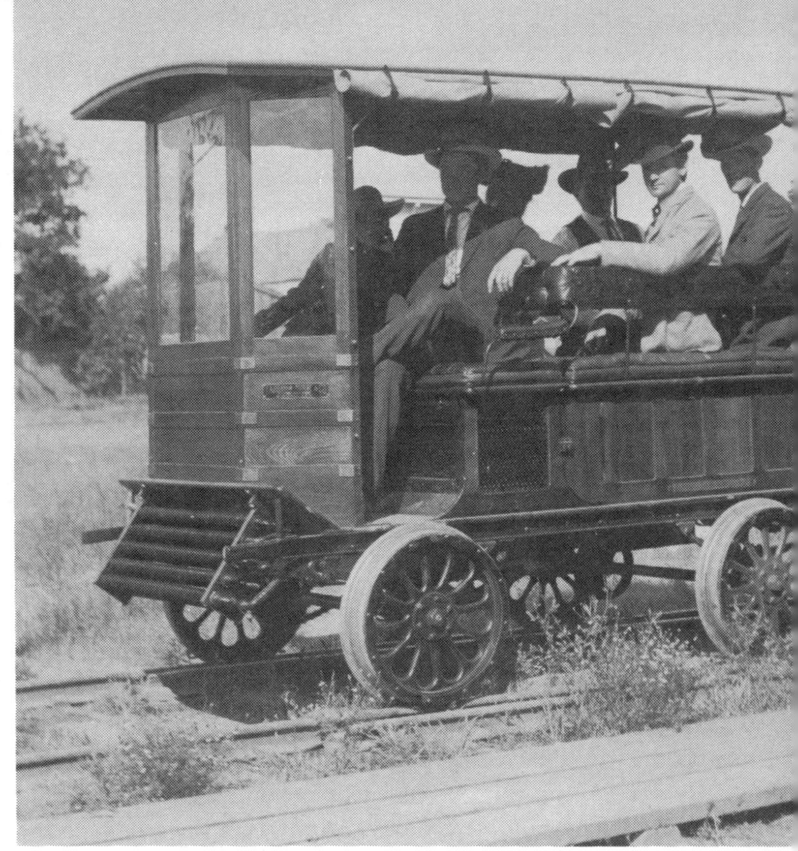

car was available for short-notice charters to anyone able to pay the fee. Its speed was managed with a movable arm applied to a large rotating wheel. When the arm was positioned against the outside edge of the wheel, like a needle on the starting edge of a phonograph record, the car moved rapidly. When a slower speed was wanted, the arm was positioned nearer the center of the wheel. The car had no springs and creaked. It was very noisy and was hard on one's "sitter," but people said it was a lot of fun to ride.

In the meantime, regardless of the various measures Barnum honestly took trying to keep his venture afloat, his railroad was just about out of business. One of the major causes: Automobiles.

Even with the jitneys that were stealing what passengers he had left, a different kind of public transportation was developing in Medford, and it would eventually *amoebae* its way into Jacksonville.

Trolley Cars

Hundreds of cities and towns across the nation had their fling with electric streetcars and Medford was one of them. The Southern Oregon Traction Company was headed by Spencer S. Bullis and was chartered for running on Medford streets in late 1913.

An article in the *Electric Railway Journal* (Vol. XVII, July-December 1913 declared:

> MEDFORD, ORE. Dec. 30, 1913—Southern Oregon Traction Company has completed 1 mile of track in Medford and plans to build 3 miles of new track within the next 6 months. It will purchase power from the California-Oregon Power Company (COPCO), Medford. This railway will ultimately connect Medford, Siskiyou Heights, Phoenix, Talent, Ashland and Central Point, according to S. E. Bullis, President.

Jacksonville was not mentioned!

Did Bullis consider the Rogue River Valley Railroad to be a viable means of public transport so his trolley cars were not needed there?

Spencer S. Bullis and his son Seth started this streetcar line by setting track in East Main Street which ran up the east hill (Medford Heights), past the present country club to end at the reservoir on Capitol and Valley View Drive. He experienced the same joys as had the "J-ville" steam railroad when it was new as just about everybody wanted to ride – 5¢.

The trolleys had been run up the east hill because Bullis believed real estate developers would flock to sell lots and build homes along his track. Indeed, the heights would become an affluent neighborhood, but Bullis was years too early. With little business on the hill, he pulled his rails and replanted them in West Main Street. This modified line then ran from about Eastwood Avenue at East Main to Oakdale on West Main Street. The desire to offer streetcar service west

ROGUE RIVER VALLEY RAILROAD

4 Daily	2 Daily	Miles	STATIONS	1 Daily	8 Daily
5 35	10.40	0	Lv. ....MEDFORD ....Ar	9 20	3 50
6 15	11.00	6	Ar......... Jacksonville Lv	9 00	3 30

Trains stop at Thomas, Harbaugh and Darisville on signal only.

MOTOR CAR SERVICE

Leaves Medford daily, 8.00 a. m., 9 00 p. m. and 12.50 p. m.
Leaves Jacksonville daily, 7.00 a. m., 11.30 a. m. and 7.30 p. m.

With the arrival of the Train-car, as he called it, which did not cost much to operate, stops and starts along the line were no longer an issue. Barnum allowed accommodation stops at farms along the way.

Barnum's passenger business had all but ceased but he was mandated to continue it by officialdom in Salem. It was reasonable that Spencer S. Bullis, and his sons, the men behind the Southern Oregon Traction Company, the streetcar line in Medford, could be successful by joining the two lines and electrifying the RRVRR. The idea was a good one but was about twenty years too late. In picture, the poles for the trolley wire are planted and the railroad is about to "go electric."

of the SP track had been a burning desire of Bullis but his effort had been thwarted by SP. It was a matter of crossing "frogs" where the car line would cross the railroad's track. Southern Pacific had a tradition for being very uncooperative about track crossings, especially with a streetcar line.

As a considerable number of residents on Medford's east side attended the Presbyterian Church at W. Main and Holly Streets, Bullis' streetcar could stop there for passengers – *business*– right in front of the church *if* he could put his rails on West Main Street. In time, SP granted crossing rights under very strenuous conditions, so the car line was extended westward to Oakdale.

As we have seen, Barnum was not making any money on his Rogue River Valley Railway. Plausibly he dreamed of some kind of a deal between him and Bullis. The later had hawked that electric trolleys would run throughout the valley but in his pronouncement, he had never mentioned Jacksonville. Was now the time for Barnum to ask Bullis if Bullis wanted to expand into Jacksonville? No record has surfaced to indicate who asked whom but the answer seems obvious.

Somehow, rumors became rampant that a merger between the Jacksonville Railroad and the trolley line was in the works. In answering questions about how soon his streetcars might run to Jacksonville, Bullis let it slip, that "just as soon as we can make arrangements … we want to get it electrified as soon as possible."

In due course, agreements were reached whereby the Southern Oregon Traction Company would buy Barnum's railroad for $125,000. This would be part in cash and part in a mortgage to be held by Barnum. It was the summer of 1915.

Barnum was probably feeling great relief to realize he was now out from under the burden of the railroad which had been stooping his shoulders for a decade and a half. But the Oregon Railroad Commissioner got in its last jab with a directive that while electrification was being done, workers would have to step aside to allow eight trips every day for the steam locomotive and its single passenger car to pass, as service had to be maintained, so ordered the Commissioner.

> **The first through streetcar from downtown Medford that ran all the way to Jacksonville started January 1, 1916.**

To connect with the Jacksonville track, Bullis had to lay track a few more blocks on W. Main Street to Elm, then south on Elm to 8th Street on which the steam railroad operated. As there was still occasional freight for Jacksonville, it was decided to install a switch between the car line and the railroad. The trolley line was electrified from town, through the switch then west to Jacksonville. There was no trolley wire on 8th Street east of Elm.

---

* For a complete look at the Medford streetcars refer to *Single Track to Jacksonville* in bibliography.

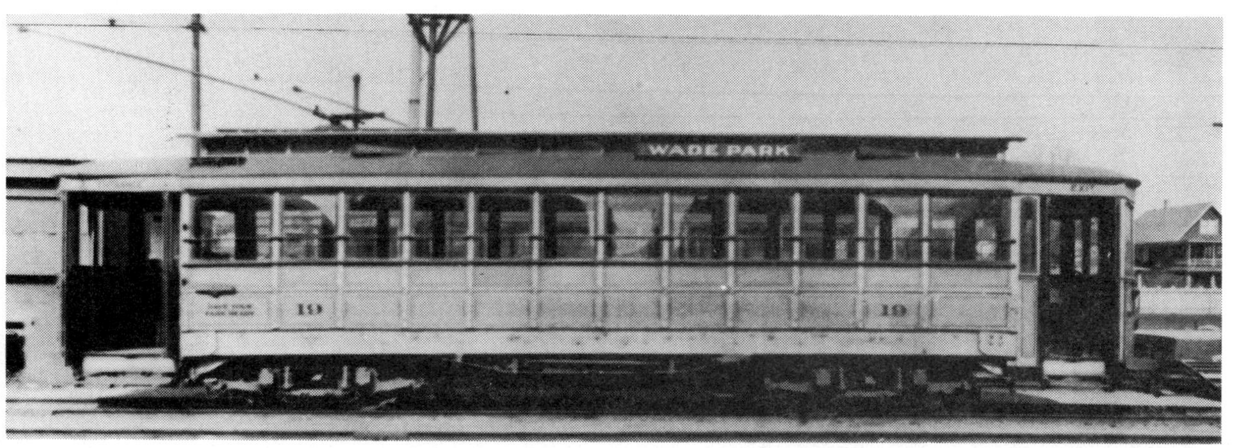

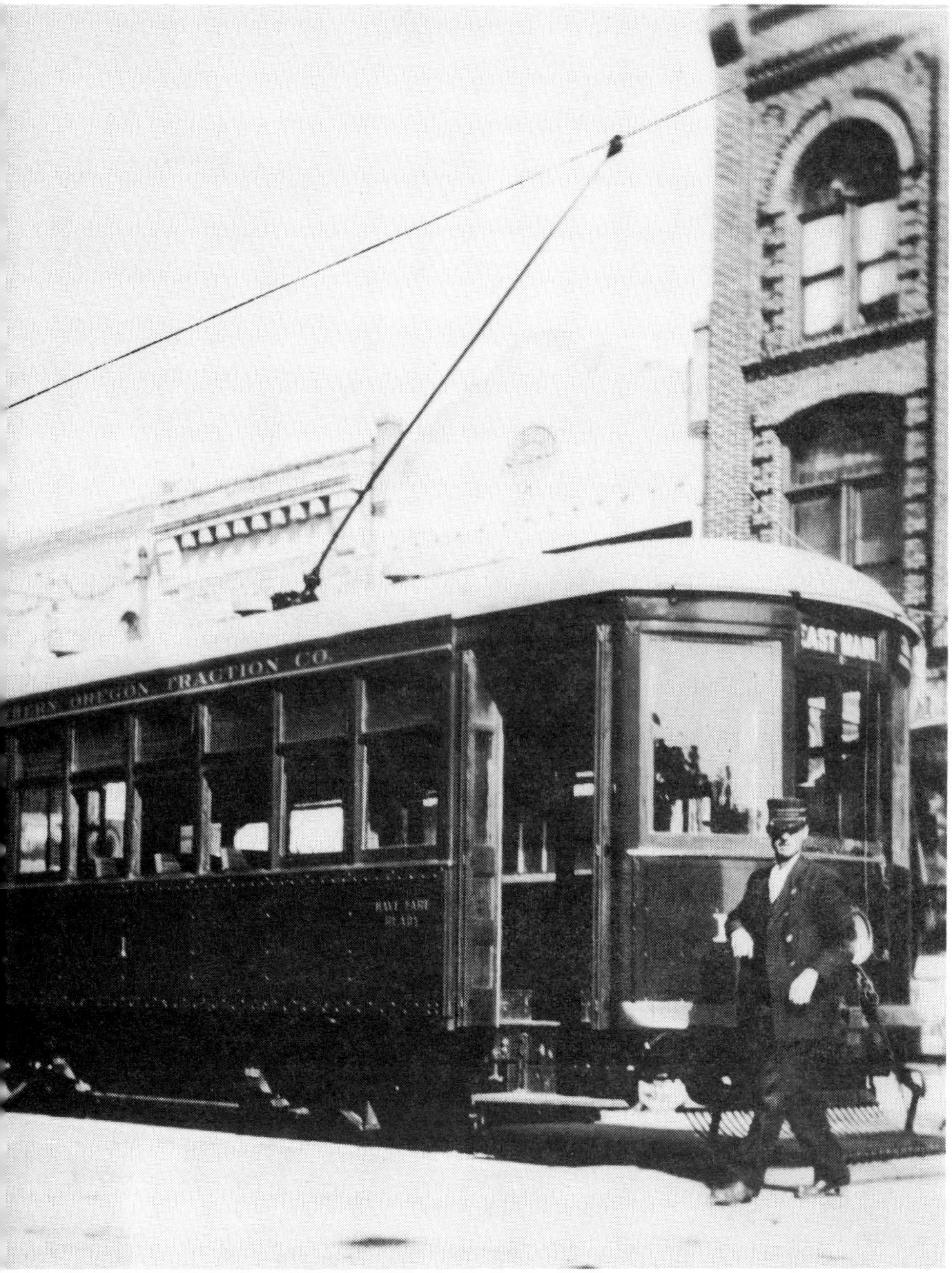

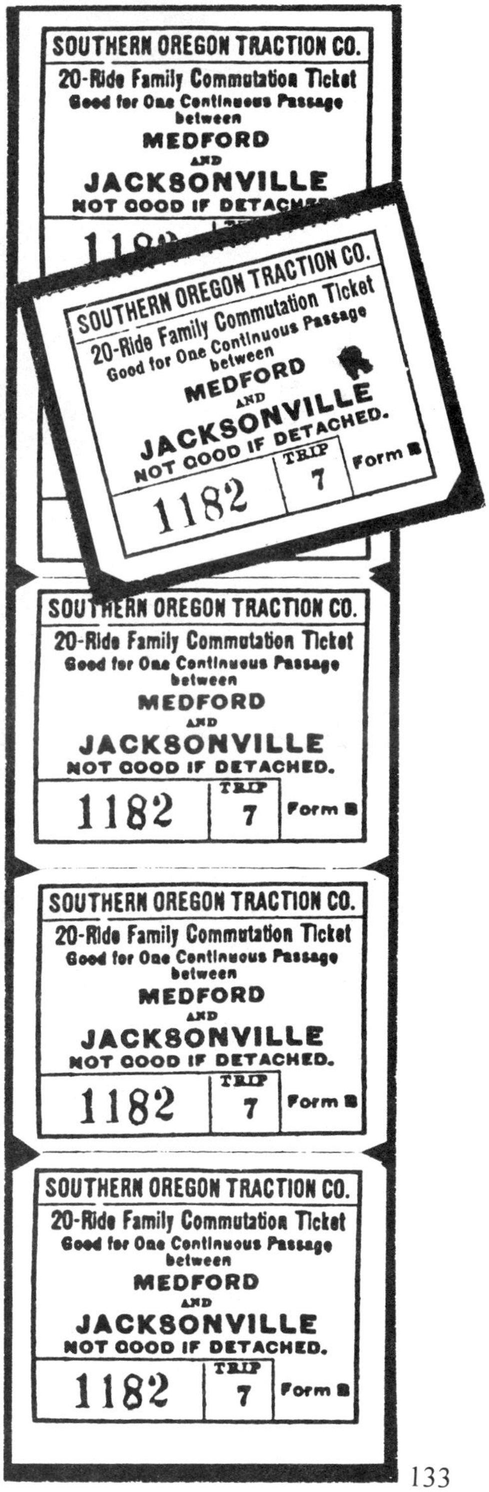

SOUTHERN OREGON TRACTION CO.
20-Ride Family Commutation Ticket
Good for One Continuous Passage between
MEDFORD AND JACKSONVILLE
NOT GOOD IF DETACHED.

SOUTHERN OREGON TRACTION CO.
20-Ride Family Commutation Ticket
Good for One Continuous Passage between
MEDFORD AND JACKSONVILLE
NOT GOOD IF DETACHED.

1182	TRIP 7	Form B

SOUTHERN OREGON TRACTION CO.
20-Ride Family Commutation Ticket
Good for One Continuous Passage between
MEDFORD AND JACKSONVILLE
NOT GOOD IF DETACHED.

1182	TRIP 7	Form B

SOUTHERN OREGON TRACTION CO.
20-Ride Family Commutation Ticket
Good for One Continuous Passage between
MEDFORD AND JACKSONVILLE
NOT GOOD IF DETACHED.

1182	TRIP 7	Form B

SOUTHERN OREGON TRACTION CO.
20-Ride Family Commutation Ticket
Good for One Continuous Passage between
MEDFORD AND JACKSONVILLE
NOT GOOD IF DETACHED.

1182	TRIP 7	Form B

(TOP) Large city streetcar, purchased 2nd hand in Cleveland, Ohio, was shipped to Medford for use on the inter-city line. (LOWER) Single-truck Brill-Birney car was common sight on Medford's Main Street before arrival of the larger car.

| SOUTHERN OREGON TRACTION CO. | | SOUTHERN OREGON TRACTION CO. | | SOUTHERN OREGON TRACTION CO. |

SOUTHERN OREGON TRACTION CO.
TIME SCHEDULE NUMBER 2
EFFECTIVE OCTOBER 18, 1916.

Subject to change without notice.

Lv. Jacksonville	Leave Medford end of paving E. Main
7:30 A.M.	8:00 A.M.
8:30 "	9:00 "
9:30 "	10:00 "
10:30 "	11:00 "
11:30 "	12:00 See below.
1:00 P.M.	1:30 P.M.
2:00 "	2:30 "
3:00 "	3:30 "
4:00 "	4:30 "
5:00 "	6:00 "
7:15 "	Leave Riverside Ave.
	10:00 P.M.

The 12:00 car from Medford lays over at Highland Park thirty minutes. Cars pass waiting room going out East Main ten minutes before above schedule and going to Jacksonville eight minutes after.

R.S. BULLIS, Gen'l Pass'r Agt.
Medford, Ore.

SOUTHERN OREGON TRACTION CO.

EFFECTIVE JUNE 1, 1917.

Subject to change without notice.

Lv. Jacksonville	Leave Medford
7:30 A.M.	8:00 A.M.
8:30 "	9:00 "
9:30 "	10:00 "
10:30 "	11:00 "
11:30 "	12:00 NOON
1:00 P.M.	1:30 P.M.
2:00 "	2:30 "
3:00 "	3:30 "
4:00 "	4:30 "
5:00 "	6:00 "
7:30 "	10:00 "

R.S. BULLIS,
Gen. Freight & Passenger Agent

SOUTHERN OREGON TRACTION CO.
TIME TABLE No. 5
EFFECTIVE AUGUST 23, 1917.
Subject to change without notice.

Lv. Jacksonville	Leave Medford
7:30 A.M. daily except Sunday	8:00 A.M. daily except Sunday
7:50 A.M. Sunday only	8:30 A.M. Sunday only
8:30 A.M. daily except Sunday	9:00 A.M. daily except Sunday
9:00 A.M. Sunday only	10:00 A.M. daily
9:30 A.M. except Sunday	12:00 Noon-daily except Sunday
11:30 A.M. daily except Sunday	2:30 P.M. daily
2:00 P.M. daily	3:30 P.M. daily
3:00 P.M. daily	4:30 P.M. daily
4:00 P.M. daily	6:00 P.M. daily
5:00 P.M. daily (Note 1)	10:00 P.M. daily
7:15 P.M. daily (Note 2)	

R.S. BULLIS,
Gen. Freight & Passenger Agent

SOUTHERN OREGON TRACTION CO.
TIME TABLE
EFFECTIVE FEBRUARY 23, 1919.
Subject to change without notice.

Lv. Jacksonville	Leave Medford
7:20 A.M. daily except Sunday	8:00 A.M. daily except Sunday
8:30 A.M. daily except Sunday	9:30 A.M. Sunday only
10:00 A.M. Sunday only	9:45 A.M. daily except Sunday
11:30 A.M. daily except Sunday	10:38 A.M. Sunday only
2:00 P.M. daily	12:08 Noon-daily
3:45 P.M. daily	2:45 P.M. daily
5:00 P.M. daily	4:30 P.M. daily
7:15 P.M. Wed. & Sat. only	6:09 P.M. daily
	10:00 P.M. Wed. & Sat. only

R.S. BULLIS,
Gen. Freight & Passenger Agent

Southern Oregon Traction Company did not become an "interurban," according to the classic definition of an interurban line, just because it bought the Rogue River Valley Railway which ran between two towns. For all practical purposes, SOTCO remained a city street traction company merely with an extended line into the country. Although there were true "interurban" railways in other parts of the nation with short milage runs, those short hauls were often parts of greater inter-city systems. The Sausalito - Mill Valley line in California, just north of San Francisco, and the Medford - Jacksonville line were the same length—six miles. This Mill Valley line was part of the Northwestern Pacific, a true interurban, which had half-a-dozen routes from the Sausilito ferry dock to points to about 25 miles away. The Market Street Railway of San Francisco, with hundreds of miles of track in the city, had a similar situation with the Jacksonville line. MSRY's San Mateo line was only an "extended line into the country" even though the distance was about 20 miles between the two cities.

Southern Oregon Traction Company's operation between Medford and Jacksonville was a mere trifle if compared with other electric lines in Oregon. It served its purpose but never very well not having been built until after the peak of inter-city electric rail development had passed. The line was far too short to be able to collect high enough fares to show any profit. It has been classed as one of the "worst examples"* of financing and operation in the country and was forced out of business by progress—automobiles and a paved highway. Elsewhere in Oregon, the Portland—Oregon City line, about 25 miles, carried passenger service longer than any other interurban in the United States—65 years.

*The Electric Interurban Railways of America. pp. 37-38.

The streetcar used in Medford was a single-truck Brill-Birney that was a double-ender meaning it could be driven from either end. Bullis, in the meantime, had bought a second Brill car and also bought a second-hand full-size double-truck Kuhlman standard car. Before shipment by rail to Medford from Cleveland, Ohio, the Kuhlman was converted to one-man operation, was made double-ended and had two trolleys. It had been built in 1902 and it was definitely secondhand in some of its features. But it seated 56 passengers and about 40 more could stand. He particularly sought it for interurban service on the Jacksonville end of his line.

Just as soon as the electrified line was operational, people once again flocked to ride the "interurban" between Medford and Jacksonville. The fare was a dime each way.

While the Rogue River Valley Railroad had only

one scheduled stop, Perrydale Station, a streetcar can make many stops with no "fuel" troubles as occurred with the steam train. A hand-drawn map shows 6 streetcar stops, evenly spaced between towns. Number 1 was not named but stop 2 was "Thomas," 3 was "Harbaugh," 4 "Davisville," 5 County Court House at C and 5th Streets in Jacksonville. Stop No. 6 was the terminal and depot at Jacksonville. The map did not show that Perrydale was continued as a stop, but that was probably presumed. (See map page 118)

There was a short parking spur west of Lewis Avenue where Bullis parked his out-of-service cars. The stop was unlisted on the map but trolleys stopped there on flag to drop off and to pick up motormen – the term used for streetcar men who drove the cars.

That the electric line to Jacksonville was a success in the early days there is no question. But like all other rail ventures in the Rogue Valley, the initial "happy faces" turned sour with time.

National politics were blamed for Bullis' decision to give up the trolley line and let his whole package revert to Barnum who held the mortgage.

Barnum, in his uncanny wisdom, had foreseen that the streetcars would not succeed because automobiles and trucks were now so firmly entrenched in the valley that the county was on a "good roads" building spree. Barnum had just about "bottomed out" earlier when he was able to sell to Bullis. When Bullis quit, Barnum received a working, electrified railroad which was in considerably better shape than it was when he sold it. He toyed with its operation for about one year when he had a chance to unload it again.,

J. T. Gagnon, a local man, bought it but again left the mortgage with Barnum. Gagnon incorporated using the name Medford Coast Railroad.

Streetcars, if not regularly maintained, have a tendency to burn out controllers and motors. Because of frequent breakdowns, the trolley schedule was abolished and the cars ran when they worked. This outraged the public but there was nothing anyone was able to do about it *except* jitney operators. A fellow with a couple of 6-passenger touring cars went into business to fill the obvious need. Gagnon, trying to catch his breath with his hands in the air, toughed it out until 1922 when a man named John W. Opp, a successful miner with his stake west of Jacksonville, wanted in.

Opp told the newspaper he planned on extensive upgrading and promised a regular schedule. But before he had a chance, there was a fire in the substation that fed the 600 volts to the car line. This COPCO power station was apparently not needed by other customers, so the electric utility did not rebuild it. Opp suddenly had in his hands an electric streetcar

Interior of street cars was fairly standard although each manufacturer had variations. The object was to haul as many people as possible at a time. When seats were full, the hold-on handles steadied standing passengers from loosing their balance as nearly all cars jerked at stops and starts. —Photo by authors at Seashore National Trolley Museum, Kennebunkport, Maine.

and interurban system that would not work as there was no power. Early in 1923 he dumped it all back on Gagnon and silently walked away.

All this was noticed by the Medford City Council which had granted franchises for use of its streets to the trolley car interests. In its use-it-or lose-it threats, the city ordered SP to remove the switch that served the J-ville line in front of the SP freight depot. This would mean an end to the trickle of freight service to Jacksonville, whose people promptly complained. SP did nothing about it (plausibly because the switch was on SP land-grant property not under the jurisdiction of the city). The city seems to have forgotten about it. That switch remained until 1995 when Central Oregon & Pacific Railroad pulled up all the excess track in downtown Medford in a general cleanup sweep.

Although Gagnon promised to get the streetcars running, it didn't happen. He didn't pay his note to Barnum and Barnum found himself once again owing this troublesome and challenging enterprise.

Disposition of the three streetcars is a little foggy.

One of the Brill-Birney cars had a burned out motor so it could not go anywhere under its own power. Some say it derailed near the Bear Creek Bridge and landed with one end in the creek where it was abandoned though no hard evidence such an event occurred has been found. The other 4-trucker had controller trouble so would operate only on the "slow" speed. It could be used, but riding on it was no joy to passengers and running it was a bore to the motorman.

Its use proved impractical unless fixed, which it was not, but a dealer in used streetcars learned of it and bought is "as is, where is." It is plausible that the dealer fished the other Brill out of the creek, if that is where it was, and took it also.

Gone Forever

(TOP) **Antique, light-weight rail, believed to be 56-pound stock installed by SP for the use of SP and RRVRR, for mutual switching of freight cars between the two lines was seen in the Medford switchyard for generations. As shown, was called the "caboose parking track," but heavy GP-38 and GP-40 diesel-electric locomotives also rested there. Shown parked in lower picture is a flanger, a light-weight snow plow. After SP sold this part of its system to RailTex in late 1994, much "non-essential" track was chosen for salvage and this stretch was one of the choices. Although there were "stops" at the ends of the rails at edge of pavement (LOWER), the old track was under the 6th Street pavement where it remains at this writing. (INSET) Mis-matched rail is common on some sidings.**

The once majestic-in-its-day Kuhlman car also suffered with a burned out motor, but its last motorman was able to crawl it to the West Medford parking spur before it quit. Over the years it was vandalized, and with continual exposure, the weather aided in the car's deterioration. Some say its metal was picked up for salvage during a national scrap metal drive early in World War II.

ooOOOoo

Bill Barnum still owned the system. His streetcars were gone. He owned a dilapidated steam engine that didn't work very well. The City of Medford was almost constantly on his back with one complaint or two or three others. The City of Jacksonville wanted some action on the "service" it was supposed to be getting from its franchise agreements. With all these "assets" put together, the only thing William S. Barnum was getting was one grand headache. He petitioned the Oregon Public Service Commission for a permit to stop everything, pull up his rails and sell them for scrap iron. He made the statement that the line had not operated since April 1, 1924, that the system was inoperable and he was pleading for relief. But the state would not let him off that easily.

Barnum was directed to sell to whomever might want to buy the line as an operating entity but his price could be no more than the scrap value. He was further directed to make his firm decision no later than November 10, 1925.

Marching at quick-step with the state, the City of Medford passed an Ordinance (No. 1791) which authorized it to buy out Barnum for $11,000. In 1925 that was big money. But it was nowhere near the book value of the property in question. Nevertheless, any object is worth only what one can get for it.

Barnum took the deal because he had no choice. The anti-climax for this man who had spent years as a railroader, was that due to the fact that none of his rolling stock would roll, he had to walk home. <>

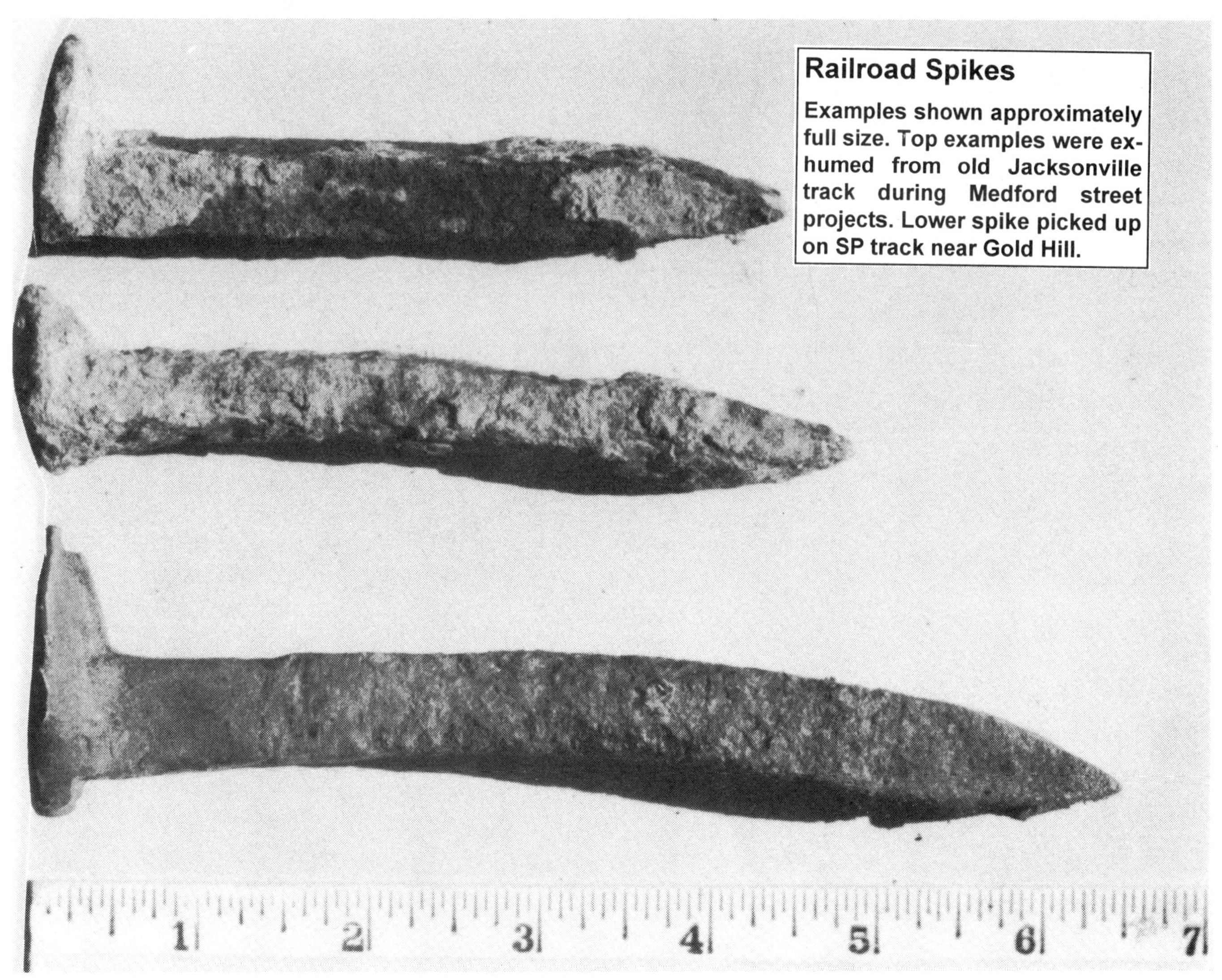

Steamer "Old No. 19" of Yreka Western Railroad getting ready for excursion in autumn 1996.

Chapter 12

Yreka Railroad

January 9, 1889 - July 12, 1933
Yreka Western Railroad - August 24, 1933 –

THE HISTORIC YREKA WESTERN Railroad's Baldwin locomotive, built in 1915, is the featured pulling power on the "Blue Goose." This excursion train operates seasonally between the Yreka depot and Montague, California, about 7 miles east. Montague is a historical railroad town on the Central Oregon & Pacific Railroad (formerly the Southern Pacific).

The locomotive is a 2-8-2 Mikado, construction number 42000 and is spot No. 19, of the Yreka Western. Its primary job is to pulls the "Blue Goose" Stream Excursion Train.

The success of the tourist excursions is evident by the smiles and laughter of the passengers, many who are repeat riders.

On many of today's nostalgic steam train excursions, the tourist trips may be a last gasp for life in a dying railroad. It is true that the Yreka Railroad, which started in 1889, had its ups-and-downs, and sometimes it was pretty far down, but today's operation is exciting, worthwhile, and profitable.

The excursion train has a usual configuration of four coaches. There are two 1923 Harriman cars with Southern Pacific markings, and two from 1948. The 1948's are off the famous Milwaukee, Saint Paul & Pacific line's crack train the "Hiawatha." A 5th car, an open car with protective rails built on a flat car, has a permanent "sun-roof" – no roof at all. This car is jokingly called by many, the "cattle car."

The train capacity is approximately 350 people. In the "cattle car," although there are lots of benches, nearly everyone stands ohing and ahhing the countryside as the train chugs along at a comfortable 10 mph. The train is named "Blue Goose" and there is indeed a blue goose. It is a hunter's decoy painted blue, mounted in a field about 25-yards off the side of the track in a meadow. (One might wonder how many thousands of snapshots of the decoy help Kodak's bottom line?)

The train creaks, clanks, squeaks and groans as traditional older stream trains have traditionally complained. The "Blue Goose" covers the 7.32 miles in about an hour on mostly 75-pound rails along a line that also regularly hauls freight cars – both empty cars inbound and those loaded with lumber and wood chips outbound, from two large mills along this line.

Hazel Thompson remarked, "That engine is as old as I – 65." She posed for picture with No. 19 at Montague terminal.

Steam Locomotive Heads Freight Trains

At times, when the EMD's are not available, the steam engine goes to work. As far as is known, this is the only steam locomotive in the country today pulling revenue-generating freight trains. On one occasion, when there were locomotive inspection officials in the area and learned of it, they rushed to Yreka to see this rare situation with their cameras clicking.

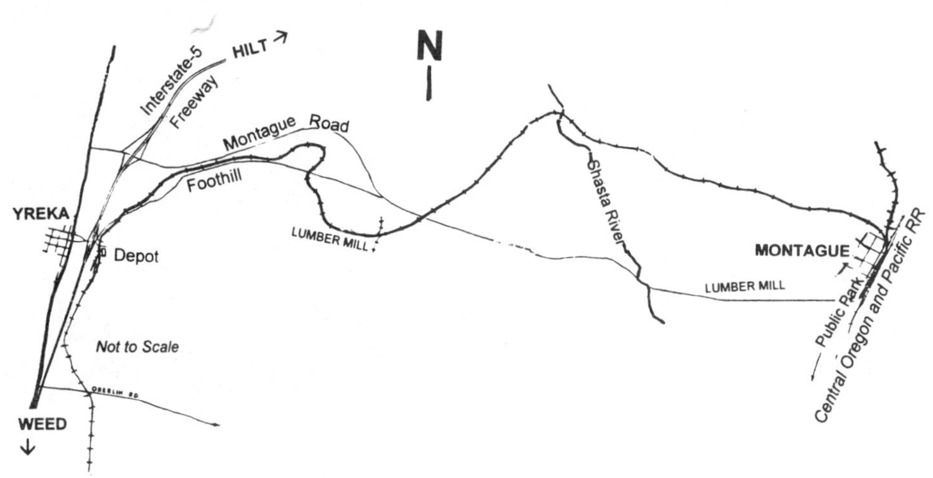

140

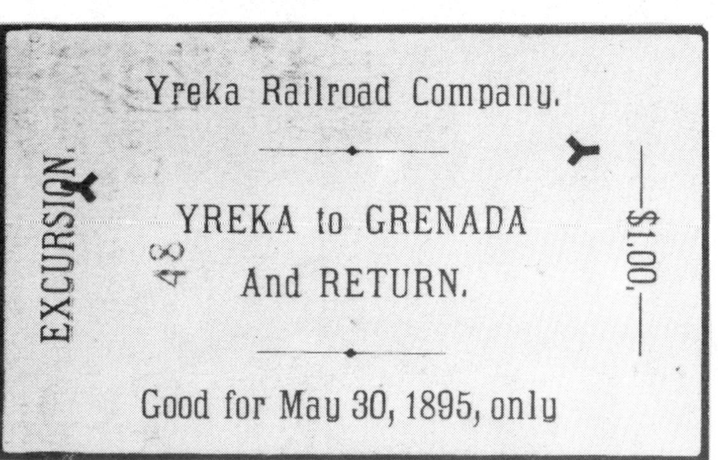

(TOP) **Gasoline powered car of Yreka Railroad. This is the first car of 23 build by Hall-Scott. As on other railroads, the self-propelled car was lower cost to run than a steam train.** (LOWER) **Conductor on "Blue Goose" excursion train, pulled by steamer No. 19, in 1996, punches ticket (below) of passenger Ben Truwe.**

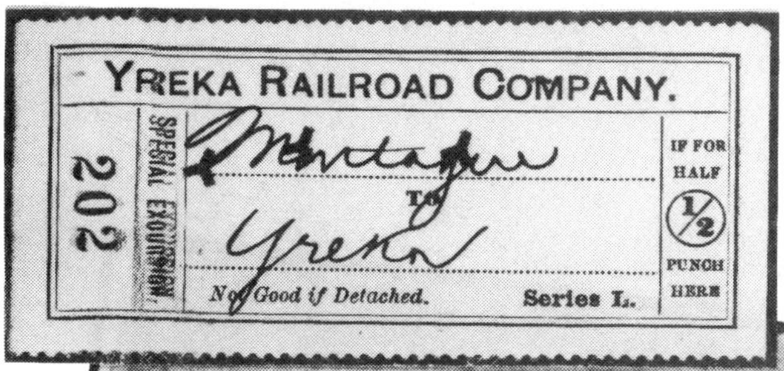

"Business Offices"

(TOP) The control room (cab) of No. 19. (CENTER) The company office at Yreka Depot. The antique desk was in the room when building was remodeled, will not fit through a door. (LOWER) Ticket counter for "Blue Goose" excursions, Yreka Depot.

Classic 3/4 front view of "Blue Goose" excursion train at Montague, California.

In 1995, the line handled 330 cars but a huge jump in the lumber business realized 1,000 cars hauled on a five-days-a-week schedule in 1996 and 1,500 in 1997. For this work, the cars are tugged and shoved by the line's two EMD SW-8 800 horse power diesels. These 1953 model locomotives were acquired from Southern Pacific and rebuilt in 1979.

The Yreka Railroad opened on January 9, 1889 as a short line to link the mainline track of the California and Oregon Railroad (later the Southern Pacific) and Yreka. The C&O had placed its mainline north-south road east of Yreka in the Shasta Valley because of better terrain – a similar circumstance in the Rogue Valley of Oregon where Oregon & California Rail Road surveyors missed Jacksonville.

Yreka is on the southern edge of the Siskiyou Mountains and was on old Highway No. 99. For the most part, this road is today's Interstate-5. The railroad's yard and depot can be seen from the freeway.

The first track put down was 40-pound rail. It was known to be light, but was considered sufficient to get the line going and, that weight was what could be afforded.

The initial depot was in town, near 2nd and Main Streets. But the frequent flooding of Yreka Creek caused damage to the trestle over the creek, therefore, in 1910, a new site for the depot and engine house and shops was found east of the creek on higher ground. The present depot was built in 1910. This new depot follows the same design as the original building but it is larger.

Taking on water at Yreka before trip. Locomotive burns recycled engine oil discarded by motorists.

"Blue Goose" excursion train under way.

pounds weight, to the Brooks 2-8-2 of 1920 weighing 176,000 pounds.

The power unit roster also shows a gasoline fueled 1929 Plymouth. But the Plymouth was always too light for the loads it was expected to pull. This was regrettably discovered on the Yreka line as well as on the WCTU (which see).

The first unit built of the famous Hall-Scott self-propelled combination express/passenger car was purchased by Yreka Railroad in 1909. (See Appendix A)

At one time, the line operated a Lima Shay geared logging locomotive which the firm bought from Long-Bell Lumber Company.

There have been several of diesel engines. The Yreka Western had an S-4 Alco 1,000 horsepower diesel on its freight runs but that was sold when the EMD's were acquired.

But it is the line's No. 19, 178,400 pound antique steamer, that folks love to see and hear. Its bell clangs. People cover their ears when its whistle pierces the air with steam escaping into the heavens when the train leaves the depot for another "Blue Goose" excursion.

Locomotives

Three locomotives were acquired from the opening in 1889 through 1906. Over the years, there have been 21 locomotives. Of these, eleven were steam and range from the original Baldwin 2-4-2T of 52,000

(TOP) **Ben Truwe takes close look at worn out ties and derailer on unused go-around track near Yreka. Manager Larry Bacon says the railroad does not want to pull out this track as future operations might need it, at which time it will be rebuilt.** (LOWER) **View of passengers in the "cattle car" seen from roof of Dan Wilkinson's Santa Fe caboose.**

Passengers in (TOP) **"cattle car"** (LOWER) **in coach.**

(TOP) **Montague, California is a very quiet village in winter, but bustles during steam train excursions in summer.** (RIGHT) **Passengers re-boarding train at Montague for return to Yreka.** (LOWER) **Ben Truwe in doorway, enjoys view of Shasta Valley from Dan Wilkinson's reconditioned Santa Fe caboose.**

Dan Wilkinson, Grants Pass, owns this fully restored and operating 1927 Santa Fe caboose. By special arrangement, this bright red caboose is kept at the Yreka Western's terminal in Yreka. It sometimes runs on the Blue Goose for special events.

Weyerhaeuser No. 100 pulls log train on run from forest into Sutherlin.
—Doris Hubbard collection

Chapter 13

Weyerhaeuser Timber Company

Sutherlin Operations - January 17, 1949 - January 16, 1961

ONE OF THE LARGER timber operations in the Pacific Northwest, Weyerhaeuser, had approximately three dozen locomotives with most doing duty in the woods and feeder lines in Washington state. In Oregon, Weyerhaeuser had mills, with associated railroads, serving Beatty, Klamath Falls, Springfield and Sutherlin.

A construction company was given a contract to build a standard gauge track using 75-lb rail from Camp Sutherlin, south of Springfield, to Sutherlin. The distance was between 17 and 20 miles depending on one's source. The woods camp was just east of the confluence of Coon Creek and the Calapooya River. The train's route made its way west of the hills passing over at least 10 bridges to get to Sutherlin.

The plan: Logs would be hauled from logging sites in the woods by truck to the railroad then reloaded to a log train at Camp Sutherlin. The log train, with a company locomotive (#100), would be taken to Sutherlin then switched at the Sutherlin yard to await a northbound Southern Pacific train. SP would pick up the full cars and take them to the mill siding in Springfield.

(The Weyerhaeuser railroading operations in Sutherlin and in Springfield are closely intertwined. Springfield also had a woods camp and reloading area onto a train for the run to the mill.)

On return from the Springfield mill, empty cars would be placed in a holding yard near State Street in Sutherlin. Here the cars awaited the arrival of the company's locomotive which would push the cars back into the woods.

Weyerhaeuser acquired locomotive spot #100 in 1937 and it is presumed it was used in Washington until operations opened near Sutherlin in 1948.

Locomotive #100, a Cooke, 2-6-2, builder No. 62965 has 50-inch drive wheels and it weighed in at 127,500 pounds.

Recollections of old timers claim the minimum train was 25 cars but up to about 60 cars could make the run.

This engine pulled the first and last loads of logs into Sutherlin, originating in the forest at Camp Sutherlin, starting on January 17, 1949. The final load was on January 16, 1961 – 12 years of service on this line. The railroad crew that worked the first load, was brought back with some ceremony for the last train.

After the line was converted to diesel locomotion some time in the mid-1950's, "Old #100," as the locomotive was called, had to be kept in reserve for when

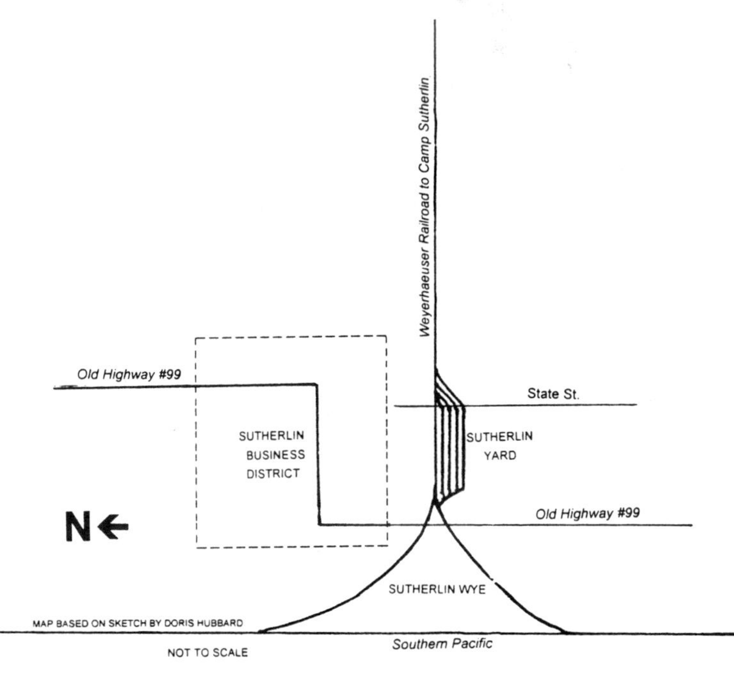

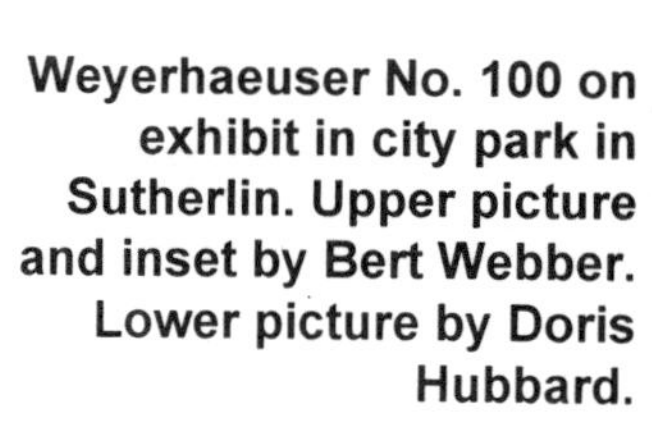

Weyerhaeuser No. 100 on exhibit in city park in Sutherlin. Upper picture and inset by Bert Webber. Lower picture by Doris Hubbard.

the diesel "had a headache" the work proceeded on schedule by firing up the old steamer.

One major factor caused the closing of the Sutherlin Railroad. The branch, and SP, had been hauling logs 80 miles to Springfield by way of Sutherlin which is south of the unit in the tree farm that was being logged, and the mill. When Weyerhaeuser bought a Cottage Grove mill, all the branch timberlands were connected. It was more economical to haul logs by truck just 35 miles to the Cottage Grove mill.

Weyerhaeuser was no different than many other railroad logging outfits. When a rail line no longer served a purpose, they took up the track and the ties and reinstalled them elsewhere. Such was the case when the Sutherlin Railroad was closed. If the owners didn't have a use for the salvaged parts, they were sold to someone who did. There was always a waiting line of buyers for good used rail. This is still true to the present time.

Above Wendling, the major part of the Weyerhaeuser line was 54-lb light-rail with heavier rail on some curves. Eight of the 11 miles of that track were rerailed with the 75-lb rail from the Sutherlin road. The rejuvenation of that line was assisted by 8,000 second-hand ties from the Sutherlin Railroad.

Doris Hubbard, wrote: "We purchased property east of Sutherlin and the old raised roadbed where the railroad was, separates our property."

After retirement, "Old #100" and its caboose were presented to the City of Sutherlin where they can be seen in the city park.◇

(TOP) **Loading yard of Weyerhaeuser's Springfield and Sutherlin operations were practically identical. Scene is of Springfield.** —Doris Hubbard collection (LOWER) **Railroad right-of-way was on raised ground in shadow-line of trees, is property line of Hubbard property.**
—Bert Webber photo

Chapter 14

Kinneyville Spur

January 1, 1901 - Autumn, 1903

THE VAST MAJORITY of locomotives at the turn of the 19th-20th Century were fueled with wood. As a result, there was a huge demand for wood which had to be cut and split to railroad specifications of maximum 48-inches by 8-inches.

In Oregon, there were hundreds of thousands of acres of trees. Quite a lot of this would become fire wood for the trains. Trees, being a "crop," would grow back, but there seems little reason to believe wood-cutters thought of this at the time.

Initially called "Stump-town," this community was later named Kinneyville for J. J. Kinney, one of two men, the other being D. T. Cox, who together had a contract with Southern Pacific to supply fire wood to fuel SP trains.

The contract called for Southern Pacific to build a spur into the woods where this partnership hired up to 300 men to harvest trees to make fire wood for the railroad. The men needed to be housed and fed therefore, in short order, a community sprang up. In Kinneyville, a hotel was quickly established along with several eating establishments, a blacksmith, a general merchandise store, a livery, as well as bath and boarding house and a barber shop.

This village site was in Josephine County between Leland and Tunnel #9 on the railroad.

Larry McLane, writing in his book *First There Was Twogood*, reported that by late in January 1901:

There was wood piled as far as the eye could see … [they] clear-cut all private timber in the Tunnel Creek area leaving only bald hills and flats in their wake. (Some fifty years later that same area was logged again.)

It would be April before the first trains arrived to haul the fire wood as they had to wait on the laying of the track. Once the deal got going, Southern Pacific ran regular "wood trains" into Kinneyville where all this cut fuel was loaded then hauled away for use on the main lines of the railroad.

This boom-town thrived for about two years until the available wood to cut became limited after which time the woods' crews moved on and the town died.

Kinneyville did not have a post office and is not listed in *Oregon Geographic Names*. Details of the town and a map are in McLane. ◇

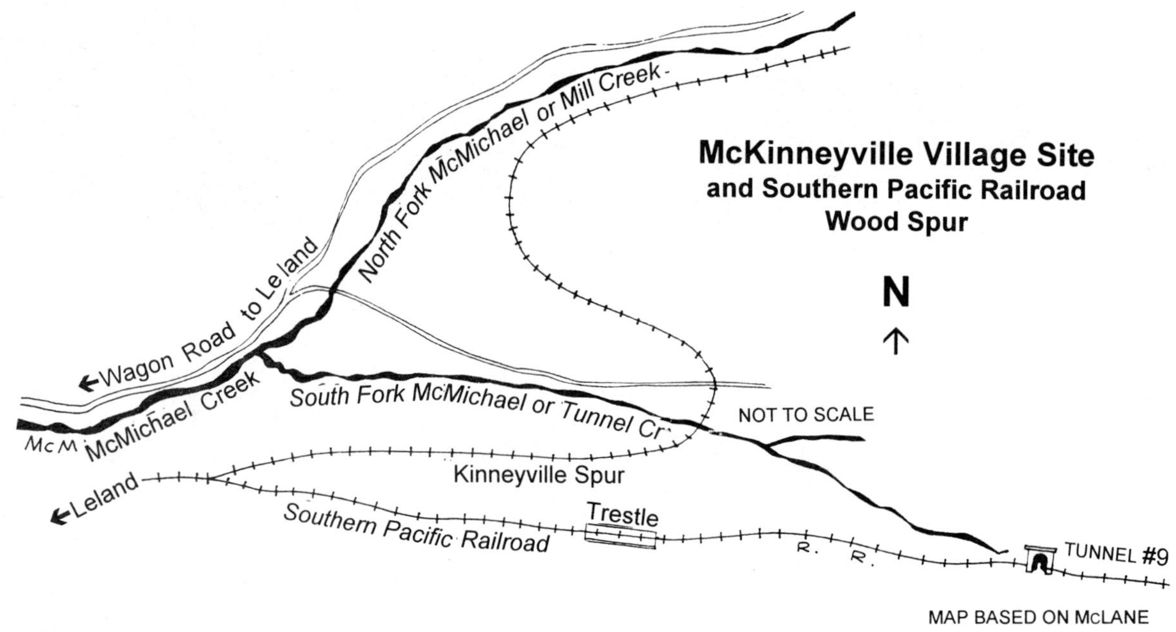

Interurbans Along the Siskiyou Line
Builders: Ferry, Hall-Scott, McKeen

IT SEEMED WEIRD to the author, at about age 8, who certainly knew what a train looked like with its puffing locomotive, to see what looked like a passenger car from a train roaring along a track with no obvious means of locomotion. It was many years later before he realized what he had seen.

In a relatively short span of years, over a dozen firms went into the business – then out of it – designing and constructing rail cars that were self-propelled.

The production of three of those companies meets our interest. These are:

The Ferry Garage Company, San Francisco
> Apparently only one car built (Road No. 2). Used on the Rogue River Valley Railway between Jacksonville and Medford

McKeen Motor Car Company, Omaha
> Cars Numbers 26, 64, 98 (Road Nos. 9, 63, 55) of 152 built, were used on Southern Pacific between Ashland and Grants Pass.

Hall-Scott Motor Car Company, Berkeley
> Car No. 1 (Road No. 5) of 23 built, was used on the Yreka Railroad between Yreka and Montague, California.

ooOOOoo

The Ferry Garage Company

The Rogue River Valley Railway, or "Jacksonville Line" as it was called, came about when the Oregon & California Rail Road by-passed Jacksonville and built its own station and town, which became Medford, 6 miles away. The people in Jacksonville felt slighted so a short connecting line, The Rogue River Valley Railway, (Chapter 11), came into existence. In an effort to cut operating costs, William Henry Barnum, who was the younger son of William

Sign in depot, California State Railroad Museum, Sacramento. All depots had similar signs.

S. Barnum, owner of the "J'ville" line, designed a gasoline-power single car in which he planned to haul his passengers for less cost than operating his steam train.

Young Barnum is believed to have been the vice-president and treasurer of the builder, which was a business interest separate from the railroad in Oregon.

The "train-car," as it was called, was a combination car with the front third dedicated to hauling express, mail and small packages. This express portion had a door on each side of the car. The back two-

Rail car in San Francisco before being shipped to Jacksonville.

Ashland end-of-track for McKeen cars. All signs of this are gone today.

Ferry Garage Company gasoline rail car on flatcar being readied for shipment to Medford on Southern Pacific. San Francisco Ferry Building in rear.

thirds was divided into two compartments. There was a six-seat smoking section and a 22 passenger capacity general coach. This section had a single door on the right side.

Although there was a No. 1 end, the car had controls at both ends, and there was a "cow-catcher" on each end. Barnum planned his car with these features as there was no wye, turntable or loop at either terminal to reverse his train-car.

The car was equipped with a squawking horn that was powered with exhaust from the 70 horsepower four-cylinder Brennan gasoline engine. Of course, if the engine was not running, the horn wouldn't work. Drive chains from the engine to the front axle propelled this train-car which had only two axles and four wheels. The rear axle was mounted at the end of the 10-foot wheel base.

The body of the car was frame and it was mounted on a steel chassis. For a bell, the builder bought a standard San Francisco-type cable car bell. The bell was on the roof, just as it was on the cable cars, and had a rope protruding through a "roof port" (hole) the rope dangling near the engineer's head. He rang the bell by yanking on the rope.

This unique and apparently one-of-a-kind car, was built in 1910. Its cost was believed to have been about $5.000.

Although the Ferry Garage Company's train-car was a technical success, the folks from Jacksonville who used it to commute to and from Medford didn't care for it and said so. Owner Barnum was always short of cash and apparently did not maintain his track unless he was faced with some dire emergency. The track was light on ballast, its spikes were loose, and there were heaves in the bed with every spring thaw.

Due to track conditions, the car could never reach its best cruising speed therefore its jerky slowness did not permit it to outrun the exhaust from its engine. Passengers declared the train-car "stunk like a skunk."

Without any notice, Barnum ran his train-car into the garage and there it stayed. The excuse presented when he was asked, was that it was being serviced, or he was waiting for parts. But no record has been found to indicate what happened to it.

Hall-Scott Motor Car Company

The first Hall-Scott interurban constructed went to the Yreka Railroad because of a family connection. John ("Al") Hall and Bert C. Scott decided to work together for the purpose of building racing cars in a shop in Berkeley. Hall was the engineer. Bert Scott's father was a partner in the Yreka Railroad. The Yreka line sought a self-powered car for its passenger busi-

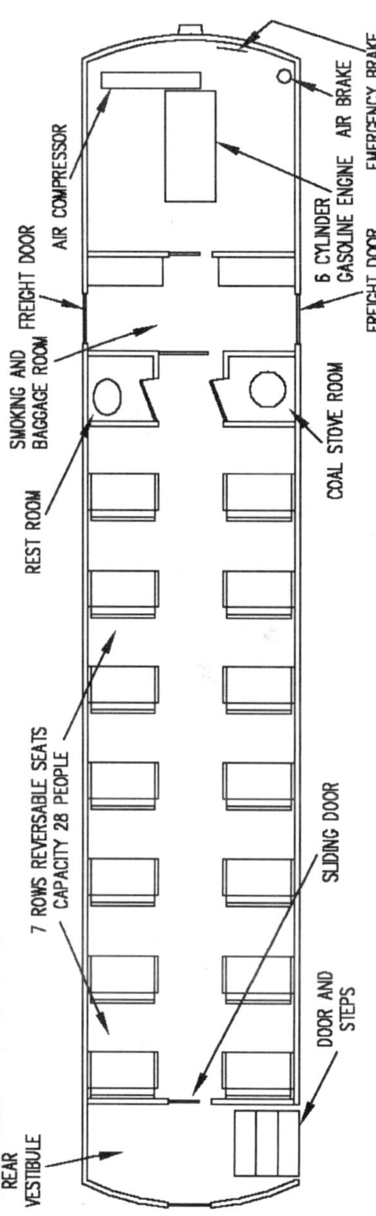

The only preserved Hall-Scott car is the "YERINGTON" in California State Railroad Museum, Sacramento. Pictures made May 25, 1997. (TOP TO BOTTOM) **Rear view of car (front end obscured). Passenger coach, seats 28. Baggage compartment with two fixed seats for smokers.** (RIGHT) **Pencil sketch by author redrawn using computer-assisted mechanical drawing** (AUTOCAD) **by Richard Webber, Stratford, NJ.**

(TOP) **Engine and driver's compartment.** (RIGHT) **Two views of 6-cyl. engine. Air compressor in front of engine (see drawing page 155).** (LEFT) **Coal stove heated car. No provision for summer ventilation.**

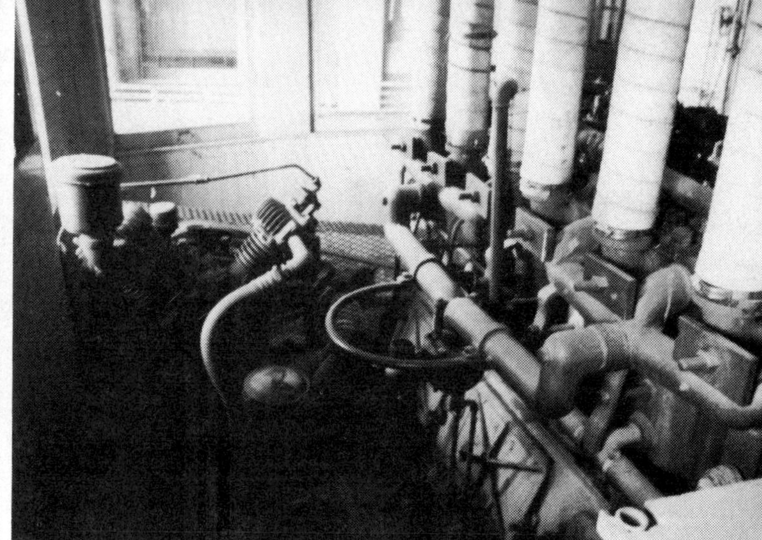

ness that would haul more people than its tiny Fairbanks-Morse "dinky." Hall was an expert engine designer. Hall and Bert Scott, at Scott's insistence, bought tickets and went for a ride on a new McKeen interurban that was running a 10-mile stretch for the Southern Pacific between Sacramento and Roseville.

As successful as the McKeen cars became, Hall observed limitations in the McKeen and decided to design and build a better engine, clutch and drive mechanisms. This was because the McKeen was intended as a single train-car that had very limited pulling power for trailers. It would not pull an empty freight car let alone one with a full load. Scott's idea was that a Hall-Scott car be powerful enough to haul its load of passengers as well as several loaded freight cars. With such a specification, this car could be used on the Yreka Railroad at considerable less operating costs than conventional steam trains.

Hall designed a 4-cylinder, 8-inch bore with 10-inch stroke valve-in-head 100 horsepower engine. The power from the engine would get to the wheels with a regular propeller shaft through a 4-speed transmission on the front axle of the back truck.

Holman Company, a San Francisco railroad car builder, got the job of supplying the trucks and wooden body.

After some test runs on the SP tracks next to the shop, Hall-Scott No. 1 was hooked into a northbound freight and delivered by SP to Montague, California, the Yreka Railroad's eastern terminus.

With some celebration, the new interurban, bearing Yreka spot No. 5, went into service in 1909. Its seating is estimated to have been about 30.

Hall-Scott was heavily involved in many other ventures and apparently did not promote its interurban business. Nevertheless, it built 23 units with lengths from 40 to 60.5 feet with various engines. These units served in Canada, Hawaii, and China with domestic use primarily in California and Utah; one in Texas. The final Hall-Scott interurban was produced in 1921.

Shop No. 5 (Road No. 21) the "Yerington," 54-feet long, completed in November 1911, was bought by the Nevada Copper Belt RR and operated for many years. It is the only Hall-Scott interurban preserved and can be viewed in the California State Railroad Museum in Sacramento.

McKeen Motor Car Company

McKeen interurban "wind-splitters" saw service between Ashland and Grants Pass, Oregon as early as 1908 but the date the McKeens were discontinued in the Rogue River Valley seems elusive.

The first McKeen rail car was rolling in March 1905 on the Union Pacific. It was a little 31-foot experimental unit build in the Union Pacific Omaha shop. The 152 cars eventually built ran on many railroads of which Southern Pacific bought 49 new, then picked up an additional eight as second-hand. The Oregon Short Line and the Oregon, Washington Railway and Navigation Company used McKeens. This versatile interurban was employed far and wide across the United States, Mexico, in Canada, in Australia and one to the Alaska railroad and one in Cuba.

McKeen No. 9 served in the Rogue Valley between Ashland and Grants Pass.

The McKeen was a most "awkward looking and spine-shaking contraption," wrote a critic, but the writer agreed that this single car interurban served its purpose calling it "functional."

The inventor, William R. McKeen was a university trained engineer and in 1902, found himself as Superintendent of the Union Pacific Railroad's Motive Power and Machinery Division with office in the Omaha UP shop.

Edward H. Harriman, the railroad magnate, held substantial interests in UP and in SP. He sought to cut operating costs on his branch lines so in 1904, he requested McKeen to work on it. McKeen came up with the idea for a self-propelled passenger car and had the UP build an experimental full-size following his specifications.

This inventor's mind sought a design that was non-typical of all existing railroad cars. He wanted a design that would be instantly recognizable as well as effective thus was born the "wind-splitter" front and rounded tail. These cars, sometimes called "torpedoes," were considerably lower to the ground than so-called standard passenger cars. The McKeen car was an early effort at "streamlining."

A New Jersey firm built the 6-cylinder 100-horsepower engines for the first cars. The transmission was two speeds forward and one reverse and was controlled by an Octoroon friction clutch. To start the car, compressed air was fed into three of the cylinders to turn over the engine.

With much fanfare, the red-headed and red-bearded Bill McKeen saw his little single-truck marvel, shop No. M-1, running the rails in the Omaha yard on March 7, 1905.

Southern Pacific did not acquire any until 1908 and it was just as well. The M-1 had just about everything go wrong with it that could go wrong from a slipping clutch, an unreliable carburetor, blown gaskets, snapped engine mounts, and you name it – it happened.

Nevertheless, the idea of a self-propelled train-car was snapped up by many railroads and orders came in. The cars were so successful that McKeen resigned from UP and formed the McKeen Motor Car Company of Omaha, Nebraska. Harriman, completely sold on the design, felt that the unreliability of the first models would dissipate with time. He saw to it that his lines, UP and SP, invested heavily in McKeens.

The interior was utilitarian but with a touch of class. The floors were hard maple and were laid on noiseless sheet steel. The walls were polished mahogany. There were fresh air vents in the floor – natural air conditioning – for summer cooling, and heating coils in the water line inside the car for winter comfort as the floors were always very cold in winter.

"Smoking" and "No Smoking" sections were walled off and each section had its own "W.C." On doors of these telephone booth size "bathrooms" was the admonition:

DO NOT FLUSH THE CLOSET WHILE THE TRAIN IS STANDING IN THE STATION

McKeen No., 63 pulls in for stop at Gold Hill Depot. —Gold Hill Historical Society collection.

These early rail cars had a 6-cylinder gasoline engine with the fuel fed from a 120 gallon tank. The drive wheels, the front pair, were 42-inch diameter and the trailers were 33-inch. Great pains had been taken to shield the passengers from engine as well as track noise, especially the notoriously loud "clicks-and-clacks" that were heard every time wheels rolled from one rail to the next.

The car was sleek in appearance. It had a compressed air driven horn that was reported to "awaken every sleeping range steer and curdle the milk of all dairy cows within one mile."

Bill McKeen was a showman and had his demonstrator car painted bright red. His hawking was hard to beat when he piped that a steam "locomotive requires 14 tons of fuel and 7,000 gallons of water while the McKeen car, to run the same distance, needs only 50 gallons of gasoline."

His 31-foot first car with 25 seats proved the point of practicability so he went for cars as long as 70-feet and engines as high as 300 horsepower. He purred that his car could literally "fly" on good level track up to 50 miles per hour. Some sat as many as 83 passengers.

McKeen No. 84, factory-fresh in October 1910, was operated on the Chicago & Great Western and lasted longer than all other McKeens chalking up a 40 year record. It finally went to the car-breakers in October 1950. If there is a McKeen "wind-splitter" on public display anywhere today, the authors have not learned of it.

We have noted that the McKeens did very well on "good level track." They also did well on slight inclines as occur between Ashland and Grants Pass. But the Southern Pacific learned the hard way that level track in the mid-western plains, where Bill McKeen did his evaluations, did not compare with operations in the foothills of the Sierra Nevada Mountains. On the run between Sacramento and Colfax, the steepness of the grade caused power failures, slipping clutches and strandings on the main line that proved detrimental to the regularly scheduled passenger and freight trains.

McKeen No. 9 was a specific example of this. It is presumed that No. 9's troubles happened after being pulled from the Grants Pass - Ashland service, for on an undetermined date, this McKeen is reported to have been sold to the Virginia & Truckee Railroad. One record says it was scrapped May 21, 1923. But was it? About forty years later there was a McKeen dutifully serving as a roadside diner south of Carson City which is in Virginia & Truckee RR country. No. 9?

The "Whiskey Local"

Three McKeen cars, Numbers 9, 55, and 63, were hauled to Ashland for local service. Passenger seating was 71, 75, and 62 respectively.

These heavy-duty, all steel cars were 50 feet long (Nos. 9 and 63) and 70 feet long for Number 55.

As we have seen, when Mr. McKeen designed his coaches he put in two "johns." Some probably long-

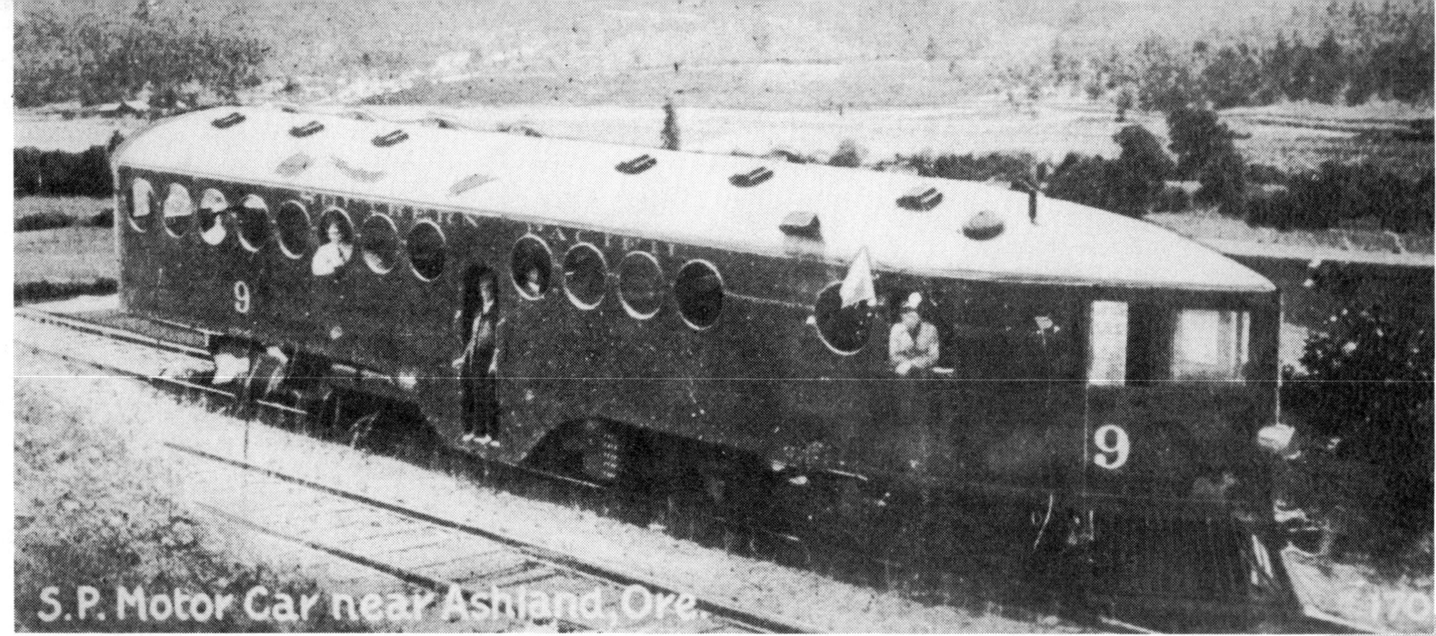

buried statistic must have established that one telephone booth size rest room was enough for so many people, because when rest rooms were first included in passenger cars, the cars sat about 40 people. As the McKeen cars accommodated more people, the "2-john" models apparently became standard and "Oh, so convenient," recalled 91-year old Jameson Parcuch. He had been a "young sport" as he called himself, who worked in a hardware store and lived in Grants Pass The author talked with him when the two accidentally met at the California Railroad Museum in Sacramento about 1980. He recalled:

> We would leave home [Grants Pass] on the Friday supper-time commuter train and go to Ashland to have a lively weekend. The ride to Ashland was uneventful but the trip back could be something else. The one-car train banged and clanked on some pretty rough sections of the track. The too much booze and the jerking and sway made some fellows, including me, sick, and both 'johns' were usually occupied all the way back to Grants Pass.

In those days, Grants Pass was a "dry" town and Ashland was "wet." The train was a "local," and made all stops picking up Medford and Ashland-bound passengers at nearly every stop. After living it up in Ashland over the weekend, the fellows straggled to the depot for a ride home on the Sunday evening runs.

The exact dates of the McKeen operation in Southern Oregon seems elusive but we know that No. 9 was scrapped in 1923. No. 55 met the same fate in early 1934.

Many folks in the Rogue River Valley would like to see commuter service restored on the rails between Grants Pass and Ashland. Some want the service to run as far as Yreka, California. Such a trip, especially on the scenic railway through the amazingly attractive Siskiyou Mountains, might no longer be called "The Whiskey Local," but it could be a tourist's dream trip on a sunny summer day. ◇

W r e c k s
Railroading Can Be Hazardous to One's Health

IT WAS ONCE CLAIMED that the safest place to be was as a fare-paying passenger, properly seated in one's assigned place, on a passenger train in the United States. And maybe it was.

But there were occasions when open switches, storm-weakened trestles, wild or domesticated animals on the track, land slides, drunks and hobos and any other of a number of obstacles were encountered, including violation of operating rules, which wrecked trains.

In recounting the history of railroads, it would seem an obvious error of omission not to include some wrecks, for news of these incidents filled newspapers whenever they occurred. Today, the TV reporters with their scanners, are usually the first on the scene of a wreck and first to tell the public about wrecks. Space permits only a sample of what's in the public record.

—Data from *Biennial Reports* of the Railroad Commissioners of the State of Oregon and from newspaper accounts.

ooOOOoo

Two firemen were killed when their locomotive ran into a slide in the Cow Creek Canyon south of Riddle.

In the Ashland yard, a brakeman, intending to make a running switch of a car, leaned down to pull a coupling pin. The train jerked as the engineer cut off steam. During the lurch, the brakeman grabbed the handle on the door at the end of the car instead of grabbing a ladder rung or a grab iron. The door came off and both the man and the door fell to the ground. The brakeman died exclaiming, "The door did it"!

At Leland, in Josephine County, a brakeman was properly walking the top of box cars in mid-train when he fell off the train as the train lurched. He died of a broken neck.

Two men were killed when a freight train collided with a steer as the train passed a switch. The animal was thrown off the track by the cow-catcher, hit a bank beside the track and rolled back and derailed a car which, at the switch, split the train sending some cars into the ditch. In the wreck were also bodies of two men who had been stealing rides. The Board of Inquiry found neither the company nor its employees responsible for the wreck.

At Glendale station:

...he was one of a party of men who were beating [hitch-hiking] their way, and in attempting to swing from a truss-rod onto a truck when the train was pulling out, he lost his hold, fell under the wheels of the moving train and was crushed to death.

Possibly the worst accident of early day operations was on an original O. & C. trestle in 1890. While crossing a 2,500-foot long structure over a shallow lake, the trestle collapsed. In all, five people were killed and about 100 were hurt.

The train was "loaded to its fullest – two sleepers, one tourist car and two day coaches" plus baggage car, Railway Post Office car, and express car. The train, bound for California, came upon the trestle at about 20 miles per hour, the posted speed. Suddenly the engineer applied the airbrakes about 600 feet from the north end of the trestle, which caused the trestle to give way. Engine, tender and mail car went into the water on the east side of the trestle. The express and baggage cars were hurled at right angles as the trestle collapsed. The weight of the loaded passenger cars caused additional collapse although these cars remained on the track.

Tampering was suggested. Investigations revealed a rail was misplaced and a claw-bar and track-wrench were found in nearby bushes. But the trestle was very old and weak in places. The foundation was judged to be "spongy." The investigation was lengthy and detailed and required 174 pages of single-space type in the official report.

Between Grants Pass and Woodville (now City of Rogue River), the engineer of a freight train saw the body of a man on the track. Investigation revealed that the night before a man had been seen walking the track in an inebriated condition. The report:

> The finding of a body the following morning frightfully mangled, was evidence that he had been run over by the northbound passenger train though the crew of that train knew nothing of the incident. The Board of Inquiry determined that the deceased was on the track intoxicated … was run over and killed with no negligence on the part of Southern Pacific or its employees.

There are many incidents where persons crossed rivers on railroad bridges against posted

NO TRESPASSING

signs, tried to out-run approaching trains and lost the race. Walking on tracks, bridges or other railroad property is trespassing and is prohibited.

The most shocking of all wrecks in Southern Oregon was on October 11, 1923 when three brothers, the DeAutremonts, stopped a train high in the Siskiyou Mountains for the purpose of robbing the mail car. The men murdered all the train's crew and in dynamiting the mail car, killed the Railway Mail Clerk, a federal employee. The plunderers, scared, left empty handed. There was no money in the mail car.*

---

* The entire story, with dozens of original on-scene and current photographs, are in the book *Oregon's Great Train Holdup; Bandits Murder 4; Didn't Get a Dime. See bibliography.*

Responsibility

Near Greens, a station three miles south of Roseburg, there is the record of deaths and great damage due to operation without clearance. This incident wrecked two locomotives, killed three men and injured four others.

A conductor had forgotten his briefcase of tickets and papers on leaving Roseburg. As there was no telegraph office at Dillard to report the situation, he directed the engineer to cut the locomotive from the train and go back to Roseburg. The engineer pointed out that such could be done only "under flag rules." In the meantime, the telegraph operator at Roseburg sent a message to the Portland office that the conductor had left without his papers.

The Roseburg dispatcher issued train orders for a light engine to carry the papers and catch the earlier train which would be stopped at Myrtle Creek and held there. At a point south of Greens, the two engines collided head-on.

The light engine had the right to the track. The locomotive returning to Roseburg, proceeding under flag, had the responsibility of seeing that the way was clear. Rules called for a complete stop no less than half-a-mile from an obstruction to the engineer's view thus, a flagman must be sent ahead, on foot, and the train would not proceed to within one hundred yards of a curve before dropping the flagman. Just at that moment, the light engine rounded the curve and struck the returning engine.

The Board of Inquiry judged the conductor and engineer (both injured) of the flagging (returning) engine were responsible. (The deaths were in the light engine.)

(TOP) **No. 2639 a C-5 Baldwin 2-8-0 built in 1902 and No. 2357, a T-31 Baldwin of 1912 vintage 4-6-0 smashed noses. Both were rebuilt. The former served until scrapped on August 7, 1935. The later until May 5, 1953.** (CENTER) **Another head-on at Gold Hill on March 25, 1903 caused the usual havoc. One train was alleged to be carrying dynamite so the crew jumped before the crash. One train was carrying rolls of newsprint.** (LOWER) **Oooopps! The folks near Ashland walked to this wreck to gander at damage. Date unknown but quite early as track not yet with ballast.**

"Slugged" Train Stops Abruptly, Wrecks Cars

On Sunday, March 17, 1985, there was a 15-car derailment on the S. P. White City Branch east of the Tolo Junction wye.

S. P officials said the actions of an elderly woman motorist caused 15 cars of a 68-car freight to jump the track at the Kirtland Road crossing.

Trainmaster Mike Healy declared the railroad would not press charges. He announced that the woman, whom S. P. declined to name, had stopped at the crossing's stop sign but proceeded onto the track without looking to see if the way was clear. It wasn't.

The train, mostly empty box cars, was moving about 8-miles an hour on a curve, having just switched from the main line to the spur leading to Medford Industrial Park at White City.

The engineer saw the car move from stopped onto the track and immediately slugged the train to EMERGENCY STOP. The car's driver backed her car off the track as the heavy train screeched to a stop with all wheels locked and missed the car by a bare three feet.

There were no injuries but the cost of damage to track, and the rerailing of the cars was estimated at about $15,000. The sudden stop, in combination with the curve, caused the empty box cars to derail. Some cars were on their sides, two were pitched at high angles and several were merely derailed.

Because of the large number of spectators at the Kirtland Road incident, as well as a full array of TV reporters and scroungers , uniformed S. P. Police were summoned to the scene.

It was a pleasantly warm June day in 1996 when railroadmen and track repair crews assembled on the Central Oregon & Pacific Railroad's scene of a derailment about five miles south of Ashland. An Eastbound freight had rolled along the track in a seemingly usual manner when suddenly empty freight cars derailed in the middle of the train. One of the cars that broke loose and jumped the track shoved dirt from the bank near the rails as a bulldozer blade shoves dirt. There were no injuries. Officials told TV reporters that the wreck was caused by worn wheels on a boxcar that had avoided detection at Black Butte Junction when the car was accepted from Southern Pacific.

When a west-bound Central Oregon & Pacific freight train derailed some of its cars and leaked about 500 gallons of formaldehyde, the day was saved by quick thinking rural fire district personnel. The Colestin Rural Fire Department personnel dug emergency dikes for containment which prevented seepage into Cottonwood Creek.

It was Saturday July 20, 1996 around 6:20 in the morning. The derailment occurred on the California side of the Siskiyou Mountains near the entrance of a Tibetan Buddhist monastery in the Cottonwood Creek Valley. The leak came from an overturned tank car. Other involved cars carried cement and lumber.

The "syrup-like gooey mess" was contained in a pool about 4 feet by 12 feet about 50 feet from the West Fork of Cottonwood Creek.

Track crews had been replacing old ties a few days earlier at the site, which is about 3,500 feet elevation on a steep section of the line.

A rail safety inspector for the Oregon Department of Transportation said "deferred maintenance" by the line's previous owner, Southern Pacific, contributed to recent mishaps along the Siskiyou line.

It took a longer time than earlier anticipated for special crews, a few weeks later, to remove all contaminated earth and right the tank car that had leaked some of its formaldehyde. The several derailed cars were again on the track and had been locked with chain to the track awaiting pickup by a regular train, when, apparently, unknown person or persons managed to release the cars. These cars promptly rolled down the track to crash. There were no witnesses and no injuries. The use of the track, which had been closed for weeks because of the original derailment, was further delayed until the new wreck could be removed.

Wrecks are a part of railroad operations just as wrecks are part of maritime operations. No one in the business likes to see wrecks because wrecks often take lives, hurt people, break equipment, damage the earth

Cab-First Locomotives

SP 4018 Cab-first
Baldwin No. 36491 Class MM-4
(1911) 2-8-8-2. 57-inch wheels.
Scrapped June 30, 1947.
—Photographed near Ashland *ca* 1915

Locomotives called "cab-first" models, because the engineer's and fireman's cab was on the front of the fire box rather than behind it, were developed for use in the snow sheds in the Sierra Nevada Mountains. This way, the smoke, which trailed past the train, was behind the men instead of their being enveloped in it in the sheds.

Officials of the Southern Pacific quickly observed that engineers obviously had a better vision of what was in front of them by looking through a window on the nose of the locomotive instead of always fighting the "blind spot" trying to look around the fire box. As a result, cab-first locomotives became common sights on most all lines of Oregon and California.

On the Siskiyou Line, and on the Cascade Line via Klamath Falls, these locomotives were the choice of engineers.

These engines were quite powerful as they were "articulated" having two sets of drivers in tandem. But they were expensive to operate.

Even these big-boy locomotives required helpers in the Siskiyous if the trains were long.

These engines were kept at Eugene where they were switched onto trains going to California over either line. They were exchanged for so-called "conventional" locomotives at the yard at Dunsmuir.

After an explosion of a cab-first (No. 4017) in the Siskiyous, SP limited the use on that line of this model allowing only as far south as Ashland.

SP Cab-first Class AC-1 - 12 1909-1944
First as 2-6-6-2 (No. 4000) then 2-8-8-2, then 4-8-8-2. Final was Baldwin No. 70092-101 63-inch drive wheels. (1944) SP No. 4294. This ran on the Auburn - Sparks run, retired 1955 and is exhibited indoors in California State Railroad Museum, Sacramento.

Cab-first engine No. 4294 is only such model preserved. It can be visited in California State Railroad Museum, Sacramento.

or the sea, and cost a lot of inconvenience and money. Lack of safe practices can cause wrecks. The byword among all railroaders is *Safety.* ◇

The Explosion of a Cab-first Locomotive on the Siskiyou Line in 1929

The long freight train, with cab-first locomotive #4017, was northbound. It passed Bailey Hill then descended to Hilt, and started the long bore uphill to tunnel 13 [3.67 percent grade]. It passed through the tunnel still uphill, then started down the other side after clearing the tunnel's north portal now with both dynamic & auto brakes due to the steep grade [3.40 percent]. The train entered tunnel 14. After the head-end rounded that big loop, the train entered and started to emerge from the 258-foot long tunnel #15 — crew could look up and see the caboose just entering tunnel #14.

As the train continued down-grade, apparently between the Steinman and Mistletoe sidings, after passing the north end of Dollarhide fill (formerly a trestle) the fireman, Halley Head, climbed out of the cab and on to the running board. This was alongside the firebox. He proceeded to beat on the boiler check valve with a hammer as the water glass in the cab had indicated the boiler was not getting water.

It was common for calcium in the water to clog the lines and plug a valve. When calcium is very hot it is a soft sludge (when cold looks like oyster shells). With this thick silt, the check-valve won't lift to allow water to flow. This meant there was insufficient water on the crown sheet. Accordingly, it was only a matter

of time before Engine #4017 blew up.

The explosion blew off the smoke box door. The steel door flew through the air and on hitting a tree in the forest, broke the trunk of the tree. Because the fireman was outside the cab, the concussion blew him off the engine and onto the side of the hill near the broken tree. He survived and continued work for Southern Pacific until he retired.

The engineer, Ira Bateman, was not so lucky. The explosion knocked the huge locomotive off the track and down the slope. Whether it was the blast that killed the engineer, or his being pinned under the engine is not known.

After this wreck of #4017 in the Siskiyous, Southern Pacific discontinued using these locomotives in these mountains.

Locomotive #4017 Baldwin MM-4 Construction No. 36490, 2-8-8-2, was rebuilt, and served until scrapped on June 14, 1947.

Asbestos was a hazard on these locomotives, was 4 inches thick around the fire box. When overhauled, the chunks of asbestos would drop out and land at workers feet to be kicked out of the way with dust (particles) arising. Dozens of men were paid hundreds of thousand of dollars in claims, and most all are now dead, so stated Harry Smith, one of the mechanics, to the authors.

> **Engine #4017 was a shop-mate with #4018 in the Baldwin factory in 1911. No picture has been found of #4017. For a photograph of #4018 see page 165.**

Siskiyou Line Wreck July 14, 1906

[We were on the southbound train and] stopped at Ashland for the evening meal before continuing over the Siskiyou Mountains. This evening, the Pullman section had been left in Ashland and we were in the chair car section. The [conductor], who had been looking out of the window exclaimed, 'What's this'? as the train started to go backwards [returning] to Ashland.

A heavily loaded freight train had run wild down the mountain, jumping the track and freight cars were piled up on top of each other. The fireman had jumped and sprained his ankle badly but the engineer, who had stayed with the train was badly burned. He was scalded and bad off. [Men] laid him on the warehouse floor and did all they could do. As he lay, my husband heard him telling about his family. [The engineer] said 'For me this doesn't matter but I hate to have to leave my family.'

At the wreck [rescuers] found two 18-year old boys pined under the sacks of sugar and Tonppah gold ore, which the train was carrying. There was enough [spilled] oil to drown them. The rescuers pulled the [boys] out and fortunately they were not injured. They had been stealing a ride on the rods beneath the car. A farmer and his wife came to the wreck in an effort to help. He gave his overalls to one boy and his wife gave her apron to the other. The [boys] removed their oil-soaked cloths then they were taken to Ashland where they were put in the caboose with the engineer and taken to Portland. But before they left, they were escorted through the Pullman section and [passengers] donated enough money to clothe them head to toe, including a pocket handkerchief and fifty cents spending money. The engineer who had been burned in the wreck died before they reached Portland.

The train we were on was held up until the track was repaired [then] we passed the wreck and could see cars which had been smashed into kindling wood and piled up in a heap.

—From memoirs of Phoebe Nye Lister by David Lougee

<u>The *Ashland Tidings* reported:</u>

Two Killed in Train Wreck

Locomotive Engineer Robert Steiger and Brake-man C. D. Lockerman are dead and the Brakeman Sam Wylie was severely injured as result of a wild runaway, the derailment and wreck of SP freight train No. 222 a few minutes after noon on Saturday, on the north side of the Siskiyous, just south of Ashland. The wreck is the most disastrous in the history of railroading on the Siskiyous.

The other members of the train's crew, Conductor Louis Hiltry, Fireman Galbraith and Brakeman Ranse Morris, were more fortunate than their companions and came through the frightful experience without injury. Two hoboes riding between the cars behind the locomotive had every stitch of their clothing torn off from their bodies but were otherwise uninjured.

Nichols, the SP operator at Steinman, was on the runaway train and escaped without injury. He was on the caboose platform and held himself there on the mad ride down the grade.

The body of Brakeman Lockerman was taken to Chico, California, his home, fro interment. He was about 35.

The train, drawn by engine No. 2629, one of the big mountain

climbers [Baldwin constr. No. 19855, built 1901 Class C-5 2-8-0, Vauclain compound] was comprising 17 cars was piled into an indescribable mass of wreckage at the east end of the siding at Clawson, five miles south of Ashland. Railroad men declared the wreck to be the most complete they ever saw, the cars being double up and twisted into one-third their length, jammed and packed and split into kindling wood. The engine, in the cab of which brave Bob Steiger was pinned down and scalded, lay dismantled on its side, back of it was a tank car of oil upturned with its trucks in the air, and there, tossed upside-down and sixty feet from the track was the engine tender. The great steel rails were curved and twisted and twirled in a scene that beggars description.

The big wrecking outfit came from Roseburg and the great mogul No. 2629 was put back on the track and brought into the Ashland yards.

Section foreman Williamson was eating dinner with his gang at Steinman Station, half way down the Siskiyous and 10 miles from Ashland at 12:20 p.m. when he heard the wild whistling of the freight train whose engineer was calling for brakes. In a moment, the men were horrified to see a complete freight train coming like a whirlwind. Scarcely had they glanced at it before it had disappeared around a curve. The gang took their hand car and started down the rails after the train as Foreman Williamson says, "just to see where she will pile up." The crew pumped on their handcar five miles to Clawson switch and found the wreck.

In the cab, engineer Steiger was pinned at his post and scalded. The doctors have him morphine which tended to ease his pain. A special train was made up to take the injured to a hospital in Portland and was ready to leave by about 5 p.m. Just before reaching Roseburg at about 7:30 p.m., Steiger was relieved from his agony.

(TOP) **This wreck in 1898 during an early morning fog in T. R. Sheridan's field was about one mile south of Roseburg. Engineer Sam, Hendrix was killed and Fireman Ed Riddle lost a foot. The Brakeman, E. T. "Buck" Morian was not hurt. Note "C.P." for Central Pacific on the box car body and on the car door, and Southern Pacific "Ogden Route" in the SP Logo. The locomotive with either 6 or 8 drive wheels, was also marked "C.P." on tender.** (LOWER) **Central Pacific engine No. 2187, built in CP shop, Sacramento, in 1888, toppled off new unballasted track near Ashland on unknown date. This was a Class T-6 (old Class DF) and was a 4-6-0. It survived this crash, was rebuilt and worked until January 12, 1927, when it was scrapped.**

Wrecks in the Gold Hill area. (TOP) **Wheels and axles are nearly always salvageable, box cars not always. Lumber had to be off-loaded before car could be moved. When a wreck is "extra bad" and there would be long delays in the cleanup to clear a track, a "jack-track" might be built around the obstructions so trains can continue to operate.** (LOWER VIEWS) **Each appears to be head-on wrecks.** —Gold Hill Historical Society collection

(TOP) **South portal Tunnel 13 in Siskiyou Mountains the day after the infamous murder of trainmen and dynamiting of mail car killing the mail clerk by three DeAutremont Brothers. This was October 11, 1923. Bodies of dead (arrow) yet to be removed.** (LOWER) **What's left of Railway Post Office car shown parked on White Point siding, later towed to Ashland yard. This, "The Last Great Train Holdup of the West" is chronicled in the book *Oregon's Great Train Holdup Bandits Murder 4 – Didn't Get A Dime!* (See book list page ii.)**

Box cars of CORP lost their footing in Cow Creek Canyon and landed in the creek. Years earlier, the O&C had so much trouble in this canyon they abandoned a long stretch of track. For the story seepage 61.

Engine No. 4348 lost its footing while on a curve on May 7, 1943 between Oakland and Sutherlin – one mile from the Sutherlin yard. The engineer, J. H. Corbett was accused in the official investigation of excess speed. He died here. Fireman Ira. L. Smith was burned in hot oil but managed to crawl from the wreck. No. 4348 was Class MT-4 4-8-2 with 73-inch drivers built in SP Sacramento shop in 1926. It was re-railed, hauled back to the shop for refit. No. 4348 worked until scrapped on March 3, 1953.

Trouble on the Yreka Line

An automobile lost the argument with old No. 19 back in 1957. Whatever happened to the car is not known but No. 19 is still puffing away.
—Yreka Western Archives

Incident near Yreka with Engine No. 19 of the Yreka Western on October 23, 1957.

TELEGRAM

AT 8:30 A.M. DATE OUR TRAIN INVOLVED IN GRADE CROSSING ACCIDENT WITH AUTOMOBILE AT CROSSING 47-3.9. FOUR AUTOMOBILE PASSENGERS INJURED.
—Yreka Western Archives

Steve Avgeris, Chief of
the Colestin Rural Fire
District, headed the
containment project,
was praised by officials
for prompt attention.

The July 1996 incident of an upset train involved spilled formaldehyde near Colestin. At risk was the potential leak of the chemical into Cottonwood Creek. Prompt action by the Volunteer firemen contained the "flowing goo" with no damage to the creek. Many cars were derailed, and some were "totaled" in the affair. (LOWER) Hazardous materials ("HASMAT") team members and railroad men hold track-side conference at Colestin. The occupants of the Buddhist monastery about one-half mile away, were notified to prepare for evacuation if the wind turned and sent chemical fumes their direction, but the evacuation was not needed.

The Enigma of Buck Rock Tunnel in Siskiyou Mountains

SILENT AND ALONE in a wilderness of trees, the all but forgotten hole in the side of a mountain called Buck Rock Tunnel is hard to find even for those who think they know where to look.

Buck Rock Tunnel was the original "Tunnel 13" in the Oregon & California Rail Road's plans for laying track through the Siskiyou Mountains. But for reasons never told, when the Central Pacific (later Southern Pacific) took over the bankrupt O&C, the SP engineers changed the route.

At the time of the driving of the golden spike near Ashland, the matter of the O&C's planned route compared with the route chosen, sparked arguments among railroad engineers that still persist.

There were people at the ceremony who contended that the Buck Rock route surveyed by O&C engineer John A. Hurlburt was the better of the two. The facts are these:

- Buck Rock route is a little longer than the one chosen
- The grade does not exceed 2 percent to the summit
- The route lay in a sun-drenched exposure resulting in less trouble with snow
- The route would be less expensive to build and maintain
- Trains cost less to operate when the climb is not so steep.

On the route that was built:

- The track, from Point A to Point B is 2.60 miles shorter
- The grade is steeper being as must as 3.67 percent
- The track is heavily covered with snow in winter that has little tendency to melt as it is on the north side of the mountain.
- The route was more expensive per mile to build
- Trains require more power to climb to the summit which increases operating costs

The decision resulted in the abandonment of the drilling of the 1,650 feet long Buck Rock Tunnel which was about 25 percent along.

With the advantage of hindsight, it has been speculated that the difficulties encountered after the trains were running in the Siskiyous, was a contributing reason that the Natron Cutoff in the Cascade Mountains was built to get away from that steep, twisting, expensive Siskiyou climb.

Between the preliminary survey and the construction, 24 years elapsed. The delays were marked by bankruptcy, changing companies, several surveyors, and debates over the O&C land grants.

The first two preliminary surveys of record were by Simon G. Elliot in 1863 and Colonel Charles Berry

(TOP AND CENTER) **East entrance bore penetrates Buck Rock 312 feet.**
(LOWER) **West entrance extends about 100 feet.**
Is shown on topo maps as "mine."

Buck Rock Tunnel and Southern Pacific Final Route

Researched and Drawn by Mark E. Lawrence Feb. 19, 1966

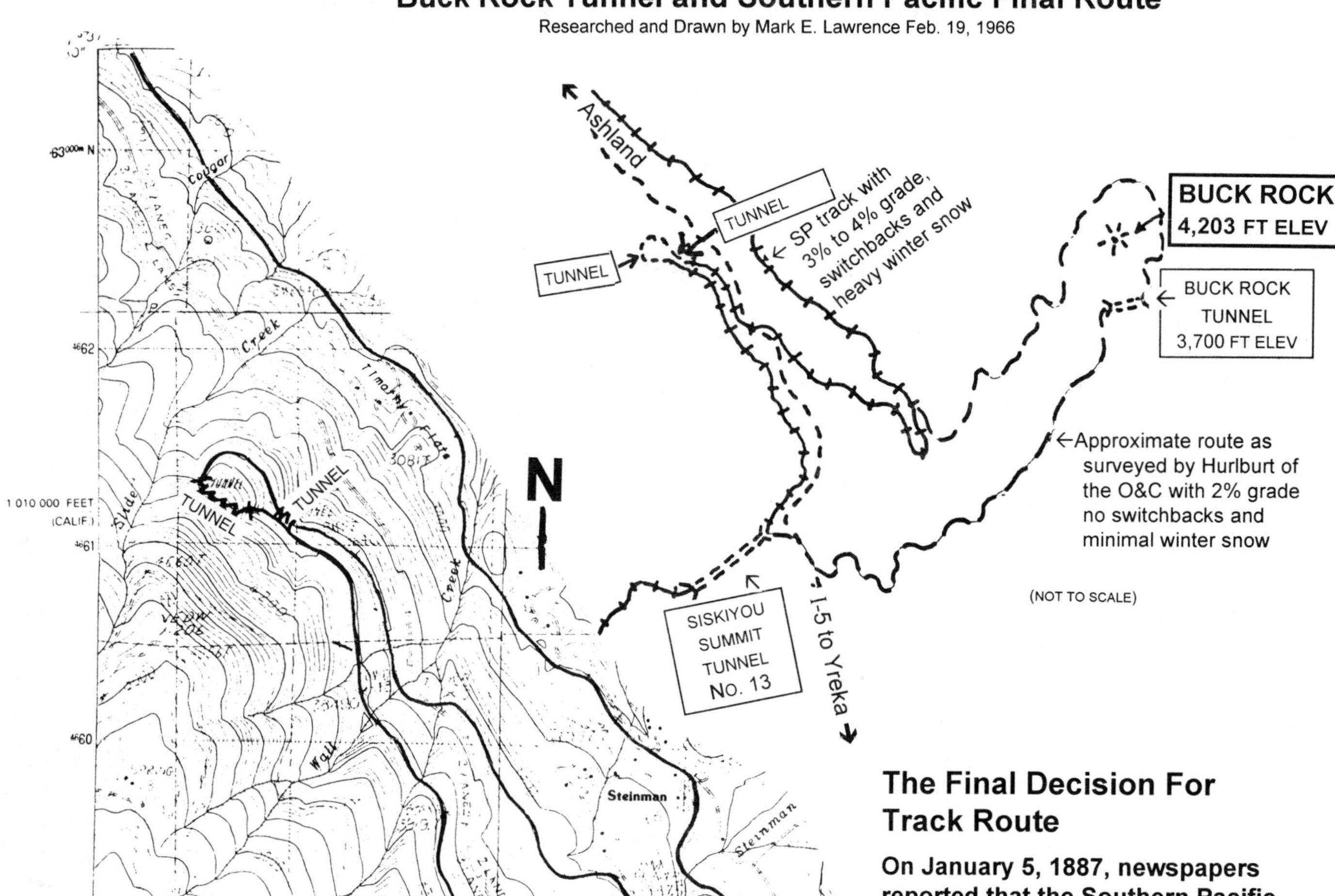

The Final Decision For Track Route

On January 5, 1887, newspapers reported that the Southern Pacific secured possession of the railroad and, we find that their engineers were still probing the Siskiyous as late as February 2 to eliminate the Buck Rock Tunnel either by a longer and lower Siskiyou Summit tunnel or by using a heavier (steeper) grade. No reasons are given for the proposed route change, but the engineers were looking for the shortest and fastest possible route. At this time, a decision was made to complete the summit tunnel as originally located and eliminate the Buck Rock Tunnel by jumping the grade to 3.3% up to almost 4% and come down the mountain on a big Z with switch-backs and high trestles to get over the rough country. From this time on, Crocker, his Chinese laborers, and the crew members, pushed the road through to completion by the present route.

Riding Down to the Last Spike Celebration

YREKA, CALIF. DEC 21, 1887—The road takes the shady or north side of the canyon from the summit which all people in that section contend is not as good a survey made by the Oregon surveyor John A. Hurlburt, claiming that the road by Buck Rock Tunnel was of much easier grade and less liable to become blocked by snow in winter. Going down the mountain, there is even more winding around forward and back stretches than on the California side. The train, after running a few miles from the summit tunnel, passed through a tunnel with a 14% curve swinging around again and through a short tunnel almost under the tunnel above. The lower tunnel could have been an open cut but, it would have weakened the foundations of the upper tunnel. Near these two tunnels are trestles 90 feet high and 164 feet high. After arriving at Ashland and the usual round of speeches, Charles Crocker, Vice President of the Southern Pacific, drove the golden spike with a silver hammer. California and Oregon were linked by rail at last.

—*Yreka Journal*

in 1864. In 1881, John A. Hurlburt searched the Siskiyous for a route and he determined that the best way would be to drill a tunnel through Buck Rock.

By 1885, another engineer, Tasheira, seemed to be trying to eliminate the Buck Rock Tunnel although drilling had started from each end.

Newspapers, on January 5, 1887, reported that the Central Pacific had obtained possession of the O&C. Immediately, as Central Pacific wanted to finish the route in a hurry, engineers were sent to probe the Siskiyous, as late as February 2, in an effort to locate a site for a lower Siskiyou (summit) tunnel or develop a steeper grade to the summit tunnel which was also partially drilled.

(In 1885 the *Yreka Journal* declared the Siskiyou summit tunnel was "too high in grade" and although it was half-finished, it was "likely to be abandoned." Work had stopped.)

The elevation between the Buck Rock site and the elevation at the summit site is 1,400 feet. One observation was that a train would creep to the top in a somewhat easy manner using the Buck Rock route or, with the use of helper locomotives, steam its way to the top on a much steeper and twisting route with high trestles and extra tunnels. If this route, with its famous switch-backs was chosen, Buck Rock would be eliminated. The steep route was chosen. Why the abandonment of the work on Buck Rock Tunnel in favor of the steep, twisted route with the famous **Z** switchback, remains a mystery.

Buck Rock Tunnel was also stripped of its number, "13." The number was reassigned to the Siskiyou Summit Tunnel. ◇

Short Takes From the *Yreka Journal*

May 11, 1887 — Vice President Crocker of Southern Pacific says rails over the Siskiyou Mountains will be laid from the California side. He said within 10 days he expected trains will be running to a point 8 miles north of Hornbook to a new station to be named Cole.

May 29, 1887 — At lower Coles [*sic.*] the road takes a long turn westerly thence back toward the south end of the Siskiyou Tunnel on a 15 degree curve making about 7 miles of track to gain 3 miles of the old stage road. All work camps will be moved to the Ashland side by July 4. [Some] tunnels not over 300 feet long will be needed .

July 13, 1887 — July 4 the work was at Tunnel 14. The contractors are not doing sufficient work and have been relieved of their contract. Tunnel 14 is about 1½ miles above Major Barron's place. The tunnel is 1,200 feet long and will be the last to be completed. It is cut through very peculiar rock and requires men of great experience. Two camps of carpenters moved here on July 4 for timbering the tunnels.

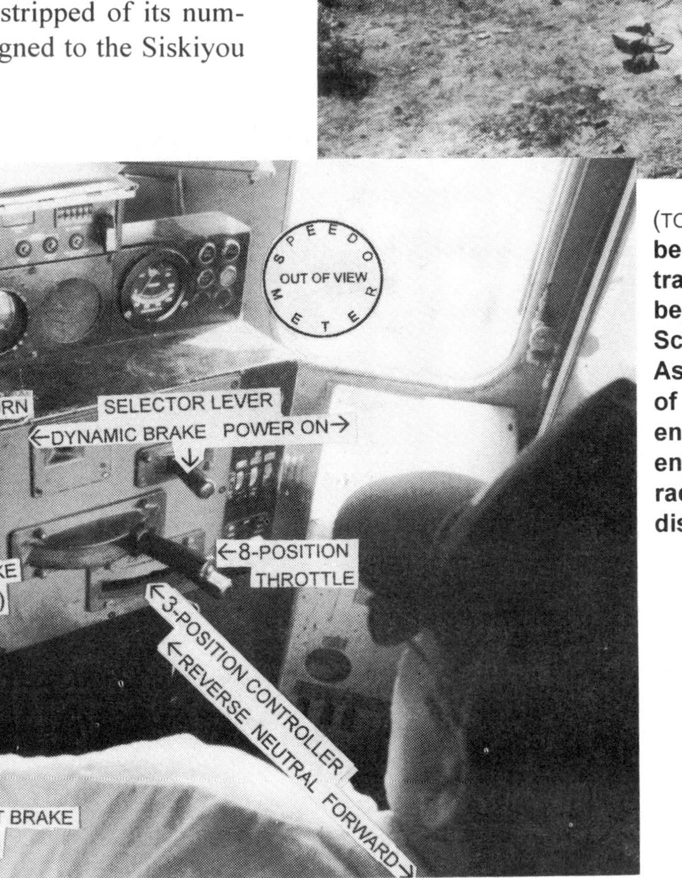

(TOP) **Camp sites have been common along tracks since the beginning of railroads. Scene southeast of Ashland. (lower) "Office" of a GP40 diesel-electric engine. Tom Moore, engineer, is talking on FM radio to Roseburg dispatch.**

Motel With No Rooms – Just Cabooses

Unique concept at Railroad Park, south of Dunsmuir within sight of Castle Crags.

Lonesome Cabooses
Cabooses No Longer Used by Railroads

WHEN RAILROADS DISCONTINUED attaching a caboose to the end of every freight train in the nation, thousands of cabooses were put out of work. The cabooses were "fired."

What became of them?

Railroads, aware of the cost of breaking up obsolete cars, at one time gave the cars to scavenger firms or sold them for a pittance of their original cost. Cars destined for the car-breakers oftentimes had more than a million miles on them and many of them were just plain worn out.

The salvage firms helped the railroads by taking old cars off their hands, removed salable parts then teams of workers armed with cutting torches reduced the cars to jagged-edged sheets of cold metal. This scrap iron was sold for market value. It was a convenient arrangement. The railroads got rid of obsolete and worn out cars, and the car-breakers made a few bucks from sale of the scrap.

There were many scavenger firms around the country but the authors are aware of the car-breakers who worked on an SP spur at Lincoln, California. On one visit, the cars being put to the torch were passenger cars. But on two sidings, were 14 cabooses each awaiting its turn.

The majority of decommissioned cabooses were relics of the past. Many were not in good condition and some were barely able to pass inspection to be used at all. These went to the car-breakers.

The railroads found certain tax advantages in giving away cabooses, and other relics of their once

(LEFT) **Home made 2-axle caboose used on Weyerhaeuser Sutherlin line in Sutherlin park.**
(ABOVE) **Dan Wilkinson and his reconditioned Santa Fe caboose, often runs between Yreka and Montague on "Blue Goose" excursions.**
(LOWER) **Burlington Route antique caboose at Medford Railroad Park.**

proud fleet, to historical societies and to city parks. Many are the old steam locomotives, tenders, boxcars and cabooses on permanent exhibit in parks.

But there were also the "Friends of the Railroad." Some retired cabooses went to retired employees who had a suitable place to put a caboose and let management know of their interest. Other "friends" were permitted to buy a caboose for scrap value – a few hundred dollars. And there were special cases where a caboose, possibly one that had been damaged in a smashup, was reconditioned by volunteers then donated to selected individuals or presented to historical societies and parks.

The authors did not have to look very far to find retired cabooses many places. Pictured here are but a few of them. ◇

(TOP) **Ken Beebe, orchardist, great friend with SP, has caboose among his fruit trees near Central Point.** (BELOW) **Norm VanManen waves from caboose in park in Cottage Grove.** (LOWER) **Older caboose awaits reconditioning in Medford Railroad Park.**

Bert and Margie Webber at south portal Tunnel 13 while researching on their book *Oregon's Great Train Holdup*.

About the Authors

BERT WEBBER traces his earliest interest in writing to when he was caught laying out a newspaper front page while he was supposed to be doing arithmetic in the 5th grade. Today, as a Research Photojournalist, he writes books mostly specializing in subjects that occur in what he calls "the fantastic Pacific Northwest."

During World War II he served in the Army and in the Air Force, then returned to the Army as, among other duties, a Signal Corps Photographer serving in Alaska, England, Scotland, Belgium and twice in France.

Before returning to school, Webber owned a commercial photographic and camera shop business. Later with Remington Rand, he graduated from the National Sales Training Institute, Fishers Island, New York, at the top of his class.

He earned a degree in journalism from Whitworth College then the Master of Library Science after studies at Portland State University and the University of Portland. He taught History of the Pacific Northwest and was a librarian in Washington state and in Oregon schools.

Bert has photographed more subjects, over fifty years, than he can remember and he has contributed hundreds of articles to newspapers and magazines. He has nearly sixty books with his name on the title page. He is listed in *Who's Who in the West,* in *Contemporary Authors* (twice) and he was awarded the *Degree of Merit* in *Men of Achievement* in the International Biographical Centre, Cambridge, England.

For fun, Bert plays Euphonium in the Southern Oregon Concert Band where he also serves as the Vice President for Administrative Affairs.

MARGIE WEBBER is a retired Registered Nurse who earned her baccalaureate degree in Nursing from the University of Washington and did post-graduate work at Oregon State University. She worked in a variety of professional nursing positions in Washington and in Oregon including Public Health. She has been a consultant in nutrition and skin care.

She assists her husband of more than fifty years in field research, photography, earlier in the photo-lab, and serves as a Senior Editor. Margie Webber is co-author with Bert on a number of books.

The Webbers make their home in Oregon's Rogue River Valley in the town of Central Point where they often hear the horns on the Central Oregon & Pacific's diesels as the trains purr along *The Siskiyou Line* in the night. <>

Bibliography

BOOKS

Abdill, George B. *Pacific Slope Railroads.* Superior. 1959.

Austin, Ed. and Tom Dill. *The Southern Pacific in Oregon.* Pacific Fast Mail. 1987.

__________ *The Southern Pacific in Oregon Pictorial.* Pacific Fast Mail. 1993.

Bancroft, Hubert Howe. (Vol. XXX) *History of Oregon* Vol. II 1848-1888. History Co. San Francisco. 1888.

Beebe, Lucius. *The Central Pacific & The Southern Pacific Railroads.* Howell-North. 1963.

Best, Gerald M. and David L. Joslyn. *Locomotives of the Southern Pacific Company. Bulletin No. 94.* The Railway & Locomotive Historical Society, Inc. (Boston, Mass.). March 1956.

Burkhardt, C. Jesse. *Backwoods Railroads.* Washington State Univ. Press. 1994.

Culp. Edwin D. *Early Oregon Days.* Caxton. 1987.

__________. *Stations West; The Story of the Oregon Railways.* Caxton. 1972.

Hald, Chris and Bert Webber. *Camp White Oregon; The 91st (Fir Tree) Infantry Division – Documentary.* Webb Research Group. 1994.

Hauff, Steve and Jim Gertz. *The Willamette Locomotive.* Binford & Mort. 1977.

Keilty, Edmund. *Interurbans Without Wires; The Rail Motorcar in the United States.* Interurbans. 1979.

LaLande, Jeff. *Medford Corporation, A History of an Oregon Logging and Lumber Company.* Private print. 1979.

Lewis, Oscar. *The Big Four [Huntington, Stanford, Hopkins, Crocker and the Building of the Central Pacific].* Knopf. 1941.

McArthur, Louis L. *Oregon Geographic Names.* (6th Ed.) Oregon Historical Society Press. 1992.

McLane, Larry L. *First There Was Twogood.* Sexton Enterprises (Sunny Valley, Ore.). 1995.

Robertson, Donald B., *Encyclopedia of Western Railroad History – Oregon - Washington.* Caxton. 1995.

Stephens, Kent. *The Yreka and Western Railroad; A Centennial History.* private print. 1992.

Walling, Albert G. *History of Southern Oregon.* Walling. 1884.

Webber, Bert and Margie. *FLOOD! Ashland Devastated – New year's Day 1997 – An Oregon Documentary.* Webb Research Group. 1997.

__________. *Jacksonville Oregon; Antique Town in a Modern Age.* Webb Research Group. 1994.

__________.. *The Lure of Medford; An Oregon Documentary.* Webb Research Group. 1996.

__________.. *Oregon Covered Bridges – Expanded Edition.* Webb Research Group. 1995.

__________.. *Over the Applegate Trail to Oregon in 1846.* Webb Research Group. 1996.

__________.. *Railroading in Southern Oregon and the Founding of Medford.* YeGalleon. 1985.

__________.. *Single Track to Jacksonville; The Rogue River Valley Railway and the Southern Oregon Traction Company – An Oregon Documentary.* Webb Research Group. 1990.

__________.. *This is Logging and Sawmilling – Documentary.* Webb Research Group. 1996.

NEWSPAPER ARTICLES

Dodge, Dani. "Chemical Cleanup Continues; Creek Pollution Still Possibility " in *Mail Tribune.* July 22, 1996.

__________. "Spill Frets Colestin Residents in *Mail Tribune* July 23, 1996.

__________. "Trains Will Resume Siskiyou Run Today" in *Mail Tribune.* Sept. 11, 1996.

Enriques, Alberto. "Spill Stops Short of Creek; Colestin Crews Swoop in After Tanker Car Tips Over" in *Mail Tribune.* July 21, 1996 p.1.

Fattig, Paul. "Old Engine Gets Refit; S. Oregon Train Enthusiasts Restore No. 8" in *Mail Tribune.* Sept. 22, 1996.

"High-tech Train to Have Test Run in Oregon" in *Mail Tribune.* Apr. 26, 1997.

Macomber, Paul. "RailTex Likes Small Shippers" in *Mail Tribune.* Dec. 7, 1994.

__________. "Freight Trains to Roll South Over Siskiyous Once Again" in *Mail Tribune.* June 2, 1995.

__________. Train Reconquers Pass; Siskiyou Run as Challenging as Ever" in *Mail Tribune.* June 6, 1995.

__________. "Cause of Derailment Eludes Investigators" in *Mail Tribune.* July 23, 1996.

__________. "Rails Trace Lines Back into History" in *Mail Tribune.* Sept 22, 1996.

"Railroaders' Dream Failed to Materialize"[Medford & Crater Lake RR] in *Mail Tribune* June 6, 1985

GOVERNMENT DOCUMENTS

Abbot, Henry L. "Report of Lieut. Henry L. Abbot, Corps of Topographical Engineers, upon Explorations for a Railroad Route from the Sacramento River to the Columbia River, made by Lieut. R. S. Williamson, Corps of T.E. assisted by Lieut. H. L. Abbot, Corps of T.E. [in] 1855 to Ascertain the Most Practicable and Economical Route for a Railroad from the Mississippi River to the Pacific Ocean made under the Direction of the Secretary of War in 1854-55 according ot the Acts of Congress of March 3, 1853, May 31, 1854, and August 5, 1854," in *Senate Executive Document No. 78.* 33rd Congress 2d Session, 1857.

PERIODICALS

Gaston, Joseph. "The Oregon Central Railroad" in *The Oregon Historical Quarterly.* Vol. III. Mar. 1902. pp. 25-27.

__________. "The Genesis of the Oregon Railroad System" in *The Oregon Historical Quarterly.* Vol. VII. No. 2. June 1906. pp. 105-132.

__________. "The Oregon Central Railroad" in *The Oregon Historical Quarterly.* Vol. III. No. 2. pp. 133-144.

"The Story of the Beginning of the Southern Pacific; Building of Oregon Lines That Are Now a Part of the Southern Pacific "in *Southern Pacific Bulletin.* Jan. 1930. pp. 10-14.

Taber, Thomas T. "A Large Gasoline Motor Car for the Oregon Short Line Ry. [McKeen cars]." *The Train Sheet.* Wellsville, NY. 1910(?)

Index

Page numbers shown in **bold,** *italic* as *45* are photographs and maps
Major subjects as "Southern Pacific" and "Central Oregon & Pacific" are not generally indexed

**Diesels head freight train emerging from
north portal, Tunnel 13**

Solar-powered block signals.

Yreka Railroad's No. 1 was called "Old Betsy." Shown on new bridge over Shasta River.
—Yreka Western collection

Hi-railer's are assigned to many tasks including track inspection, special trips to meet or catch a train, etc.

High-efficiency, and high speed, commuter trains have proven themselves throughout the nation often running close to 100 mph. Several models are being tested in selected areas in the Pacific Northwest at this writing. Pictures made in McMinnville in May 1997 by Bert Webber.

—NOTES—

—NOTES—

STRUCTURAL TRAPS V

COMPILED BY
NORMAN H. FOSTER
AND
EDWARD A. BEAUMONT

TREATISE OF PETROLEUM GEOLOGY
ATLAS OF OIL AND GAS FIELDS

PUBLISHED BY
THE AMERICAN ASSOCIATION OF PETROLEUM GEOLOGISTS
TULSA, OKLAHOMA 74101, U.S.A.

ISBN: 0-89181-586-4
ISSN: 1043-6103

Available from:
The AAPG Bookstore
P.O. Box 979
Tulsa, OK 74101-0979

Phone: (918) 584-2555
Telex: 49-9432
FAX: (918) 584-0469

Association Editor: Susan Longacre
Science Director: Gary D. Howell
Publications Manager: Cathleen P. Williams
Special Projects Editor: Anne H. Thomas
Science Staff: William G. Brownfield
Project Production: Custom Editorial Productions, Inc.